GRACE'S RESCUE

DEBBIE WATKINS

KINGSLEY
PUBLISHERS

First published in South Africa by Kingsley Publishers, 2023
Copyright © Debbie Watkins, 2023

The right of Debbie Watkins to be identified as author of this work has been asserted.

Editor: Anna Cullen

Kingsley Publishers
Pretoria,
South Africa
www.kingsleypublishers.com

A catalogue copy of this book will be available from the National Library of South Africa
Paperback ISBN: 978-1-7764254-5-7
eBook ISBN: 978-1-7764254-4-0

This book is a work of fiction. Names, characters, places, and incidents are either a product of the authors imagination or are used fictitiously. Any resemblance to actual people living or dead, events or locales is entirely coincidental

.

With special thanks to my husband and children for their belief in this book. Without them, I would not have understood the true meaning of grace.

For the grace . . .
    that redeemed me

Author Note

According to Freedom United (the largest anti-slavery movement in the world), there is an estimated 45.8 million people sold in some form of slavery worldwide. * Most of the world's child labourers live in Asia. It is also estimated that forty percent of African children aged five to fourteen work as servants, miners, factory workers, weavers, prostitutes, and in various other industries. This is also true of some countries in the East where a similar number of girls are employed in manufacturing businesses, or used in the sex trade. Thousands of women and girls become victims of human trafficking in one form or another every day.

This stain on modern civilisation is a matter of urgency. It has extensive consequences for our society as a whole, as it impacts people both socially and economically, notwithstanding the psychological and emotional trauma victims must endure. Thankfully, there are many global organisations trying to eradicate human slavery, but their task is monumental and these crimes still persist.

The author of *Grace's Rescue* hopes to inspire Christians all over the world who so believe in a just God that they would answer the call to pray for the deliverance and freedom of the oppressed. As you read through the pages of this novel, the author's prayer is that you would lift a burning torch for those who are orphaned and hurting. Perhaps there are some among you who feel the burden to engage in such a righteous obligation that you will physically or materially pursue aid for those in need.

The prophet Isaiah declared the acceptable year of the Lord, our Saviour, who came to set the captives free by bearing in his body their pain and sorrow: *Because the Lord has anointed Me to ... heal the brokenhearted, to proclaim liberty to the captives, and the opening of the prison to those who are bound ... To comfort all who mourn ... To give them beauty for ashes, the oil of joy for mourning ... That they may be called trees of righteousness... (Isaiah 61:1–3).*

Dear reader, we are living in the acceptable time of our Lord. Let us take his light to the dark places.

*www.freedomunited.org

PART I

That which is has already been, and what is to be has
already been; and God requires an account of what is past.
Ecclesiastes 3:15

1
South of Colombia, South America
The Cielo

The rik-tik-tik of the fan poised above the woman's bed played a dull duet with the throbbing in her head. She held a thin hand to her brow as she gazed at the ceiling, her body drenched in perspiration. Instinctively she questioned the images entering and exiting her mind like strong tides on a quiet shore. She recognised them—the long march, the siege, people running like wild deer from a mad hunter, and the tall man who had shown her compassion. She could still feel his hands in the clefts of her arms lifting her to a position of safety. Within the maze of her shifting thoughts, the woman saw herself surviving an arduous ordeal; yet here she lay—she knew not where—safe and cared for.

The shuffling of little feet close to the wooden door that barred her from the outside world nudged her awake. The door partially opened, and a young boy stood there, wide-eyed and staring—his tanned face radiant in the falling rays of the afternoon sun. Perhaps it was the way the gentle light trickled into the room or the way the old door hung comfortably in its frame, she could not say, but the woman sensed she was somewhere special. Then, just as strangely as the appearance of the boy, a second person arrived.

'Ah! There you are Sebastian.' The voice was deep

and masculine.

The woman struggled to see the new person. Indistinct images frustrated her attempts to focus. As soon as they cleared, she saw a tall man make his way in.

'I see our niño has found you.' The speaking face was foreign, yet familiar. It smiled at her as it voiced an endearment in Spanish to the youngster, then shooed the child away.

The man was moving towards her now, his actions reassuring. He addressed her with an apologetic gesture. 'You must excuse Sebastian. He's, what you would say, our inquisitive one. Sometimes he forgets his manners.'

The woman focused easier, warming to the man's calming tone. She eyed him closely. Her thoughts cleared as she intuitively calculated his age—mid to late thirties. He walked quietly to her bed and seated himself beside her. *Had she died?* she wondered. *Was this man the heavenly seraph sent to carry her away?* She began to drift again. Quick to observe her withdrawal the caller drew closer. He spoke softly, 'You've suffered greatly, Señorita. We were all worried for you and have sent many prayers to our Saviour for your recovery.'

Then, as if sensing her exhaustion, the man gently squeezed her arm and lowered his voice to a calming whisper. 'I know you have many questions, but the time for answers will come. We must get you recovered first.'

His comforting words sanctioned Grace Kellerman's need for sleep. She closed her eyes, almost instantly returning to her earlier nightmare.

***

Somewhere East of the Tropical Plains

'Señorita, get a move on!'

The jungle air descended on Grace like a blanket. It gagged her senses in its cauldron of thick foliage. Her captor barked his command in a coarse Colombian accent, the timbre of his voice vibrating through the vines of the jungle. They weren't many, those who made up their party of prisoners. Too tired to talk, Grace was at least able to convey that she was the only European; the rest were poor locals—mostly young men. Only one stood out—a boy who could not have been older than sixteen.

Grace sensed she was holding the group back. After suffering for months at her ruthless husband's villa, she did not have enough strength to cope with the physical demands of the journey.

She felt weak. Her scrawny arms clutched onto every bit of outgrowth to aid her forced march through the bayou. Grace recalled having been hauled onto the back of a truck. One of her captors had grabbed her by the waist to steady her landing. Noticing the scars on the insides of her arms, he had shaken his head in disgust. 'Another European slumming on the spoils of our country!' he had mouthed silently. The man eyed her staggered retreat to the back of the vehicle—how pathetic she must have seemed. The truck had sped towards the forest that bordered the edge of the extravagant home she had lived in.

Jolted by the harsh commands of the group's leader, Grace forced her thoughts back to the present. How she would keep up with their fast retreat into the jungle would be a miracle. To make matters worse another complication had reared its head. Grace was injured.

She had sustained a gash to her leg while leaping from the villa's balcony. Her wound, however, seemed to go unnoticed by her captors.

Finally, the exhausted crew reached a small clearing next to a stream. Grace crumpled her body against a tree. Its formidable height rose above the jungle and spread a hazy canopy over them. Although they were not able to feel the sun through the thick cover of scrub, the heat and the torture of insects became insufferable. Grace swatted the air around her. She began to feel faint. Her injury seemed to attract more forest attention than she could endure. The armed guards remained vigilantly close. One of them, in what appeared to be a fleeting moment of kindness, handed her his bandanna. Reluctantly, Grace took the rag.

As the leaders of their group discussed the trail ahead and where they would finally settle, Grace took the opportunity to examine her kidnappers. She wondered what they were going to do with her. Dipping a leaf in the clear water, she patted her forehead and arms with its coolness.

Grace knew she had been captured by a group belonging to a powerful revolutionary organisation. Her husband had rivalled them in illegal drug trafficking. Although she was born in Colombia, Grace had attended an English school and had trained as a teacher at an international university. She thought she had a sound grasp of the Spanish spoken by most in her country; however, Grace was barely able to interpret the rapid dialogue between her captors. The guerilla groups had adopted new ways of using their mother tongue. They refused to use the language of the "imperialists" who ruled over them.

As she rested against the tree, Grace felt she needed to take her mind off her frightening predicament. She searched, as she had on countless occasions, for answers to the many questions that had troubled her. Of one thing she was certain: like so many radical campaigns of revolutionary factions, noble ideas soon slide into lawlessness. Grace had always had a good understanding of the political unrest in her country. Because of her husband's involvement in the drug trade, she knew what she was up against.

The People's Army had emerged out of the ashes when Colombia was thrust into a civil war in the 1940s. Peasants branded as liberals became enemies of the conservative partisans. Each opposing faction protected their land and their people. Inspired by Bolivarianism, they were a peasantry to be reckoned with. The liberal forces funded their operations by distributing illegal drugs and kidnapping for ransom. It was widely accepted that the guerilla warlords committed human rights crimes while holding people hostage in the Colombian jungle. Probably one of the saddest aspects of the war was the recruitment of minors to be trained as soldiers and informants. The ensuing years of political mayhem were therefore aptly referred to as *la violencia,* meaning "the violence".

Like late snow falling in early spring, futile attempts to reconcile differences between the parties dissolved before any promise of change could be established. By the 1950s the Revolutionary Army had entrenched itself as a communist guerilla group, looking for complete power. Grace's parents had been young then. They had experienced firsthand the political consequences of the resistance. Grace realised that unlike some of her fellow captives, she was not "interchangeable", and possibly had a worse fate awaiting her. The guerilla groups used this term to describe political detainees who could be traded for the organisation's prisoners held in Colombian jails.

Nearly all of the kidnappings by the drug lords were politically motivated. Grace suspected that most of her fellow prisoners were victims of a war that had spun out of control. It dawned on her that it was most likely rural workers who had not accepted the rebels' tyrannical rule. However, because of her husband's disloyalty towards these radicals, unlike them she was expendable—a worthless asset without a return. The potential consequences of his betrayal overwhelmed Grace. She had heard stories of people captured by the liberal forces who never escaped the jungles of Colombia. Most of them became fatalities of the heinous minds behind the abductions.

Grace's brief rest was interrupted as the prisoners were ordered to fall into line. Their captors rallied them together while giving further directions for the way ahead. As they trudged along, they were suddenly ordered to slow down. Grace guessed they were nearing their location. In a short while they reached the base camp, and the men busied themselves with plans to secure their captives. Grace found herself, yet again, holding up the pace of the group. Following the other prisoners closely, she frantically grabbed onto one of them to steady herself. Her hair, damp with perspiration, clung miserably to her face. Her rasps for air were the only sounds of desperation rising above the jungle.

Finally, the men forced their prisoners into makeshift cages barricaded by steel bars. The enclosures were strategically placed in the center of the camp. Grace mimicked the tentative motions of her new friends, till she finally settled on a straw bed slightly apart from the others. Curling her body into a tight ball, she tried to rest and ease the ache in her muscles. She tightened the bandanna around her wound. As she lay there, she found that more than her ordeal, her greatest challenge was to reign in the unbridled thoughts that recounted with remarkable clarity the events leading to her capture.

***

A Villa in Pasto, South of Colombia

Tears trickled into the mouth of the woman who lay on a stony pathway that led to a luxurious villa. She could hear the loud pounding of quick-moving footsteps—three, perhaps more, militia moving towards her. With all the strength she could muster, Grace Maria Kellerman clawed at the broken stone. The gravel had served as a frightening landing pad and was now the only leverage she had to lift herself. Her right leg hurt as she pulled herself over a hedge crammed with jasmine flowers. The sweet-smelling shrub separated her from the villa's gate and the outside world.

    Grace glanced up at the villa for the last time. The place that should have been a haven for her had become a prison. She could feel freedom within her reach. Just a little way now and she would meet Gloria at the end of the road. Her escape had been meticulously planned over a period of time. Now, with the militia intent on investigating her husband, her intention to flee had come sooner than expected. Grace hoped that Gloria, her housekeeper, had followed her instructions carefully: *if chaos broke out, they were to immediately go ahead with their plans.*

From the outset Grace had married without love. It was an arranged union, forced upon her to save her family from financial ruin. Grace's father, Jake Kellerman, was a drug runner in Colombia. He was an Englishman who, as a young man, had ventured to the República de Colombia to find his fortune. Jake was no fool. He had used whatever schemes he could to further his success at pilfering money. Jake shamelessly played both sides—the government and the drug cartels always rallying for the highest bidder. He quickly gained a reputation and became known for his muscle and charm, swashbuckling his way through courts and countryside.

It was in the breathtaking mountains of rural Colombia that Jake met Grace's mother, Maria, the daughter of a cartel leader. Maria's father grew cocoa plants for the sole purpose of procuring trade in Colombia's illicit narcotics market.

The glory days of opulent living off dishonest deals melted when political unrest gripped the state of Colombia. Tension developed between the drug lords. Competing for bigger profits increased. It was at this critical moment that Jake ran into difficulties with the heads of the cartels. Grace was a young woman by then, enjoying her first years as a novice English teacher. She taught at a poor Colombian school by choice, enduring her father's disappointment. Maria was a good mother. She supported her daughter's passion for teaching. The woman did her best to protect her only child from her husband's illegal actions. Sadly, Maria's good intentions were not enough to shield Grace from inevitable consequences.

***

Grace did not see the truck that pulled up beside her till a pair of burly arms plucked her from the road and lifted her onto the back of the closed lorry. Her housekeeper was nowhere to be seen. The truck's loud engine vomited strong fumes, deafening Grace's cries for help. Darkness engulfed her as the heavy doors of the vehicle slammed shut. The truck rambled towards the forested hills that bordered the opulent country suburb. She could hear the frightened whispers of her fellow prisoners—some pleading to be released, others silent, just breathing. Her mind conjured strange images, speckled with distorted faces—voices shouting, footsteps advancing.

While Grace spent her days in the cage, she noticed that her fellow prisoners avoided her. The few times she was allowed to take care of her personal needs were the only moments she could think clearly. To keep herself sane, Grace recalled a psalm her mother had frequently recited to her when she was just a child. Grace had always been afraid of storms and the flashes of lightning that accompanied them. For as long as she could remember, the psalm's reassuring words had helped to calm her fears. The sudden recollection of it surprised Grace because she had long since renounced the existence of all things spiritual. This recall, however, was not an uncommon act of God. Little seeds planted in one's heart along life's way present themselves like special gifts at the right time.

Grace recalled her mother cuddling her as they gazed at the moon together. Here they explored a world of new words, rhymes and songs. Together they watched as starlit shadows danced across the silvery pan which hung elegantly in the halls of space. The words of the psalmist, strung poignantly together during his own time of suffering, came back to her...

The Lord is my shepherd; I shall not want. He makes me to lie down in green pastures; He leads me beside the still waters. He restores my soul; He leads me in the paths of righteousness for His name's sake.

Grace could not remember more than the first few lines of the psalm. It was enough, though, to make her feel that she was not alone—to give her some hope of being rescued. Unbeknown to her, a greater power was in fact at work. Grace reached for the soiled cover that lay loosely at the edge of her straw bed and pulled it over her body. Sleep, however, eluded her. Then, to her surprise, Grace heard new voices drift towards the camp. They were faint at first, then close enough to hold her attention. There was singing too. Grace raised her body from the mattress and stretched her neck, to see a small band of people make their way through the thick undergrowth. Their machetes ripped a pathway as their voices rose melodiously above the jungle buzz—a striking unison of faultless notes strung together in perfect harmony. Grace shuffled closer to the bars of the cage. From her vantage point she could see the strong, yet fluid movement of the group. They were led by a male who appeared taller than the rest. The newcomers were undoubtedly not part of her party. Grace sensed there was a courageous air about them. This in itself was unusual. If the merry band had known who they were approaching, they would certainly not have ventured this far.

The group stepped into the clearing where Grace and the other prisoners were kept in the cage. Grace edged closer to get a better look. The rebel leader, a middle-aged Colombian dressed in militia clothes, had rushed forward when he heard the singing. He looked troubled and seemed determined to prevent the foreign party from further intrusion. Then, to Grace's surprise, the man's face broke into a broad, welcoming smile. He appeared to be relieved. *This can't be good*, she thought. *More perpetrators to persecute us*. Still, there was something different about their latest company.

'Ah! Father Joseph. What brings you and your troop of holy minstrels to our neck of the woods?' The man spoke with a thick accent, swaying slightly on his feet—he had been drinking. He flung his arms wide as if to embrace the newcomer he referred to as Father Joseph. Still, he continued to taunt him, 'How've you been, my old friend? Have you come to harass us with your chastisement? To tell us how wayward we've all been?'

A guttural laugh accompanied the rebel's words. He swayed towards the intruders while clutching a glass bottle half filled with an amber liquid. His mocking tore through the jungle and tailed off into the endless ocean of formidable green.

'José! It's good to see you, my brother.' The stranger's reply was unaffected.

Grace moved as close to the bars of the cage as she could, straining her ears to hear more.

'We're here only to bring food and share our Saviour's love. Of course, we've also come equipped to help those who need medical attention.'

A compassionate smile broke across the stranger's face as he spoke to José. He casually waved a hand over the camp as if what was happening there was quite irrelevant compared to the benevolence they had brought with them. The man was clearly familiar with the rebel leader. He maintained a fearless stance while addressing him. Grace suspected that a game of cat and mouse between the two men had begun.

The strangers grouped to sing again. José responded, 'Forgive me, Father. As you can see, we're all resting now. If you don't mind, I've certain indulgences that help me cope with my own mission.'

Lifting his arms, still clutching the half empty bottle, José flung an apology at the stranger. He bowed in mock compliance, welcoming the visiting group.

From where she crouched like a terrified bird poised for flight, Grace could see that José was calmed by the promise of food and medical help. The group got to work quickly and Grace, who barely acknowledged the existence of God, said a silent prayer. Her injury needed urgent attention. She prayed that despite his drunken stupor, José would not forget her. There was something, however, that alerted the visiting group's leader. Grace's bleeding wound had created a tiny trail from the men to her enclosure.

The stranger spoke with calculated patience, 'José, my friend, I notice one of your men is injured. Perhaps it's one of your prisoners.'

The stranger bent down and gently touched the darkening flecks. Then, just as surprised as their first discovery, they were amazed to see the young woman crouched in the cage.

José squinted at first, as if he did not recognise Grace. Then he recalled the English lady with the golden hair. Grace froze—her heart thumping loudly in her chest. Her gaze was fixed on the two men as she clung to the bars of the cage. The man they called Father Joseph seemed surprised that one of the rebel's prisoners was a European woman. Grace noticed that Joseph tried to hide his discovery. It was as if he knew that his finding would place her in further danger. The man distracted José by casually asking one of his helpers to assist the woman in the cage. José summoned one of his men to unlock it while he kept a wary eye on Grace.

Then, just when Grace felt her prayers had finally been answered, the sound of heavy artillery raked through the air for the second time in just a few days. A flurry of people from both groups scattered to seek cover in the shadows of the undergrowth. They were being assailed by a rival drug gang who appeared to have stumbled upon the path leading to their camp.

Anguished shouts and the smell of gunpowder permeated the air. The green haze which permanently hung over the selva opened with sharp flecks of orange.

Grace stayed in the cage. It had been unlocked but she was too frightened to leave. Overcome by waves of panic, her heart pounded. It was becoming increasingly difficult to breathe. 'God, if you are there,' she prayed from lips that struggled to speak, 'help me.'

Then, in what seemed like a dream, Grace became faintly aware of strong hands lifting her. They carried her to a place, far and safe.

***

A village Orphanage, South of Colombia
The Cielo

The gentle voices below her window woke Grace. It took all her strength to peel away the damp sheets that clung to her body. Her leg still ached. As she made her way to the open window, a faint breeze touched her upturned face with the morning's freshness. The small gathering of children in the far corner of the cobbled courtyard continued their heavenly chorus, oblivious of their admirer.

The children, boys and girls of varying ages, were dressed in plain clothes. Their sandalled feet tapped softly to the music they created. Their faces were turned upward—aglow with spiritual adulation. Somewhere in the distance a rooster crowed and a stray pup whimpered for its mother. Grace breathed in the comforting words of their song. She examined the space below her. There was nothing pretentious about the place that sheltered her. The ancient structural design of the stone buildings and the pervading ambiance seemed to be some sort of haven for destitute children. She wondered whether the tall man who had rescued her was the overseer. Relieved, Grace felt she had been saved from her old life where fear lurked beneath extravagance and deception.

As she stood at the window, the door to her room was suddenly pushed open by a stout woman wearing a nun's habit. Her chubbiness hid her years. She gracefully manoeuvred her large frame into the space that had become Grace's quiet sanctuary.

The nun spoke rapidly in broken English. Her eyes were warm.

'Oh, no, what's this I see, eh?' The woman faced Grace squarely.

'It's time to rise and shine, my little tomato.' The nun spoke to Grace as if they had been friends for a long time.

If this was the older woman's way of lifting Grace's spirits, her plan worked. Grace found an involuntary smile skirt the corners of her mouth.

The nun continued her introduction in a kind yet commanding way, 'We'll get you right, Señorita. Mama Sofia will take good care of you, no?'

It was the nun's gallant way of addressing Grace, her mirthful countenance and jumbled use of the English language stealing Grace's heart from the outset.

The woman patted the space beside her, and Grace lowered herself onto the unmade bed.

'You sit, Señorita. I'll feed you.'

Grace obeyed the brusque orders of the nun, who hauled a bowl of palatable soup and some crusty bread from the ghostly sleeves of her large habit. Grace was amazed at the woman's energy. She stifled a smile and relaxed with her new friend.

'There's a time, Señorita, when you must lead and there is a time when you must follow. Now is the time for you to follow, no?'

Mama Sofia lifted the spoon to Grace's lips. It was drenched in a fragrant liquid. She gave her new charge a reassuring nod. Grace was surprisingly hungry. She enjoyed the uplifting effect the place was having on her.

While the nun helped her to finish the soup, Grace contemplated the woman's words, *Now is the time for you to follow*.

Mama Sofia did not realise how this simple phrase resonated with Grace. Her journey through life had always been a rocky one, and had more often than not been fraught with disappointment. Had the time come for her to finally let go and be led by another? Grace had been rescued by these gracious people, but she did not want to become a burden to them. She had always fought her battles alone. How was she going to let go and allow another to fight on her behalf? The thought of complete surrender frightened her.

After she had eaten the soup, Sofia took hold of one of Grace's arms. She ran a chubby hand over the scars that drew a perfidious path along the inside. One particular wound was not healing well. Sofia dabbed at it with a tincture of pleasant-smelling oil. She began to hum a sweet melody, moving gently to the rhythm of her own voice. This kindly gesture touched Grace. Without asking her about her evident drug abuse, Mama Sofia seemed to understand the young woman's struggles.

As Grace basked in the attention Sofia gave her, she was able to take a closer look at her companion. Grace noticed that one of Sofia's eyes was tightly shut, perhaps the result of an old injury. She imagined the woman had not led a life without difficulty.

Sofia gave Grace a tonic, never faltering in the melody she hummed. The young woman felt herself yielding to the tender promptings of the nun. Like a wide-eyed fawn surveying its world for the first time, Grace began to understand that the gifts of love and mercy had been there all along. She had just not known how to make them her own.

Sofia's remedies began to take effect. Feeling drowsy, Grace lowered her body onto the bed. Sofia glanced at the wooden cross suspended above the lintel of the bedroom door. "Señorita, stones are only made smooth by the water rushing over them. Open your heart that it might become soft again."

Before leaving, the nun added, 'You can call me, Mama. Now sleep, my little berry.' This time she quietly closed the door behind her.

Before drifting again, Grace's curiosity got the better of her. She inspected the inscription below the cross. It read, *Come to Me, all you who labor and are heavy laden, and I will give you rest. Matthew 11:28.*

The cross that hung there was more of a spiritual symbol than object d'art. Grace began to think about her own life. She read the scripture again. She felt the sails of her own turbulent soul begin to fold and anchor in the safe harbour of the haven. With these tranquil thoughts she closed her eyes and began to dream.

In her dream, Grace was seated beside a crystal stream when a large hand, radiant with light, scooped from the water. Grace lifted her face while the hand poured the pure liquid into her mouth. Then the sky, a scintillating blue, opened. A flock of colourful birds brought small loaves of fresh bread to her. She took the sustenance and ate, thinking that it was the most satisfying food she had ever eaten. Grace felt lost in the dream's interpretation. Before she woke, however, a fleeting image of children representing various nations flashed before her—their white smiles were radiant in their smooth faces.

***

Grace spent most of her time recovering in bed. Only occasionally did she venture to her window to take in some air. This happened mostly when she heard the children singing, or when their laughter wafted pleasantly into her room like a leaf caught in the wind. She received constant care from Sofia and also the priest, who checked in with her whenever he could.

The children brought to her a stream of self-made get-well cards. They were decorated with flowers from the garden, and their messages were written in broken English. The cards helped to lift Grace's spirits while she struggled with the effects of diminishing addiction.

Grace learned that the haven was appropriately called The Cielo, a Colombian phrase meaning 'Little Heaven'. The haven was an orphanage run by an Anglican priest who went by the name of Father Joseph. At first, Grace did not see much of the man who ran the mission. She did feel, however, that it was the priest who encouraged the people who lived at the refuge to help her get better. Grace sensed that it was their constant prayers that were helping her find strength to overcome the issues she had wrestled with for so long. She was surrounded by people who cared for her. Here she felt that the freedom she had once dreamed of was indeed possible.

It was in the early days of Grace's rescue that her heart began to open to the gracious way in which the people at the orphanage ministered the love of God to her. Their unreserved affection illuminated the dark paths she had trodden. She began to see more clearly the true state of her heart. She alone could not repair what had been fractured. She knew her healing had to come from a higher source.

One morning Grace took the opportunity to revisit one of the many questions she had asked the nun. It had been a peculiar thing that since the confines of her heart had opened, so too had issues, deeply buried, start to surface. Their persistence troubled Grace, though she felt she could trust Sofia.

'Why is forgiveness so important to a person's healing?' Grace's candor caught Sofia by surprise. The nun had wondered when the beautiful señorita would open up to her. Sofia gave Grace's pillow a generous fluffing, and placed it at the head of the bed. She sat down to give the young woman her full attention.

Sofia listened patiently as Grace continued, 'How can I simply forget the terrible things others have done to me?' Grace lifted her shoulders sharply and sighed. 'What I mean to ask is, how do I just put it all behind me? I look at the children here and see that they've much to forgive those who were meant to care for them. My own troubles seem small in comparison.' Grace looked at Sofia with desperation in her eyes, then she sat beside the nun.

'My dear Señorita,' Sofia drew closer to Grace, her voice fixed with compassion, 'it is human to forgive and this we must do, but it is only God who can truly forget.'

The nun eyed Grace comfortingly. 'I think this is where we get it all mixed up, no? We want to forgive and forget at the same time. Because we find it difficult to forget, we think we have not forgiven.' Sofia patted Grace's hand before she added, 'A past not remembered is a present we must live with. The human soul is like a woman who sells her fruit in the market square. She keeps her best produce hidden under the perishing ones. Only when the sun has faded will she be ready to sell her finer produce, and at a very good price. Sometimes the woman sells this fruit when it is too early and the sun has destroyed her best intentions. You will carry the memory of your pain till you can carry it no longer. Then, when it must reveal itself, your heart will ask a high price of you. You'll either have to forgive your abusers or be crushed by the torment of it all.'

Sofia's good eye moistened as she spoke to Grace. 'Señorita, you must ask God to help you remember what it is that makes you unhappy so that he can help you to forgive. It must have no other purpose than to heal your heart and to give you a future free from anger.'

Grace listened carefully—she wanted to hear more. 'There is so much evil in this world. People suffer daily at the hands of others.'

Since she was a compassionate woman, Sofia treated Grace's questions amiably. 'Señorita, no man is truly able to forgive his abuser. Only God can do that miracle in our hearts. He is only looking for our willingness to forgive. God is able to perform in us what is impossible for us to do ourselves.'

Sofia touched Grace's arm. 'If you've already chosen to forgive but your heart tells you that you've not achieved this courageous deed, don't worry, for God is bigger than your heart. He understands all things. He'll make a way for everything to be right again.'

Perhaps it was time to tell Grace her own story. The nun had always believed that sharing a personal experience was far better a teacher than many words with little understanding.

'For me, Señorita, my appointment with forgiveness came early. I was young then and quite slim, although you wouldn't say that of me now.' Sofia winked at Grace and exhaled a light chuckle. 'You see I have only one eye. Back then I was quite pretty, with two healthy eyes. I was a good girl—just sixteen. I helped my parents raise our big family. I had eight siblings. Most of them, I'm sad to say, are not alive today—only my two brothers. The youngest is Pepe, and the second eldest is Toleda. Unfortunately, my brothers are with the People's Army who've hired them to do terrible things to our people.'

Sofia wiped a stray tear from her good eye before she continued. 'My brothers and their fellow comrades tried to persuade me to become a revolutionary. They wanted me to join them in their struggle for our people's freedom. I was, however, always wary of their schemes. Since I was quite mature for my age, I could tell they were spreading lies. They even encouraged rebellion amongst the villagers. The people in our community are poor. The leaders of the revolution were getting rich by exploiting them.'

There was a glint in Sofia's good eye. 'Señorita, I didn't hesitate to speak of my beliefs till all in our village knew I would not be a part of the People's Army. Those who supported the rebellion became angry with me. They said I was causing a revolt of my own. This wasn't the truth of course.'

Sofia's cheeks reddened.

'One afternoon, while returning from the market, a terrible thing happened to me. It had been a long day and I could only leave for my village when the sun had lost her strength. Our home was quite far from the market, so I thought to take a shortcut through an alleyway behind one of the poorer neighbourhoods. There I was accosted by two men dressed in militia uniforms. They warned me to stop spreading lies.'

Sofia's face softened. She took a deep breath before she went on, 'During the scuffle with my attackers, one of my eyes was badly injured. I didn't know it then, but despite the efforts of our village doctor, I would never be able to see from it again.'

Grace placed her hand over the nun's chubby one while Sofia continued. 'Just when I thought there was no escape for me, I heard shouting coming from the far end of the alley. A man, a stranger, ran towards us. He shouted to the men to leave me alone. The sudden disturbance of their wicked act startled them, and they let me go. I learned later that the man who saved my life that day was an Anglican priest by the name of Father Ralph. He's the old priest who founded The Cielo and turned it into a haven for orphaned children.'

Sofia had an amazing ability to change from one state of being to another in a wink. She let out a short chuckle before she said, 'Señorita, I may have lost an eye, but I was introduced to a great truth that day. It's better to forgive those who have wronged you than to walk the rest of your life crippled by an unwillingness to pardon.'

'How did you come to be here?'

'Señorita, that incident happened long ago. I've lived at The Cielo since the day of the assault. Now I help Father Joseph. He took ownership of the orphanage when Father Ralph became too old to continue his work here.'

Then, just as pleasantly hurried as she had been when Sofia first met Grace, the nun gathered her large habit and stood up. Her face was beaming. 'Señorita, I must declare that all this talk about forgiveness is making my head spin, and when Mama Sofia gets dizzy, she must have something to eat, no?'

Grace laughed.

'I think, Señorita, the time has come for you to join us all in the dining hall. I'm sure you will enjoy one of the delicious pies Roberto sends to the orphanage every Friday. Let me help you get ready.'

Grace gave in to her new friend's nudging. She agreed to join the family in the dining area. This would be the first time she would share a meal with everyone.

She made her way down the wooden stairs with Sofia firmly at her side. A ray of light streamed through a gap in one of the windows. Although the building should have felt cold, it was strangely warm. As Grace entered the cozy place, the children stood together and welcomed her with sheepish grins and bashful stares. Father Joseph stayed longer on his feet, then he made his way towards her. Grace was still unsteady—the trip from her room had left her feeling shaky. The priest quickly closed the gap between them and steadied Grace as she sat in the chair at the head of an unusually long table which was fenced by wide-eyed onlookers.

'There now,' Joseph said reassuringly.

Grace thanked him, feeling a little conspicuous. She realised that his kind gesture was not intended to embarrass her, but rather to give her special recognition in the haven's family.

'You're looking much better today, Señorita,' Joseph offered. 'What would you like us to call you?' The priest's eyes scanned the inquisitive audience before returning to Grace.

'Grace. You can call me Grace.' Grace's shyness faded as she relished the warm smiles of her new friends.

'Then that's what we'll call you.'

There was a twinkle in his eye before Joseph continued. 'Grace is the perfect name, Señorita, specially chosen for you.' His voice trailed, as if he knew something she did not. The priest's words sent beams of white smiles around the table. Grace had not felt like this in a long while. She settled then, feeling less self-conscious and more at ease with her new companions.

The children were surprisingly well-mannered. Grace sensed that they had a deep respect for Father Joseph and Mama Sofia. Other adults gathered at the table were volunteer helpers. Grace's meal was pleasantly interrupted from time to time for the priest to introduce them to her.

Joseph offered to help Grace to her room when she had finished her meal. At first there was an awkward silence between them as they ascended the stairs together. It did not take Grace much, however, to realise that her chaperone had an amazing gift of making one feel at ease. Joseph smiled frequently at her while he steadied her slow climb with his hand. He seemed to be inviting her to speak. While his eyes were fixed on her, Joseph accidentally stepped on her long, cotton dress. He gave her a deep grin and mumbled an apology. Before he left her, Joseph encouraged Grace to continue to call on Sofia, who was only a door away. He added that she should continue to rest as much as she could and that he was happy with her progress.

Finally, Joseph said what Grace felt he had wanted to say all along. 'Señorita… Grace, I know you lost your husband in that terrible incident at your villa. This is a great burden you carry alone. We see you've suffered much. Do you want to talk about it?'

Grace turned slightly from Joseph. She took a deep breath and then replied, 'Thank you, Joseph, but right now I see only an empty space in front of me. Where I know there should be grief, I feel nothing. I don't think I'm ready to speak about it all just yet.'

Grace paused before continuing. 'I do want to thank you, though, for rescuing me and for all the love and care the people here have shown me. I feel so much better already and don't wish to burden you all any longer.'

'You'll never be a burden to us. This is what we are here for—to help those who are hurting. You'll stay with us as long as God intends.' Joseph placed a comforting hand over hers.

Grace noticed the dark lashes that touched the

priest's face as he closed his eyes for a millisecond. Her husband had been good-looking, with an annoying sense of self-importance. Although Joseph was not particularly handsome, he was strong in stature. The self-confidence he carried was clearly not acquired through material wealth but rather from an inner strength fortified by the compassion he showed for the suffering.

While she stood there, contemplating the extraordinary person beside her, Grace unexpectedly felt her defenses weaken. As if sensing her unease, the priest bent politely across her. Taking care not to touch her, he opened the bedroom door with a promise to check on her later. Before turning to leave, he added, 'You can call me Joseph.'

With that he was gone.

The rest of the day slipped by quietly. Near evening, Grace had fallen into a peaceful sleep. She did not notice Sofia check on her, nor did she see the nun turn away with the satisfaction that Grace would not need her medication that night.

This ritual characterised Grace's rehabilitation at The Cielo, which continued for many days under the watchful care of Sofia and Joseph. There was never any mention by either of them of the suffering she had experienced. Her addiction began to release its hold on her and although withdrawal was a part of her healing, Grace sensed that the people at The Cielo were continuously offering prayers for her full recovery to the one they called Saviour.

2

As the days turned into weeks, Grace was in awe of all things at The Cielo. Usually, she shared breakfast and other mealtimes with her new family. Some of her meals, though, were taken up to her when she felt too tired to venture out. Occasionally, when Grace had small lapses she stayed in her room to be cared for only by Sofia and Joseph. During these moments the nun and the priest read to her from a small book carried on their person.

Grace was quick to learn that the people at the haven had a connection with each other that she had not experienced in her own relationships. Treasuring every minute together, those at The Cielo used mealtimes to gather for prayer, and work as a time to worship. God was presented as a merciful and loving Father. Everything they did was an expression of their devotion to him.

Grace could feel that she was beginning to put the pieces of her troubled life back together. Her detoxification routines were going well, and she felt a long-buried sense of urgency to embrace life with all her being. The devotion of the people at the orphanage to her recovery breathed fresh hope into her.

One morning Grace woke early to the sound of native birds chirping in the overhanging trees outside her window. She had become an admirer of the treetops whose branches, heavy with fragrant blossoms, intertwined like young men dancing with their partners tightly in their arms. There was something abuzz at the haven. She peeped through the window hoping to confirm her suspicions when the door opened with a loud knock. An exuberant Sofia waltzed in.

'Señorita, how wonderful to see that you're awake.' Sofia wrapped her arms around Grace.

'I'm so glad you're up early, my little berry. There are many special gifts waiting for you today. I'm sure you're eager to find out what they are, no?'

Grace loved the way the nun was able to pick up on the slightest changes in her recovery and turn them into moments of celebration.

'Father Joseph has requested I get you ready for a special occasion. He believes it's time for you to join us for a day in the beautiful sunshine.' With her gentle yet firm instructions, Sofia bustled around Grace's sparsely furnished room tidying invisible items.

The thought of stepping into a world that had been threatening for so long made Grace tingle with excitement. She walked over to Sofia with a raised eyebrow.

'And what might this occasion be, Mama?' Grace placed her hands squarely on either side of her hips, pretending to threaten Sofia into an early disclosure.

'It's the annual soccer championships of El Encano. Everyone from all the villages attends. Father Joseph is the top scorer of this grand event. It's the perfect time for you to celebrate the wonderful miracle of life our Saviour has given you.'

Sofia chatted to Grace as if she were a daughter of her own. These moments given frequently by the people at The Cielo fueled Grace's desire to heal. Today would be the first of many outings with her new family. Today she would have the opportunity of feeling the sun stroke her face with the warmth of its celestial hands. Today her heart would beat to the rhythm of the children's laughter and the people's cheering.

With these pleasant thoughts combing her mind, Grace prepared herself for the trip to the village grounds. She washed her face and ran a brush through her hair. Its natural, golden streaks shone like the sun outside. Grace eyed the dresses Sofia had given her. They were printed in indigenous colours and designs. Although the frocks were clearly second-hand, she treated them as new. To her, the clothing represented the new lease of life she had been given. She put one of the dresses on, then ran her hands over the unique prints. An embroidered circle in the centre of the dress depicted the solar strength of the intense Colombian sun. A tropical bird balanced the yellow ball on the tip of its curved beak.

'No time for dreaming!' Sofia playfully hurried Grace as she finished dressing. It was not long before they were both at the entrance of the orphanage, ready for their ride to the great event.

Grace was amused to see a cart drawn by two strong-looking mules waiting lazily in the stony access. Joseph sat perched on the long wooden seat at the front of the cart. He was clearly the one in command of the ingenious means of transport. Grace silently hoped their destination was not miles away. Some of the haven's children had climbed into the nooks of the cart. Most of them, however, were quite happy to walk alongside the mules, which were clearly no competition for them anyway. Grace grinned as she met Joseph's eyes.

The priest touched the tip of his straw hat. 'Ah, Señorita, it's good that you can join us today. There has been much speculation amongst our little people as to whether you would accompany us or not.' He gave her a wink. 'I'm happy to say I've won the wager, which will be an extra bag of peanuts for me at the tournament.'

Joseph smiled broadly, 'I see Mama Sofia has provided you with the perfect dress.'

He swept his gaze briefly over her attire. Grace thought she felt her cheeks warm. Before there was anything further to say, the priest summoned one of the little girls he referred to as Cassia. The child carried in her hand a straw hat, similar to the one Joseph wore, though it was garlanded with pretty flowers loosely fastened around the edge. Cassia did not take her eyes off Joseph. It was as if she needed constant reassurance from the priest, who gave the child an encouraging nod.

Cassia handed the hat to Grace before she ran off to find her own spot in the wagon. Grace thanked them both for the kind gesture, wondering why the little girl seemed unable to speak.

Joseph patted the seat beside him, and Grace joined him before they rambled towards the soccer field. She felt like an adolescent again, enjoying the soft breeze as it touched her face and lifted her hair. Relishing the children's laughter and Joseph's protective presence, Grace felt alive and content. It turned out that the grounds were not far from the orphanage after all. Grace had the distinct impression that the priest had organised this unusual means of transport especially for her to experience their way of life.

The turf was no more than a large sandy area interspersed with patches of dry grass. It did not, however, deter the people who had gathered there. Grace's first impression of the rural folk were that they were an animated, colourful, and lively group.

She scanned their tawny faces. Some sported wide, toothless smiles; others imitated the heroes and heroines they followed on their television sets by dressing like them. It was a coming together with one purpose in mind—to contribute, and to be partakers in the celebrations. The tournament was a good reason for them all to enjoy the music and food together.

The wonderful day filled with joyful exchanges amongst the competitors and spectators eventually drew to a close. Father Joseph's team won the impressive trophy and, as predicted, the priest had scored the winning goal. The victory cup was nothing more than a giant, brightly coloured rooster made from traditional fabric and straw. Grace later discovered that the trophy was freshly made each year by Mama Sofia. Although nothing extravagant, the prize depicted the humble yet soulful wealth of the folk who attended the annual event.

Finally, the victory emblem was flung into the air by the jubilant crowd. The priest was, in no quiet way, hoisted on the shoulders of the village folk.

Grace was overwhelmed by the popularity Joseph engendered. He was clearly loved by everyone. She could not help but feel a twinge of sadness; all her life she had fought for such a love. Putting the thought from her mind, she took a deep breath. The smell of roasted peanuts, empanadas packed with ground beef and cilantro, and cheese breads, filled the air. Grace lifted her eyes to the azure skies, thinking that the day's events could certainly have been a slice of heaven.

They arrived at The Cielo as the sun began to retreat behind the low hills of the countryside. It had been a long day for the children. They were given their dinner and instructed to turn in. The nun had arranged for Joseph and

Grace to have a light snack on the patio. Grace noticed a mischievous twinkle in Sofia's good eye. The older woman closed the wooden doors that led from the terrace to the house.

Grace sat under the umbrella of a fragrant climber and waited for Joseph. The moon began to sway casually behind the tall trees that surrounded the expansive garden. The smell of nighttime flora traced a scented path near her.

The priest stepped onto the terrace, his dark hair still moist from his shower. Grace was ravenous. She had refused the many Colombian delights offered to her at the tournament. She mused that this was much like the old Grace—living without a thought for her own needs. At one point Grace noticed Joseph frown at her, but he had quickly turned back to engage the volunteer he was with.

Grace's thoughts turned to the man now seated beside her. There was so much she admired about Joseph. He was someone who could clearly have had it all, yet here he was, the overseer of an orphanage for abandoned children. The priest was as content as the steely moon behind them—at ease with his purpose in the great cosmos of existence. He had shown Grace that a person's spirituality was indeed a way of life—deeply affecting others.

Questions continued to churn in her mind. *Why had Joseph chosen to be a steward to those whom the rest of the world had clearly rejected? How had he come to personally know the God he freely served?*

As if reading her thoughts, Joseph surprised Grace with a striking statement. 'It's grace who found me, Señorita.' His voice was soft.

Grace contemplated Joseph's words. She believed

that although they were plain enough, they were profoundly significant for the man with her.

'You speak of grace as if it were a person.' Her eyes were wide and inquiring.

'Grace *is* a person, Señorita. It is Christ, the most merciful act of God towards humanity. It is the gift of his Son to the world.'

The priest looked at her. His voice filled with compassion. 'It will always be about grace finding you. The human heart has a natural inclination to wander from the path that leads to life—a battle for self-preservation. Oftentimes it sets itself up for ruin. The heart does not naturally want to do things God's way. That's why, like the gentle cooing of a dove, God calls you and me, mostly in the dire moments of our lives, to be rescued by him.'

Grace thought of all the battles she had waged throughout her life, and particularly her latest one. She would have been dead had it not been for the priest.

'My father taught me to fight for everything I wanted. He said there'd always be others ready to take from me that which I couldn't hold onto. Sadly, he didn't show me how to fight for love.'

There was a flicker of sympathy in Joseph's eyes. 'We all feel we must fight for what we need, Señorita. We seldom know what's really good for us. A boat sails in the ocean deep, allowing the wind to blow it wherever it wishes. It's only the strong and sturdy hand of the skipper that will keep it on course… and help it reach its destination.'

Joseph leaned forward before he continued.

'I'll explain by means of a story. If you'll pardon me, I use simple illustrations—they help the children understand truths hidden in God's Word. Nonetheless, I believe you'll find the tale quite intriguing.'

He cleared his throat before he began, 'A wealthy man set out on his horse one day. He hoped to find the purest bride for his only son. He searched far and wide for such a prize. In return, this bride would be loved unconditionally by his son. She would have at her disposal many beautiful things. Her children would also bear his name, and all his wealth would be theirs. Although the man was rich and could have whatever he wanted, in all his searching he could not find the woman he desired. One day he came across a village called Plentiful. The man was told that here he would find the finest women in the land. The first woman he saw was indeed beautiful. In fact, there were many like her, but the wealthy man could see by the way they behaved that their affection for the material things of this world would be more than their love for his son.'

Catching his breath, Joseph continued. 'The man had all but given up. He was ready to leave the village when his eye caught the figure of a young beggar woman sitting in the street. The woman cried out to him, imploring the man to have mercy on her. It was quite plain to see that this woman was not worthy of the rich man's attention. Her only hope was that by some miracle the wealthy man would take pity on her.'

Joseph straightened his shoulders. 'Señorita, grace is an unjustifiable gift. It is an example of the most extravagant love given by the God of our universe to the undeserving. Grace is for those who will call out to him when they cannot fight their own battles any longer. It is for those who will completely surrender their hearts to him.'

Before ending his story, the priest turned to look

at the moon. 'The rich man was filled with compassion. He lifted the shabby woman onto the back of his horse and took her to his palace. There his maidservants meticulously prepared her for the great wedding day where she would be united with his son. A simple tale, Señorita, the way the grace of God should be explained.'

Grace reflected on the beautiful story for a while. She turned her attention to the irresistible glow of the night sky. There they were, just the two of them, looking up at the moon together as if it were an intermediary. Grace had never felt more at peace.

'You share this story as if it were a romance—a narrative of your own. My experience of religion was the exact opposite until I came here. I was always surrounded with people who debated faith till the argument was more important than the intended message.'

Grace looked at Joseph. 'I've not heard it shared the way you have… where God comes looking for us. It is as much of a mystery to me as you are, Señor.'

She lowered her gaze. Grace was afraid her eyes would betray the deep gratitude she felt.

Joseph moved closer to her. He placed a hand on her shoulder, and then with the other he found her cheek.

'That's better,' he said.

Grace realised that with the priest there could be no secrets—no turning one's face away. He would always be there for her, just as he was for the entire family at The Cielo. Joseph was like an impenetrable wall, poised to shelter and protect.

Grace smiled, suddenly feeling self-conscious.

'What is your story, Señor, or were you always like this… born with an iron will and a heart as unfathomable as our beloved Colombia?'

Joseph stretched his tall frame before answering her. 'Our streets. They hold the tragic tales of many young men and women... of innocence lost. Their stones cry out for the vengeance of its children.' His voice was thick, as if at that moment he was reliving the experiences of his youth.

'I was raised practically on the streets of the poor suburbs of Medellin. Some say it's the most dangerous city in the world. I was born into a large, impoverished family—my story isn't that different from most of the young people in Colombia.' Joseph placed a firm foot on the bench in front of him and leaned toward Grace, arms casually slung over one knee. 'Attending a poor state school during the day and hustling at night is the only childhood I knew. When I was fifteen, I joined a gang and felt like a prince most of the time.'

A cautious smile crept across Joseph's face as he seated himself beside Grace again. He spoke to her more earnestly now, raking a hand through his dark hair. 'This was such a long time ago, Señorita. It's only by God's grace that I'm able to remember it all.'

Joseph went on. 'I felt the life of a gangster was all there was for me. It became like a drug. I'd be elated when I was recognised for doing something illegal, but afterwards I would feel awful for disappointing my poor mother who tried to instill good values in me.'

Grace was struck by Joseph's candid recount of his life as a youngster. 'How did you cope with all the guilt?'

'We used drugs and alcohol quite freely. We were deceived into thinking that they would help numb the shame of our crimes. I was making more money than my father and older brother who worked as farm hands in the plantations. I felt I had the power to do whatever I pleased with the cash I earned. I was also not willing to listen to anyone. I'd become so full of anger that no one was willing to instruct me in anything decent. One day, a terrifying yet remarkable thing happened to me.'

Joseph's voice lifted, finding its usual confidence.

'I was just seventeen, when my life was changed forever.'

A faint shadow of unshaven stubble appeared on the priest's jawline. Grace, who had never considered Joseph handsome, thought he looked quite striking in his white shirt and dark jeans—a mystical figure against a night of revelatory experiences.

'I dropped out of school at an early age. This is quite common amongst the high-risk children of Colombia. I got into some deep trouble. Selling drugs was always at the root of our scrapes, especially when we came up against the officials of the Revolutionary Army. Nevertheless, I became increasingly fearless, risking more lucrative deals. Our gang began to follow the drug transits, waiting for the day we could enjoy the spoils of a mission gone wrong. That day came, Señorita. Our little band of bravados managed to secure some narcotics through the botched hijacking of a truck carrying a large shipment. With it, however, came a whole bunch of Colombian police. I only realised sometime later how corrupt the whole system was. The hijackers and the police were prejudiced by their dishonest dealings with each other, and they had only one thing in mind—to get rid of us. I never saw my three friends again.'

Joseph paused before he went on. Grace could see that although the incident had happened a long time ago, the priest still kept the memory of it.

His jaw tightened. 'While one of the hijackers held

onto me, a senior member of the group discussed my fate. He was concerned about my age. They could see I was younger than my friends. Eventually, they decided to release me into a deep well that had been dry for some years in a nearby field. My disappearance would look like an accident, they said. It wouldn't cause too much of an uproar amongst the villagers, because they're quite protective of the drug cartels' influence over their children. I realised later that this was an act of God. The men seemed to know where they were taking me. Soon we were there, me and two of the men, standing in front of that old well.'

Joseph's tone became serious, 'My heart was beating so fast.' He looked at Grace, 'Señorita, I've experienced much hardship in my life, but I've never known terror as I did that day. I thought it must be the end. Suddenly from nowhere, I heard a voice—loud and powerful. It made its way towards us. The stranger ordered the men to let me go. One of the men shouted to his friends to release me. The hijacker called out the intruder's name in reverent terror, and the men immediately left me there, in a cloud of dust. Then, through the haze a lone figure appeared. It was a man holding a wooden cross in front of him. He was uttering incantations in what I assumed was Latin. The stranger helped me to my feet, and then he proceeded to greet me quite casually, as if rescuing wayward seventeen-year-olds was normal for him.'

Joseph smiled at Grace. He seemed to relax. 'I remember the man's words clearly, "So, this is young Joe. I've been praying for you and waiting patiently for the good Lord to send you across my path." He spoke to me as if we were exchanging personal stories in the market. He then said something which, at the time, puzzled me,

"I've come to give you good news, Joe. Your days of fighting are over and I'm here to help you become the young man God intends you to be."'

Joseph chuckled. 'Señorita, I asked myself, "Who is this crazy man and why does he tease me so when I've just had a meeting with death?" I was still shaken after my ordeal, but nevertheless I quietly submitted and allowed the man to help me. That was the beginning of my return. The dear priest later became a mentor and true father to me.'

Grace was intrigued with Joseph's life story. She wanted to know more. 'What happened then?'

'Well, after some time at The Cielo, and following many a rebellious wrangling with Father Ralph who, I must add, patiently carried me on his shoulders, I began to find my true purpose in life. I learned from the priest that a real man was one whose heart followed the example of Jesus.'

As Grace continued to listen to Joseph, she wanted to hear more about the love and grace that had saved him. 'Did you ever find out why your kidnappers let you go the way they did?'

'Father Ralph had a reputation for being a spiritual thundercloud, if you will permit me to describe him this way. The village folk, including the gangsters, believed he was a saint—a true servant of God. It was said that he could walk on water, heal the sick, and raise the dead. A story was once told where a small Christmas cake, enough to feed only eight people, was multiplied to feed over a thousand children when Father Ralph blessed it.'

He shrugged. 'When the old priest found me, my personal struggles came to an end. The freedom I came to know could not be bought by me. I was too weak. The price for my salvation was too high. True liberty is a gift given freely to all who will receive it. Not by what we can or cannot do, but just by simply receiving it.'

Grace listened carefully. She felt her heart begin to open to the priest's message. A sensitivity she had not felt before nudged at her. Grace looked at him, unsure of what to say.

As if sensing her struggle, Joseph changed the course of his conversation. 'Father Ralph did something quite special for me. He discovered that I had a reading problem. Letters on a page huddled like stars in a milky sky when I read! My impoverished upbringing along with the learning difficulty—well, they were a recipe for youthful rebellion… just like many boys in my position. Father Ralph patiently helped me through my education. His special attention to my challenges pulled me through. Later I went to a university and earned two degrees. After my tertiary training, I decided to return to The Cielo. Father Ralph was growing old, and I felt it would only be right for me to help him with the good work he had started here. What began as a duty, turned into a passion—it consumed my life—and now I'm here, Señorita, just as God intended from the beginning.'

Joseph's open-necked shirt accentuated his tanned skin, and for the first time that evening Grace noticed a small yet conspicuous tattoo etched on the skin beneath his collarbone. She could feel her heart beat in her chest. There was so much to learn from this man. His personal story, she was certain, was just the half of it.

The evening continued pleasantly. Grace noticed that Joseph did not pry into the affairs of her life, nor did he question why he had found her in such a life-threatening predicament. He seemed focused on getting her well again.

Joseph eventually drew the discussion to a close. 'If you'll excuse me, Señorita, I'd better turn in. Tomorrow I must leave for America. From time to time, I travel there to report to the people who support our work here. I'll return in a few weeks.'

As he made way for Grace to step in front of him, Joseph added, 'I almost forgot. I've left a gift for you, but you'll only get it tomorrow.'

This time Joseph winked at Grace, and his smile deepened.

Grace thanked him for the day. 'I had a wonderful time. Everyone has been so kind to me. I don't know how I'll ever repay you all.'

The kiss was not familiar. It came sweetly, planted on Grace's forehead, as if Joseph wished to seal his loyalty to her.

Grace made her way to her room, feeling pleasantly tired and peaceful.

***

Grace woke the following morning to some noise outside her window. Much of what Joseph had said the night before still swirled in her head. She felt an urgency to know more about Jesus—the one who Joseph knew and loved.

The priest and his personal assistant were the reason for the small commotion. Grace looked on as Pedro opened a wide gate to a spacious shed opposite the courtyard. She leaned against the window, observing the two. It was not long before she heard the engine of a seldom-used sedan as it reversed out of the shed. Pedro was driving, and Grace assumed the two were making an early start for Joseph's departure. She watched as Joseph leaned forward in his seat. He stretched his neck to look up, not expecting to see Grace standing there.

The faint morning rays silhouetted her still figure behind the window's frame. Grace's eyes, softly visible, returned his gaze. They locked for a brief moment. Joseph did not smile at her. Still, she felt her heart race.

She knew she would miss him.

Grace noticed a slight movement in a tree near her window. A male brush finch was perched steadily on a twig. The bird thrust out its densely feathered yellow-and-white chest. It was supported by a small head, masked with slick dark feathers—a gladiator readying for war. The seemingly insignificant image of a native bird looking for the attention of a female sent a special message to Grace.

Her heart, like the breast of the male bird, was ready. Today she would learn about God and the love he would show her through others. Mama Sofia had said to her that the poor in spirit were to be blessed, 'These are the words of Christ. It is his acts of love that make the human spirit rich.'

Grace got ready for breakfast. She was pleased to be the first to arrive in the dining hall. The main table stretched solidly before her, and the smell of cleaning detergent and fresh table linen hung in the air. Grace welcomed the cool breeze that drifted through the cracks in the ancient stones.

She was not seated long when Sofia bustled into the eating area. The nun smiled mischievously at her. 'Ah, there's my little lemon. You are first at the table today. This means you're hungry, Señorita. It's a good sign,' she beamed. 'The cook's helper will be happy to see you put some meat on your skinny bones.'

Grace laughed as she greeted the children. They made their way to the table, each one addressing her respectfully. Some of the younger ones sent chuckles of curiosity her way.

Grace had accepted the fact that she was somewhat of a fascination to them. She longed to get to know them better, though. Little did she know her wish was about to be granted.

After they were all seated, Sofia called for Cassia, the tiny girl who had given Grace the straw hat. She looked to Grace to be about seven years old, although she was in fact nine. The child was uncommunicative, but she edged closer, looking at Sofia occasionally, just as she had done with Joseph. Her dark hair perfectly framed her heart-shaped face. Despite her difficulties, Cassia's large, brown eyes were soft, and Grace could see that the child was happy at the orphanage.

Cassia stretched out her tiny hands which clasped a large book. She handed the book to Grace, swaying her tiny frame from side to side. It was a beautiful Bible—the gift Joseph had promised her.

Mama Sofia said the morning prayers.

Grace felt somehow that Sofia was up to something. Her suspicions were confirmed when the nun winked at Grace from across the table. This always looked odd because of the nun's closed eye. Sofia went on to tell the children that they would have a new helper with their chores. Their assistant, she confidently explained, would be none other than Teacher Gracie. Grace was a little surprised at the announcement, but then reasoned that there was no better way to get to know the children than to dive right in. After all, she had trained as a teacher and had worked with impoverished children in the past.

Grace was learning that one had little time to wallow in one's troubles at The Cielo. Most of the challenges at the haven were in fact bigger than her own.

She hurried to her room to store her gift and to dress more appropriately for the day's events. Her plain cotton attire and wide-brimmed hat would do better than any. Grace was eager and ready to meet her intrepid team of gardeners.

Mama Sofia appointed Cassia to escort Grace to the vegetable garden where they were to meet the rest of their team. It was a beautiful morning. Cassia had a permanent smile on her young face as she squeezed Grace's hand.

Grace enjoyed having her little shadow. She thought about one of the pearls of wisdom Mama Sofia often dropped her way, 'People need people to heal, Señorita. This is what the cross of Christ stands for. The vertical post is God loving you and the horizontal posts are those he sends for you to reach.'

Grace's heart went out to the child who could not speak because of what she had suffered at the hands of the adults who were meant to take care of her. Joseph had once said that Cassia's inability to speak had something to do with the trauma she had experienced when she was scarcely older than a baby. He had further explained that the development of trust with a caring adult was important when acquiring language skills. The little girl had been rejected at birth, when an infant instinctively trusts its mother to take care of its needs.

'Trust must be shared and will always involve at least two people—a giver and a receiver. It's all about giving and receiving love,' Joseph had explained. 'It means that I know another carries me in their heart even when I'm not physically with them.'

Cassia could in fact speak. However, she was selective about the people she spoke to. For now, she communicated only with Sofia and Joseph. When Cassia had first arrived at The Cielo, she was fearful and clingy, and the people at the orphanage worked hard at helping her regain the trust she had lost. Sofia and Joseph were praying for the day she would converse freely with the rest of the family. Grace wanted to help. She secretly hoped that the next person Cassia opened up to would be her.

The nun's description of how little Cassia came to be with them had touched Grace. 'Our child's story is a sad one,' the nun had said. 'Cassia lived in a migrant camp with her father. Work in Colombia, especially in the mines, attracts all kinds of people who are trying to make a living. They come from the many islands that dot our coast. Cassia's father was part of a team of men who came here to work. Sadly, Señorita, the man was also a heavy drinker.'

Sofia had wiped her face with a chubby hand before she went on. 'Cassia had no mother, and her father was the only other person responsible for looking after her. Unfortunately, her father took little care of her.'

The nun had placed her hands squarely on her hips, her body shaking in disapproval. 'The child roamed around the migrant camp every day, searching for food and human contact. But most of the migrant families have just enough for their own. They could hardly take care of Cassia as well.'

Tears had formed in Sofia's good eye. 'Cassia's father worked long hours. The two of them shared a small tent at night. The child received no education and had little opportunity to learn to speak properly. During one of our visits to take food to the workers there, we were taken to Cassia's tent by a kindly old lady. Later we discovered that it was this woman who fed Cassia her own family's leftovers. When we entered the tent, scarcely big enough for one person, we found the little girl asleep on an old mattress. She was dehydrated and she refused to speak to us when we woke her.'

Sofia had dabbed her eye. 'I've known Father Joseph for years, Señorita, and he doesn't hesitate to act quickly in situations like this. It was clear that the child had to be rescued immediately. Joseph scooped Cassia right up and brought her back here, where she has been ever since.'

Grace had listened intently as Sofia shared the tale of little Cassia's rescue. She recalled asking the nun, 'Did Cassia's father look for his daughter?'

The nun had quietly replied. 'Well, Señorita, Father Joseph went to see him the following day. He explained that if the man allowed the orphanage to take care of Cassia, he wouldn't report the situation to the authorities. Cassia's father consented. Till today, Joseph allows the man to visit his daughter.'

Sofia's shoulders had slumped at the all-too-common story of a neglected child.

***

Grace allowed her young guide to lead her through a small gate that led to a large patch of rich earth which was teeming with various kinds of mouthwatering vegetables. The Cielo's vegetable garden was vast and well-maintained. Beets, berries, spinach, pumpkins and beans sprouted neatly in straight rows, like soldiers ready for inspection. The first morning rays threw sharp shards of white light across the patches of earth. Grace pulled her shoulders back and tiptoed to reach her full height. She exhaled first and then she drew in the crisp air.

Suddenly the children rushed towards her, and nearly flattened her into the soil! Grace instinctively grabbed one of the little boys and scooped him up. She spun him around, keeping his smiling face close to hers. The smell of the clean air, the touch of the boy's warm skin, and the beauty of her new life, made Grace want to shout with joy.

Grace's first idea was to teach the children a song she made up as they went about their gardening. The children gathered around her, and they sang together as they unearthed the weeds that threatened to choke the strawberries and a plethora of green herbs.

Brutus, a strong-looking youngster and older than the rest, caught Grace's attention at the outset. The boy was agile. His coffee-brown face and small dark eyes seemed to pop up frequently behind every bed. Grace noticed he loved to play the role of overseer, keeping a steady eye on the rest of the children while Joseph was away.

Grace found that she had to be attentive with the younger boys. They loved to throw clods of damp soil at each other across the vegetable beds. These made for an exciting battlefield. Laughing, they would fall to the ground when they were struck by their enemy.

What was Mama thinking putting me in charge of this disparate little crew? Grace wondered. But she was happy. It was not long before they were all working shoulder to shoulder. Grace revelled in the feel of the lush soil smothering her hands. The earth she prodded beneath was more mysterious than the ground above.

Her time with the children reminded her of the times spent with her mother in their family garden, and of her long walks in the Colombian countryside whenever she was lonely. But for now, she was the one appointed to take care of these young ones, and Grace felt altogether proud.

***

The next two weeks passed quickly. Joseph was still away, and life at the orphanage began to turn Grace's attention to the things she had possibly taken for granted, like washing the children's clothes and helping to prepare their meals. She also provided hugs whenever they were needed.

Some of the children were more demanding than others. One young girl, Mia, needed Grace's constant consideration. Mia would make up all kinds of illnesses to get Grace to respond. If that did not work, Mia would deliberately get into an altercation with one of the other children. But when Grace learned of the child's background, her heart went out to her.

Mia was born to a mother who was an addict. When the woman died, their grandmother took care of the little girl and her five older siblings. Being poor herself, the elderly lady found it difficult to feed them all, and late one night she brought Mia to The Cielo, begging the priest to take the child in. But Joseph had already reached his capacity for taking orphans—an extra mouth to feed meant everyone would have less of the little they had. He could not, however, turn the child away. So, Mia stayed. Despite her challenges, the little one had crept into the hearts of everyone at the orphanage.

Grace came up with a plan to distract Mia from her constant need of attention. Joseph had given Grace a small digital audio player to listen to music. Grace decided it was time to share something of her own, so she gave the player to Mia. Much to Grace's delight, the idea worked. In no time, the other children helped the little girl download music onto her new player, and from then on, Mia could be found frequently clicking her fingers and singing to the lovely tunes.

Sofia was happy with Grace's progress. She decided to coax the young woman into giving English lessons to the children. Grace rose to the challenge of teaching a class of mixed ages, and each day she felt her heart swell with pride at their progress. Occasionally, she was assisted by adult volunteers at the orphanage. It was good for Grace. Her mind, her hands, and her time were constantly occupied. She barely had occasion to think of her past.

She did think of Joseph though, and wondered when he would return—she had much to share with him. Grace marvelled at the sense of belonging she felt at The Cielo. Perhaps this is what God intended for all families—a never-ending circle of giving and receiving, patience and gratitude.

Grace began to read from the Bible Joseph had given her. She sensed the hand of God in the penning of each verse. After she read, she would hold the book to her chest and reflect on what the scriptures meant to her. She felt her own heart beat in unison with the spirit of the writer.

Grace reflected on the beautiful love story of Ruth and Boaz in the Old Testament—it spoke to her of God's love and grace. Then there was the story of the Shunamite woman who helped the prophet Elisha. Here the scriptures ministered God's miracle-working power and revealed his compassion towards those experiencing hardship in their lives.

Grace saw the thread of God's redemption for fallen man in the pages of the Old Testament. She observed how his plan was fulfilled in the New Testament. She saw herself in each page—her own rebellion and the sin that had blinded her. Although she had separated herself from God, God had mercifully used the evil intentions of others to open her spiritual eyes. She found herself asking for his forgiveness, and laid her burdens at the cross of Christ where she received her new life in him.

3

One evening, while she was readying for dinner, Grace was distracted by the children's loud chatter beneath her window. *Had Joseph returned?* She thought to wait a little before she went to greet him; she would have to be patient as there were others who would need his immediate attention. Grace tucked her new experiences away like one would a special gift, until the occasion presented itself to share them with him.

She watched as Joseph stepped out of the sedan. He was finally home. This time Grace took care to avoid being spotted by him, which was unnecessary in the end as the children had already overwhelmed him with their warm reception. Although tired from his long journey, the priest still gave them his full attention. He hoisted one of the boys onto his shoulders as they laughed together.

Grace stayed in her room and read her Bible. She was barely able to concentrate. Every sound near her door distracted her. She wanted to run out of her room and into Joseph's arms to tell him how much she had missed him. That was not something she would do though. She had been raised to believe that it was improper for a woman to do what her heart wanted, so she would hold back, as her mother had always done. If she could pluck up the courage, she would tell Joseph about the special experiences she had shared with the family at The Cielo. She would also thank him for her newfound faith in Jesus.

The opportunity did not present itself, however. Instead, Grace sat quietly at the long table listening to the priest, who did most of the talking. Joseph spoke of his visit abroad and of the meetings he had had with their sponsors. In the midst of all the chiming in, Joseph added that he had missed them all. He made sure that his eyes met hers when he said this. Grace felt her cheeks warm.

The priest concluded his lively conversation with the children by announcing that he would be taking them all on a hike into the forest the following morning. They would have a picnic and swim in one of the freshwater pools there. Joseph added that he thought it a good idea for Grace and Mama Sofia to join them. He was certain that they, too, needed a rest from their work.

The children were finally bustled off to bed by Sofia and one of the volunteers, but not before each of them gave Grace a hug. In the short time she had gotten to know them they had become openly affectionate with her. Joseph was intrigued. Grace was just about to retire herself when he grabbed her hand at the table.

'Stay a while, Gracie. It's good to see you.'

The faint smell of evening-blooming cactus flowers scented the air. Grace caught a glimpse of the fragile blooms through an opening in one of the windows. They blossomed only at night, as ethereal as the moon, hiding from everyone during the day when one is unable to appreciate their furtive beauty. The flowers reminded Grace of how she had withdrawn from the world, not fully understanding the beauty that lies in serving others.

Grace flashed a warm smile at Joseph. Although he was showing an interest in her welfare, she could sense that he needed rest from his travels. Her stories could wait for another time.

'I don't want to keep you. I'm sure that beneath all your bravado you're quite exhausted. We'll talk soon. Right now, you need to rest.' Grace got up from her chair and, drawing a light wrap across her shoulders, moved towards the door.

'I see I'll not get far disagreeing with you this evening, Señorita.'

Joseph chuckled softly as he stepped towards the exit. He seemed pleased with Grace's new assertiveness. Before leaving the room, he told Grace to be ready early. He repeated that he wanted her to accompany him and The Cielo family on their excursion. Joseph added that he would be taking only her somewhere further, after they had had their picnic in the forest.

Grace climbed into bed with the smell of moonflowers still tantalising her senses and Joseph's deep voice addressing her in the hallway. She did not mind that she had trouble falling asleep that night.

***

Grace woke earlier than usual. The pale light of the fading moon still shimmered above the distant hills. She sat near the window on the small sofa that was old, yet comfortable. It had become a special place for her to read and pray and she took the Bible Joseph had given her. It was good to have him back at The Cielo. Although the orphanage could go on without him, Joseph's strong presence was the glue that held everything together. He was a true father to those who had been abandoned.

Grace thought of her own father, Jake Kellerman. It was difficult for her to grasp the notion of paternalism. Her father had seldom been there for her, but he had tried to make amends for his errant ways by showering Grace with gifts and sending his daughter to the best schools. Grace never wanted for anything.

When she was young, Grace's friends would share stories of happy times spent with their own fathers. Grace, however, felt that her father was emotionally distant. Their relationship was based on Jake's pleasure at her ability to do things perfectly, or his indignation at her inability to meet the standards he set for her.

Although Grace's mother, Maria, tried to instil in her a belief in God, Jake did everything in his power to negate his wife's sincerity. Grace remembered a time when her mother sought solace for herself and her daughter within a particular faith. Jake was against this idea. He had argued with Maria that his only child would not be raised a religious fanatic.

Jake was a self-confessed atheist. He would often rant about the perils of those who followed religion blindly. He found their rituals and prayers to an invisible God intellectually offensive. Jake would say of the devout, 'Their belief is like an old cocoa tree on a hot day. It looks ripe because of the light shining on it, but crack her pods open and her seeds are as dry as she is fruitless.'

Jake was prone to angry outbursts which were amplified when he drank. His marriage to Maria was always strained. Grace did her best to keep out of their way when they argued. Since she had no siblings, she would find comfort in the Colombian countryside—its natural beauty consoled her. Grace would chase white monarch butterflies for hours on end. Their frivolous fluttering over the tall grass that stretched for miles made her happy.

Maria struggled to maintain constancy in Grace's life. She would groom Grace carefully each day as if she were wrapping a fragile doll in plastic. A war raged in the place Grace called home. Her parents constantly argued and debated over what they thought was best for their only child.

As Grace grew older, she found the serene countryside could no longer fill the void in her heart. It was at this vulnerable time that her father succeeded in persuading Grace to marry a man who went by the name of Antonio. Jake could no longer maintain the affluent lifestyle he had secured for himself and his family. There had been too many drug deals go awry. The only way to solve his predicament was to form a strong alliance with the audacious Antonio.

Grace had learned, through the actions of her mother, to avoid asking questions and to accept things as they were. Maria would tell her daughter, 'What your eyes don't see, Gracie, your heart won't grieve.'

Consequently, Grace learned from a young age to bury the things that troubled her. Life at The Cielo was different—Grace experienced the exact opposite. There could be no secrets in a place where God was. His very nature was pure light. Confessing and forgiving was a way of life at the orphanage. In this way, the people who lived there were kept from the deceitfulness of sin. The only way the Spirit of God could set their hearts on fire was through the truth of God's love.

The circumstances surrounding Grace's marriage to Antonio remained vague. Grace remembered, however, that she had vacillated between uncertainty and compliance till her own conscience had weakened to the point where she eventually gave in to the forced arrangement.

Antonio, like many of the young men who grew up in impoverished Colombia, had learned to procure a lavish existence by dealing in drugs. He had dropped out of school early and had joined a well-known gang controlled by powerful drug lords. Because of his inclination for high-risk behaviour, Antonio rose quickly through the ranks of the cartels. His acquired lifestyle took experienced merchants years to accrue.

In those early days it was not unusual to see him in the streets of Cartagena driving luxury cars, staring down at the world through his dark shades, and always a beautiful girl at his side. Antonio's reputation for vice and corrupt behaviour had spread throughout the region. Grace's father was in awe of the young man and often spoke proudly of him at the dinner table. He would boast that the young falcon would soon be king of the drug cartels.

Jake and Antonio were introduced during the glory days of drug smuggling when a high premium was placed on profitable gains. Eventually, dealing in arms and other unlawful activities proved more lucrative for them than their original business. When Jake was overtaken by greed, he drew attention to himself—suspicions were aroused within the Colombian militia and members of the cartels. This brought trouble, and Jake began to turn to Antonio for help more often than not.

Extravagant dinner parties at the Kellermans' luxurious home were frequently held for Antonio's benefit. Jake hoped that having the young man as an ally would mean that he and his family were somewhat protected. It was at one of these sumptuous gatherings that Jake introduced Antonio to Grace. Always keen to have the close acquaintance of a beautiful woman, the young man was instantly smitten.

On one occasion, Grace allowed herself to be persuaded by her father to attend a function at Antonio's mansion. Here Grace was introduced to the liberal use of illegal drugs amongst the wealthy. She recalled how her heart had raced at the excitement generated by the people and the events that evening. Jake had meticulously planned his daughter's exposure to a life that often coexists with excessive wealth—and Grace had succumbed to it.

There was a heightened sense of anticipation as she sashayed across the marble floors that held up the cashmere-painted walls, with ceilings lit by chandeliers. Sharp shards of light and flickering shadows concealed the decadence that lurked beneath it all. People had smiled at her, but their smiles were affected and cold. They had laughed with each other, yet their mirth was like a dark cloak concealing their fears.

Soon the walls of Grace's resistance crumbled, and she accepted Antonio's hand in marriage. All Grace could recall of it was that it was a grand occasion. Beyond that, the whole event remained a blur. It was as though she held the secret to an unsolved mystery but had no way of accessing its truth. Grace knew, however—albeit in the recesses of her own heart—that the easy persuasion of her marriage to Antonio was associated with her deep need for acceptance by her father.

Just as the harsh winds blew over the Tatacoa Desert, Jake's soul was fast corroding. He continued to believe that Grace's marriage to Antonio would bode him well—the young man was sold on the idea of a beautiful wife. Jake was also happy for the support he would get from the poor whose lands he expended—with little opposition from them—to farm cocoa. The idea of Antonio becoming a family man would make Jake all the more popular.

Grace knew that her father frequently dodged the police. This was a shame she carried with solitary sadness. Grace learned to avoid asking Antonio and Jake too many questions about their illegal activities, and to accept things the way they were. Like new paint covering an old wall, Grace, like her mother, buried the pain in her life. She hid behind expensive jewellery and haute couture.

It was around this time that Maria began to withdraw from her daughter, just when Grace was preparing for her marriage to Antonio and longed for someone to talk to. Grace came to believe that her mother's evasion was because she felt she had failed her only child; that her mother could not come to terms with the fact that her daughter had been sold into a life similar to her own.

The opulent life Antonio offered Grace from his mansion in Pasto knew no limits. However, it did not come without a price, for Grace found her new husband to be a cruel man. There were times when, in fear, she would lock herself in her bedroom, with the aid of their domestic helper, Gloria. Grace's utter despair and loneliness led Gloria to give Grace small amounts of the drugs she stole from Antonio.

Grace did not tell her mother about her increasing addiction. She would conceal the needle marks on her arms by wearing long sleeves. Dark shades and wads of heavy makeup also helped to camouflage Grace's life at the villa. The day Grace heard of her parents' death in an automobile accident was life-altering for her. The young woman sunk into a deep depression, desiring more of the temporary relief that was rapidly consuming her.

Like all motives driven by greed, moral descent eventually corrodes the human soul till its scent is despised even by the unscrupulous. Antonio began to clash with cartel members and corrupt officials. The militia became aware that the young man was reaping more from his fraudulent activities than they intended. As their suspicions grew, they became vengeful—after all, it was through their sanctioning that Antonio had prospered. On that fatal day when they attacked the villa at Pasto, Antonio lost his life at their hands. During her attempt to escape, Grace was kidnapped and taken into the deep nadir of the Colombian jungle.

***

Feeling the morning warmth on her hands as she paged through her Bible, Grace tried to piece together the details of her life as a married woman. She began to realise that she could indeed overcome her painful past. Her hurt was no longer hers to carry—she could lay it all at the feet of Christ. He would take upon himself the burdens that had weighed her down for so long. This war was no longer hers to fight. Grace felt light as she closed her eyes and prayed a prayer of complete surrender to Jesus. Tears slipped from her eyes, but they carried in them a glint of hope.

The combined chime of lively voices outside her window roused Grace from her prayerful state. She closed her Bible and stretched her neck to hear the children speaking to each other in broken English. Their courageous efforts made her smile. Grace rose from her seat to prepare for the trip Joseph had planned for the family. Today would be a day to enjoy all the wonderful things God had provided through his creation. Again, God was securing a thread that had unravelled during her childhood. He was steadily stitching them all back into the fabric of her life.

Grace skipped down the stairs that led to the courtyard. The children and the helpers were eagerly waiting for the rest of the grown-ups to join them. She almost collided with Pedro who quickly stepped aside for her. He gave Grace a warm smile as she steadied her feet, and she offered the man a quick apology as she hurried out.

To Grace's relief there were no mules waiting today. This meant they would be undertaking their hike on foot. She held back a little as Joseph crossed through one of the side doors with Cassia in tow. Some of the older boys, who had trouble waking early, sauntered behind them. Like an awkward parade of circus performers, they joined Grace on the stony access.

'Good morning, Señorita!' Joseph smiled broadly as he greeted Grace. Cassia raised her eyes to greet her. There was a sparkle in them. Grace greeted Joseph warmly, wishing she didn't appear so shy, although he seemed not to notice.

'I hope it's not too early for you. The sun is quite welcoming now, but it won't be so friendly later.'

They were both wearing the same hats they had worn to the soccer event. Grace laughed easily with Joseph as she greeted the rest of the helpers. She wondered whether Mama Sofia would join them. Just as she was about to ask him about the nun, Grace heard Sofia calling for the group to wait for her. Grace quashed a smile. She noticed Sofia's face was already red from exertion, and they had barely left the haven. Sofia was mumbling a prayer under her breath. It would be one that called for the good Lord to keep them safe, but mostly for her, that she would have the courage to endure their ascent into the Colombian forest.

Before Grace could help Sofia, two of the volunteers slowed to help the nun with some baskets she was carrying from the kitchen. The items were packed with tasty snacks and sweet beverages. Sofia handed her load to the young men while playfully slapping them on their backs.

'What is taking you so long, eh? It's an honour to work while you are young, no? No matter the size of a woman, she is still a lady and you must treat her as such!'

The young men nodded respectfully and hid their smiles. They moved quickly to join the others. One of the older boys, a sturdy adolescent, led the way and Grace fell into line. She was happy to be part of the group.

This was the second time since her arrival at The Cielo that Grace was given the opportunity to venture out with her new family. She laughed as the children whizzed past her, their little backpacks jigging comfortably across their shoulders. Grace held back slightly to keep an eye on Sofia's progress behind the others. The slower pace gave her an opportunity to absorb the scenic countryside.

Grace thought about her own harrowing march through the jungle before her rescue. She had been paralysed with fear then. Now, though, her efforts were kept afloat by the joy she experienced in keeping with the disjointed line of individuals who were clearly content in each other's company.

They passed through a small village not far from the orphanage. The settlement was dotted with square dwellings that boasted white walls and red-tiled roofs. The charming little houses were reminiscent of ancient Spanish design. The homes calmly lined a dirt road which ascended sharply, then levelled before opening to a winding pathway that led to a tapering forest.

Some of the locals were out and about busying themselves with their morning's chores. They beat the dust from heavy mats while heating large iron pots over open fires. Grace waved at the older women. Their wide, toothless smiles suggested that contentment and poverty were close companions here. Grace drank in the beauty of the mountains in the distance and was contemplating how relaxed the small, rural villages of Colombia appeared when a familiar voice interrupted her thoughts.

'They paint a pretty picture, Señorita.'

Grace did not see Joseph come up behind her. His words made her feel as if he had never left her side. She moved over to accommodate him before replying.

'Their beauty, I think, is in their distinction—the contrast of these small dwellings and the looming mountains. The red earth and the tall trees with their varying shades of green... I find them so breathtaking.'

Grace turned to face Joseph. A slight breeze stole through the air, and a wisp of her hair came to rest on her cheek. The priest caught his breath for a moment. 'This is true. Beauty does have a strange way of finding you, even in the most complex situations.'

Joseph's eyes were soft. Grace thought she could hear her heart beat in her chest. Just then, an excited Cassia grabbed hold of Grace's hand. She tugged Grace away from Joseph. The child pulled at her again, determined to get Grace's attention. Cassia pointed to a large bull grazing in one of the nearby fields. Its size dwarfed the other animals. Grace noticed that the little girl was particularly attracted to the large brass bell that hung from a rope around the animal's neck.

She gave Joseph an apologetic look. Joseph nodded indicating that he would check on the progress of the others.

Grace followed the little girl to the enormous creature. She was careful to keep them both at a safe distance. Cassia stared with wide-eyed admiration at the bull. She shook her head briskly from side to side. Her round cheeks puffed into little flushed balls at the sides of her face. Grace laughed. She scooped the child in her arms and made for the path where the others were headed.

Joseph announced that they should all take a partner to help them squeeze through a small space straddled by a barbed fence. It was put there to keep stray animals out. One of the pair should hold the fence up while the other crept through the narrow yet accessible gap. It all sounded easy enough. A volunteer took Cassia from Grace. Joseph asked Grace to partner with Mama Sofia. The priest indicated that the poor nun was clearly in need of someone with a stronger dose of patience than the others. It had become quite clear to all that hiking was not one of Sofia's favourite things to do. The Lord had surely equipped her for calmer pastimes.

Grace wondered how the full-bodied woman would manoeuvre herself through what appeared to be the smallest opening—and in her billowing habit. Sofia never changed out of it except when it needed to be cleaned. She had once said to Grace that she was married to her dress. It reminded her of her loyalty to God and to the people she served.

Grace forced the wire fence apart. She used the

boot of her foot to drive the lower part of the fence as far as it would go. Sofia bent as near to the ground as she could, while uttering all kinds of spiritual mantras. Noticing the nun's struggle, Grace realised she would have to get help from the others. She was about to shout out to those ahead when she heard a loud clanging noise. It was coming from the bull Grace had visited earlier with Cassia. The sight of the beast lumbering towards Sofia, for no other reason than to enjoy its freedom, sent the nun into a panic. Sofia popped her large frame through the constricted space in the blink of an eye.

Grace laughed till she felt her sides would surely split (she later apologised to Sofia). The two friends chuckled till little tears slipped from their eyes. They embraced each other as they watched the bull nonchalantly stop before the gap in the fence to graze on some of the sweet grass.

Sofia gathered herself and wiped her face. Checking that there were no rips in her habit, she spoke quite rapidly. 'Señorita, that bull must have mistaken me for a large clover. By the mercy of God, it wasn't the end of me!'

Grace gently took hold of the older woman's arm, and together they made their way up the trail towards the forest.

'Experience is a good instructor,' Grace chided the nun playfully. 'You might want to exchange that habit of yours for something more appropriate when you go hiking next time.'

Sofia laughed, 'You know, Buttercup, I think the pupil has become the teacher. This is a good thing. Our Saviour wants us to trust in him always. He will surely deliver us from any bull at the gate.' The nun winked at

Grace's Rescue

Grace as they joined the young helpers who had come to look for them.

The little party was soon traipsing through a narrow trail which was densely canopied by lush green branches spreading over them like a gigantic tarpaulin. Grace heard Joseph call out to take care on the narrow path, and the older children were instructed to assist the younger ones. Sofia and the volunteers immediately gathered the children together, teaming each young one with an older child. Grace felt a little hand slip through her own. She knew it had to be young Cassia.

The verges of the trail were steep and slippery. The forest, which had thickened, was teeming with different species of birds. Disturbed fauna made a hasty retreat to clear the track for the explorers. Vibrant orchids and bromeliads competing for space grew from a gigantic bouquet of colour. Grace caught her breath as she examined the magnificent flora.

Suddenly, the group stopped. The trail had abruptly come to an end, to reveal the most spectacular waterfall. Excitedly they made their way to a clearing, this time with Joseph taking the lead.

The roar of the water could be heard cascading into a crystal pool above the din of the forest. Wet rocks flattened smoothly around the pool like flatbreads baking in the sun. The children squealed with delight as they elbowed each other to feel the icy spray on their bodies. Grace looked up to see whether she could spot the rocky ledge of the waterfall. It was as if the water was falling through an opening in the clouds, and in no time they were all wet. Their hair clung to their damp faces like the leaves of a tree to their stems after a heavy rain.

The children laughed and chased each other while

Sofia and Grace set up the picnic. Everything was damp; Grace felt she had entered a natural sauna. Eventually settling on one of the rocks, she watched as Joseph gave the children permission to swim. The volunteers were already cooling off in the water. Joseph dived in, only coming up for air after a long while. Grace could not take her eyes off him. Tiny beads of water like little copper pearls clung to his bronzed skin. His thick hair was hardly touched by the water.

Grace rose, and helped Sofia with the children who were quite thirsty by now. As she busied herself, suddenly out of nowhere one of the young helpers scooped her in his arms. He headed for the deep rock pool and toppled Grace into the water, sending a holler of good-humoured laughter around the pool. Grace barely had time to call out that she could not swim, when she felt the cold liquid, dense and suffocating, drag her down. Her old fear of water resurfaced. No one knew of her near-drowning as a child. If one of her father's bodyguards had not dived in to save her that day, Grace would certainly have drowned.

Although she eventually learned to swim, it was always with some caution. The unexpectedness of the incident, however, suppressed what little buoyancy Grace possessed and she began to thrash wildly. Just when she thought that no one had noticed her quandary, Grace felt strong arms circle her waist.

Joseph carefully guided Grace to the surface of the pool and helped her onto one of the flat rocks. Gasping for air, thinking she was making an utter fool of herself, Grace placed her face in her hands. The young man responsible for the incident hurried over to apologise, but the priest gently waved him away.

Grace could hear Joseph say her name. 'It's alright,

Grace. You're safe now.'

He placed his towel across her shoulders and drew her closer to him. In no time the rest of the children had formed a concerned circle around the two. Their bewildered chattering helped to lighten the situation, though. Sofia joined them—she was beside herself with worry for Grace's well-being.

Joseph quickly calmed everyone, assuring them all that Grace would be fine and that she just needed some space to catch her breath. The little group soon dispersed to leave him alone with Grace, who was feeling better already.

'Oh my, that was something.' Grace looked awkwardly at Joseph.

She muttered an apology and thanked him for rescuing her. 'This is the second time you've had to pull me from danger.' Grace laughed softly, then added, 'The circumstances are far less harrowing this time. Still, I hope this doesn't become a habit for you.' She turned to look at Joseph. He was squinting in the sun as it bore down on them.

'Well, Señorita, I will say you have a unique swimming style.'

Joseph chuckled before continuing, more serious this time. 'As for habits, I could not imagine life without–' he caught himself, his body language indicating he wished to continue that part of the conversation another time.

Bringing them back to the present, Joseph continued. 'Would you like to talk about your fear of water?'

Grace explained to Joseph the near-fatal experience she had had as a child. The priest smiled while lifting some strands of damp hair from her face.

'Yes, fear…' Joseph spoke as if it had been an old

companion of his. 'It's a thing that can enter your heart at a young age and affect you for a lifetime.'

He was quiet for a moment, contemplative, before he said, 'In God's Word we read that there's no fear in his love for us.'

For the first time in all their conversations on spiritual matters, Grace added her own thoughts. 'God loved us so much that he gave his Son to die for our freedom. That's perfect love.'

Joseph was thrilled. He realised that Grace had had a personal encounter with Christ while he had been away. He was thankful that his prayers had been answered.

'You share a great truth, Gracie. In another part of scripture, the book of Romans in fact, we find that the Spirit God gave us is one that compels us to call him Father. When we call him Father, we no longer carry an unconscious fear of feeling orphaned in this world.'

Joseph ran a hand through his wet hair before continuing. 'Your fear of water is really a fear of dying. This is quite natural. Now you understand, though, that whatever happens to you, God is in control. You're his beloved child—for him to love and always protect.'

They prayed then, the two of them. Together they believed for Grace's freedom from the fear that had haunted her most of her life.

Grace spent the rest of the morning with the children in the rock pool. They took turns in what they understood to be the important task of showing their teacher how to swim. Grace could see Joseph sunning himself on one of the large rocks. He seemed amused—the children's attempts to instruct her in their most articulate English made the priest chuckle.

Grace thought it was a marvellous thing—to let go.

She had never completely felt at ease in her own skin. She longed to be like them, to share her joy so effortlessly with others. A mounting sense of trust filled Grace as she followed the children's instructions to hold onto the rocks, and to freely explore new ways to move her body. The children swam around her like dolphins in a show.

Their morning together pleasantly concluded with a tasty midday feast carefully prepared by Mama Sofia and Cook. Grace realised that The Cielo's cook was in fact Pedro, Joseph's ingenuous driver.

There were tortillas and tacos with spicy fillings and cheese toppings. Prickly pear juice was provided to wash it all down. Some sweet fruits would finish the meal perfectly. After prayers of thanksgiving the children tucked in heartily. Grace marvelled at the stimulating effect the swim had on their appetites. Her eye caught Joseph's and they laughed together.

Mama Sofia pointed out to Grace that it was a common practice for The Cielo family to rest under the shade of the trees after a good meal. Some of the children found little spots on the thick vines, strong enough to bear their weight. Their rest included sharing the morning's escapades with each other. Grace stretched out on her towel under a tree which provided some shade. She thought of her earlier trek through the bush under treacherous circumstances. Now, the jungle with its magnificent forests was inviting. The same forest, yet they suggested two different experiences. Grace's new life was no longer beset with pain. She closed her eyes and began to doze.

When Grace woke it was to the sound of singing. The children were dancing to the timbre of their own voices. The sweet melody merged with the sound of the cascading waterfall. They danced and twirled their bodies on their little feet, splashing in the small pools of water between the mosses. The children sang the chorus to their song over and over. Clapping their hands was a natural accompaniment to their worship.

Before Grace could pull herself from her cozy spot beneath the trees, she found herself being lifted by Joseph's strong arms. He led her to the loose circle of worshippers. Together they sang as they joined the children. Their hearts united in worship to the true Creator and giver of life. It seemed as if the little group was joined by others they could not see—perhaps a chorus of angels.

Their worship continued for a while till they began to break into little groups. The children and the assistants gathered their belongings and the rest of the items they had brought along.

While they prepared to go back to The Cielo, Grace waited for Joseph's cue. She noticed him hang back to speak to her in private. Grace went to fetch her towel from under the tree when she sensed Joseph standing behind her.

'Señorita,' the priest spoke so that only she could hear him, 'our journey isn't over yet. We must go on a little—through the forest. There's someone who lives there that I'd like you to meet. Mama Sofia will see to it that the children return safely.'

The thought of them being alone together made Grace happy. 'I do love surprises. I want nothing more than to spend the rest of this glorious day with you.' Grace quickly added, 'Another experience with Mama Sofia and a roaming bull is not an attractive alternative!'

They laughed before Joseph said, 'That's settled then. I must arrange some things with Sofia first, then we can leave.'

Grace caught the twinkle in Sofia's eye as the nun busied herself with the children and Joseph. She smiled warmly at Grace. Waving goodbye, she banded her little followers together with the intention of heading straight back to The Cielo.

***

Nebulous rainclouds gathered above, but the change of weather did not perturb the two travellers in the least. The forest grew denser as they pushed their way through the narrow trails and overhanging banyans. Joseph led Grace securely by the hand. Grace did not ask him where they were headed—he seemed focused on navigating their safe passage through the bush. Grace began to wonder, *Who could live so deep in the forest, away from everyone, yet be so important to Joseph?* They continued trudging like this for a while.

Joseph was clearly a friend of the forest. He worked his way through its thickness as if he knew when to duck every overhanging branch. Grace was at the point of asking the priest about their intended destination when they came to the end of the winding trail. Joseph led her to a wide, cleared area that was interspersed with a few tree stumps.

At the edge of the clearing a faint spiral of smoke could be seen rising from a small log cabin. Although rustic, the house was neat. Some larger logs had been secured together quite cleverly, with smaller ones filling any open spaces. An older woman, a native of Colombia, was cooking outdoors over a medium-sized iron pot. She lifted her long stick out of the pot occasionally to better stir its thick contents. Grace had seen many women cooking over an outdoor fire in Colombia, and from the aroma she assumed the woman was preparing quinoa, a type of traditional porridge.

The woman broke into a warm smile when she saw Joseph approaching—she was clearly pleased to see him. Reluctantly, Joseph let go of Grace's hand to greet her.

The woman threw her arms round the priest's neck. 'Josephie!' She repeated his name several times while holding him close.

After what seemed a long while, Joseph gently withdrew from her to introduce her to Grace. 'Gracie, I'd like you to meet Francesca. Fran is like a mother to me, and I know you'll love her just as much as I do.'

Grace leaned forward and greeted the petite woman.

Francesca was reluctant to speak English; instead, she spoke rapidly in her mother tongue.

Joseph translated. 'Fran wants to know what brings me to the woods. She says she's sure it has something to do with the beautiful señorita at my side.'

He chuckled because Grace was quite at home with the native tongue herself. Nevertheless, he knew that it was not easy to follow Fran whose dialect was from a different region.

Then, just when Grace felt it could not get more awkward, the door to the little hut opened. An old man stepped out to greet them. The man's long white beard equalled the length of his hair, and flowed gracefully down the span of his tawny tunic, touching his sandaled feet.

When Grace saw him, she thought of the children at the orphanage and wondered whether the sight of the old man would have frightened them. As she contemplated their reaction, Grace was struck by the colour of the man's eyes. They were the gentlest blue. Taking her by the elbow, Joseph steered Grace towards the old man. There was a sense of urgency in Joseph, and his face lit up as he drew nearer.

'Father, it's so good to see you.'

The two embraced for some time before Joseph introduced Grace.

'Gracie,' Joseph looked keenly at the man, 'this is Father Ralph, the one who rescued me when I was a wayward youth.'

4

Grace had never asked Sofia or Joseph what had become of the old priest. She assumed that he had passed on and had left the running of the haven to the two of them. Seeing Father Ralph for the first time, Grace was more humbled than surprised. Joseph was quite right; the meeting was going to be special for her.

The priest was beaming like an excited child.

'My son, it's good to see you. Just when I thought it's time to see you again, you arrive unannounced as if you plucked my thoughts from the wind itself.'

The old man patted Joseph on the back. 'Well, no matter how you came to know my desires, I'm all the better that you're here. I see you are also in good health. Praise be to God for his mercies.'

The priest leaned forward. 'I see you have also brought with you some attractive company.' The man kept his eyes fixed on Grace for a while, as if he was seeing something she was not aware of.

Grace did not mind what could otherwise have been interpreted as impolite. The priest's humble manner made her feel right at home.

Father Ralph led Grace and Joseph into his little cabin. He called out to Francesca to fetch them something to drink. A common drink often served to visitors in these parts of Colombia is an extract taken from the cocoa leaf. Grace sat on a long bench beside Joseph, enjoying the warmth of his body next to hers.

While Joseph and the old priest caught up, Grace took the opportunity to take a peek at the quaint garden through an open window. It was filled with patches of various herbs—their pungent aroma wafted into the room.

The three chatted comfortably at the wooden table placed in the centre of the cabin. Its top was strewn with papers and books stacked unevenly, a little dust here and there. Grace noticed most of the works were of a spiritual nature. Father Ralph made a clumsy attempt to tidy the space, but Joseph interrupted him insisting that he relax.

Joseph offered the old man an apology as they sipped their tea. 'I'm sorry for not visiting sooner. I've been rather busy with some urgent matters at The Cielo.'

Father Ralph looked at Grace. He smiled warmly. The old priest clearly harboured no ill feeling towards Joseph. He seemed content with the fact that his son had come to visit him regardless.

Placing his wooden stick firmly on the floor, the priest looked up at Francesca as she entered the cabin. She carried with her a dish filled with sweet treats. The old man's eyes lit up. They ate and spoke about the orphanage—the children, and Mama Sofia. Joseph eventually centred their conversation on Grace. He explained how he had found her, and of her progress and love for the Lord. Francesca smiled sweetly at Grace as she smoothed the young woman's honey-blonde hair. Joseph did most of the talking. It dawned on Grace that Father Ralph knew all about her past life—her late father and husband, and the corrupt militia.

Finally, turning to Grace, Father Ralph spoke, his eyes filled with compassion. 'You've suffered much, my child. I can see it in your eyes. The eyes are the written pages of our souls. Nevertheless, I also see that your heart has been saved by the power of our Saviour. There's much that he has given you in strength of character, gifts, and favour.'

Grace nodded. There was a softness about her face as she listened to the old priest.

'What others meant for harm, God has turned for good. You'll be a light that'll shine where it must—for others to see. It'll be such that it can't be put out because of what God has done for you.'

Grace glanced over at Joseph. She could feel the moisture of her own tears trickle down her cheeks. The old man stretched out his hands to cover hers. 'Hush, my child. God sees every tear we spill, and he has put them in his own bottle in heaven. He does this to remind himself of the times he wiped them from our cheeks and replaced them with his joy.' Then the priest clapped his hands together, barely making a sound. He lifted them heavenward, rejoicing as if with angels.

Father Ralph turned his attention to Joseph. 'My son, you have done a good thing. God is pleased with you and the family at The Cielo.' Then quite spontaneously the four of them held hands. Father Ralph prayed. It was a special prayer of thanksgiving.

'Heavenly Father, we commit our daughter Grace to you. You have called her, like Queen Esther, to walk in your light and to lighten the burdens of others. Thank you that she has found the peace she was searching for and a safe place from all her struggles. You will fight on her behalf in the battles she may still have to face. She is now a child of your family, committed to your trust and safekeeping, O great Shepherd of ours.'

Grace wiped the tears from her face as she rose to embrace the old man. She could feel the love of God emanating from every fibre in his being. Surely the man was a seer or prophet, one who had been chosen by God and who spoke his oracles. Grace found herself holding onto him. She did not know it yet, but that brief yet powerful encounter with Father Ralph would be the first and last she would see of him.

The priest turned to Joseph as they seated themselves again. His voice took on a more serious tone this time. 'My son, I have some important information for you. It's not good news, but with God all things are given so that we can turn to him for the solutions.'

He spoke frankly. 'The militia are looking for Grace. I received this news from my brothers who work deep in the selva. I don't wish to alarm you, but you know the evil that lives in such men. They will stop at nothing to get what they want.'

Joseph's face darkened at the news. Grace, whose heart began to pound in her chest, noticed that he was instantly troubled. She gathered that the militia had been searching for her after they had heard of her escape.

Joseph was quiet. He had always trusted the word of the old priest.

'What are you telling us, Father? I've taken great care to conceal Grace's whereabouts.'

The younger man leaned in, not because he didn't want Grace to hear what he was saying, but because if it were possible, the walls would have ears. Joseph spoke in hushed tones. Grace felt her throat constrict. She realised that because of the compassion they had shown her, the family at The Cielo had had this awful situation forced upon them. Everyone was in danger—even the children.

Father Ralph waited for Joseph to finish and then, looking at them both, he patiently replied, 'My dear children, you must not forget that God has chosen the foolish things of this world to confuse those who think they are wise in their own eyes. He has already overcome the evil that exists in this world. We need not be afraid of criminals. Let us wait a little and see his deliverance in this matter.'

The priest patted Joseph's hand before he continued. 'Don't be anxious but rather give thanks to him. I will pray for guidance and your protection. The Lord will show you both what you must do.'

Father Ralph turned to Grace. He looked at her gently. 'My dear child, I see you taking a long journey. Along the way you'll meet many women, young and old. They'll come from a nation that's not like ours. There are difficult situations around the people I see you with. They have experienced unspeakable suffering and shame. I see you helping them. You will teach them about the redemptive love of Christ.'

The priest's eyes were filled with compassion. 'You must walk carefully, Grace. Although I don't know the time of this new direction for you, be aware that there'll be those who'll try to prevent you from fulfilling the plan of God for your life. Allow him to lead you by his Spirit. You'll witness many lives being set free by the power of God.'

Father Ralph appeared to be caught up in a place where God and his angels dwell. Grace did not feel afraid. She carefully processed the words of the old seer, then turned to Joseph, who sat in silence with his face buried in his hands.

Above the little cabin, Grace could hear the

rumbling of rain clouds. She placed her hand on Joseph's arm and waited for his response. As if this was the signal he had been waiting for, Joseph rose from his seat. He lifted the old priest and drew him into a warm embrace.

'Father, keep us in your prayers.'

Joseph turned to Grace and gently touched her cheek. 'We must leave now.'

Grace hugged the old man and followed Joseph out of the cabin. The atmosphere around their departure seemed quite solemn compared to when they first arrived.

Waving goodbye to Father Ralph and Francesca, Joseph and Grace headed towards the forest that held the trail that would lead them back home. They could hear Father Ralph in the distance, calling after them to take care. Joseph did not look back. He seemed deep in thought, intent on getting them both safely back to The Cielo.

***

Joseph held Grace's hand firmly, as if he could lose her at any moment. His mood was contemplative. If she could read his thoughts, Grace would have seen that Joseph was wrestling with his heart—his love for her, the possible threat to the family at the orphanage, but most of all, his inner struggle with what he had thought to be the will of God. The priest felt as though it would all tear him apart. Joseph understood that Father Ralph's words were from heaven. Even though a part of him regretted taking Grace to visit the old priest, Joseph knew he had done the right thing. It was just that he would have to surrender his own desires to God. The situation was proving to be more difficult than he ever imagined.

Grace sensed Joseph's dilemma. She longed to reach out to him. She realised, however, that the young priest needed time to think.

They made their way through the forest while heavy clouds gathered above them. The first drops of rain fell, till it was pelting. Feeling the torrent of water on his back, Joseph gently pulled Grace to shelter under some banyan leaves. Still, he did not say a word. Grace watched as the hefty plants captured some of the rain. She was instantly calmed. God would prevent any danger meant for her and her new family—she must keep trusting. Joseph had previously shared with her that perfect love drives out fear. She would pray for him to find his own peace.

While the storm raged and the rain continued to fall, Joseph's heart softened. Then, in what seemed completely out of character, Joseph pulled Grace towards him. He gently pulled her head back and cupped her face, keeping her close. Her face was small in his large hands. Grace did not resist. Instead, she felt herself melt into the closeness Joseph had arranged. She felt warm, despite the cold rain that trickled fresh streams of water down the length of their bodies.

Joseph raised her chin with his hand and gently kissed her. Grace felt the rain stream into her mouth as he let her go. The salty taste of the water was in fact from the tears Joseph had cried.

As most tropical flash storms go, their decline is as swift as their climb. Joseph led Grace to a clearing beneath some trees. The earth was wet, but it did not deter them since they were both tired and already soaked through. Grace looked up at Joseph as he settled beside her. Many wonderful and wild thoughts were running through her head, but she knew she needed time to process them all.

She no longer felt shy, though, and was the first to speak. 'I admire you, Joe.'

Joseph smiled at her use of his adolescent name.

'Most of all, I respect the strong bond you have with your people. I'm ashamed to say that the individuals I knew before I came to The Cielo used the poor as a means to an end. Their sole ambition was to increase the profits of their coffers.'

Grace lowered her wet lashes. She could feel Joseph's warm breath against her cheek. 'Well, that's only because you hung out with bad boys.' Joseph chuckled, then added, 'I'm not such a saint. I was rescued, just like you. The difference, probably, is that I feel compelled, even driven, to do the same for others.'

He turned to face her. 'Sometimes the burden of our people is like a heavy weight I can never rid myself of. It's a part of who I am. There are times, I confess, Gracie, when I must repent to God for allowing my devotion to come before my love for him. No matter how noble our earthly love is, it shouldn't replace our love for Christ. Our love for the hurting must flow from him—that is pure love. Who will the poor have if they don't have those who were once in need themselves? I think you and I share the same sentiments.'

Grace shook her head, 'I never thought I'd feel this way.'

The priest took a deep breath, as if distracted by the serene quality the rain had given Grace's features. 'The one thing I've observed about poverty is that there's a weakness within the poor to be exploited. Much like the men of our history. They ravaged the rich soil of our rivers for gold, and wildly preyed upon the wealth that was not theirs to take. Similarly, the drug lords and corrupt militia of Colombia are the predators who take advantage of the poor. They steal the gold that's to be found in human worth.'

'The poor are always disadvantaged, aren't they?'

'This is true. They are the easy targets of the greedy cartels. Even the big landholders still dictate the wages of the poor. Many of the humble farmers you see living in the villages become growers of crops that are used to produce illegal drugs.'

Grace thought of her father and late husband, Antonio. They had had an active role in exploiting the poor. This was the worst kind of malevolence she could think of. Grace did not know it then, but she was soon to be exposed to other evils in the world—and would be entering into a battle opposing these atrocities.

Joseph ended their discussion by saying, 'We mustn't forget that our own lives have been purchased at a great price. We owe everything we have to Christ.'

With that he stood up and held out his hand to help Grace to her feet. The rain had stopped, and Joseph's solemnity had abated. They began the last part of their exit from the forest in a lighter mood. Grace felt that although their paths might someday divert, she would always love Joseph.

***

The evil actions of some men sear their consciences from the morality given to all humans by God. The more they stand to gain, the greater their desire to behave in a manner contrary to human compassion. While Joseph and Grace were meeting with Father Ralph, wicked people were plotting to destroy The Cielo. The men were in search of the traitor—Antonio's wife. She would help them get back what they had lost. They came to the orphanage to frighten the people there. The men focused on the old sludge catchments overlooking The Cielo. The dams held tons of waste from the mines—long out of use. Their aim was to put pressure on the bulwarks. If they could weaken them enough, the walls would give in and unleash thick sludge down the hillside and onto the orphanage.

Eventually the persistence of the villains paid off. The dam directly above The Cielo broke. Slowly, quietly, the liquid mud trickled. Then it gained momentum and, like an avalanche of thick snow, it careened down the hill.

The children were outside, cleaning their shoes from their trip through the forest. Their laughter could be heard by Mama Sofia as she packed the picnic things away. The area where they were busying themselves was adjacent an old stone building nestled at the edge of the orphanage and directly in the path of the disintegrating dam. Brutus, the boy who Grace admired for his maturity, was the first to see the mudslide sliding like a gigantic hand towards them. The boy shouted for the children to take cover. It was not long before pandemonium erupted. Sofia and Pedro, alerted by the commotion, hurried outside to see what all the noise was about—but when they arrived, it was eerily quiet.

***

Joseph and Grace traipsed through the village near The Cielo. Grace felt content being with the man she loved. She looked forward to seeing Mama Sofia and the children. As they came to the pinnacle of the village, the two could partially see the orphanage. Then, to their surprise, they noticed Pedro running up the west side of the hill towards them. The older man appeared anxious. He was out of breath when he reached them, and struggled to speak. Joseph noticed the terrified look on the man's face, and he instantly knew that something was wrong.

'What is it, Pedro?' Still the man did not speak. Joseph took Pedro by the shoulders to shake him gently. 'What has happened? You must speak, Pedro!'

Eventually Pedro gathered himself, and blurted, 'Señor, it's The Cielo—the children! There has been a disaster. One of the old sludge dams has burst. Oh, Señor, it's terrible, you must come quickly!'

Joseph grabbed Grace by the hand and together they ran after Pedro. The priest's mind raced. He had been at the dams before his trip abroad and was assured by the engineers who worked in the area that they were safe; they would only pose a threat if someone tampered with them. This was highly improbable as nobody in their right mind would want to harm a haven for children.

As they neared The Cielo, Grace and Joseph could hear the sirens of two ambulances. The noise of their engines roared desperately. Although Grace panicked, she whispered a prayer. Joseph moved quickly. She had never seen the priest more sombre. Sofia was in tears as she ran out to meet them, engulfing them both with her hefty habit.

Grace tried to focus on the critical situation. A deluge of mud had broken through the banks of the dam's retaining structures. These had been erected years ago to keep the properties in the valley safe. The sludge had miraculously missed the main house and central buildings of the orphanage. The outbuildings, which housed the animals and important equipment, were, however, completely flattened by its strength. It was as if thick grey icing had been poured over the whole area. Thankfully the children had also been spared, except for one boy whose leg was hurt in the incident. Grace gave a sigh of relief. She counted the children—they were all safe.

Grace noticed Joseph's look of gratitude too—there could have been many fatalities.

The injured boy was Brutus. Grace watched tenderly as he was taken to the waiting ambulances. Joseph scoured the area to assess the damage as the rest of the children were attended to by volunteers. She followed Joseph as he made his way to some of the children. They were receiving medical assistance from a paramedic. It was a scene Grace would never forget—the children's faces, and the anguish on Joseph's.

Joseph rolled up his sleeves and Grace joined him. They worked quickly, making good use of the medical kits Mama Sofia sent out to them. Together they consoled the youngsters and prayed with them. Most of the injuries sustained by the children while trying to flee were minor.

While Grace worked, she quietly thanked the Lord for protecting the people at the orphanage. Then, to her surprise, she felt a tiny hand tug at the hem of her shirt. It was young Cassia. Grace's heart sunk at the thought of the little girl being harmed. She was determined, however, to focus on the miracle and not the disaster. Grace got down on her haunches to take a good look at the child. She knew that Cassia's inability to speak would make the situation more terrifying for her. Taking hold of her hand she gently asked her, 'Are you alright?'

When Grace was satisfied that Cassia had come to no harm, she tried to get the little girl to speak. 'Is there something you want to tell me?'

Grace drew closer. She felt the child's breath on her face. Cassia whispered something into her ear in Spanish. Grace desperately tried to understand what Cassia was saying. In the end she was certain she heard the child say that while the mud was sliding towards the orphanage, she had seen two men standing at the foot of the hill; the men were tall, almost as high as the hill itself. According to Cassia they were wearing white dresses and a bright light shone around them. The men were also strong. They held back all the terrible mud so that it would not hurt the children.

Grace was confident that Cassia had witnessed God sending his angels to protect the family at The Cielo. She gave the child a hug and ran her hand over Cassia's dark hair. 'You've done well, Little One. God has chosen you to witness a miracle today.'

Grace was overawed that Cassia had spoken to her. She tried to conceal her excitement at yet another miracle. How incredible, she thought, that God had prevented a human tragedy and at the same time had helped Cassia to converse with her. The child buried her head in Grace's shoulder. They stood there for a while, holding each other tightly.

Grace took Cassia by the hand while she made her way to Joseph and the others. She noticed he was in deep conversation with an important-looking person who had been sent to investigate the situation. Grace thought it best to leave him to talk to the man alone. She would share Cassia's experience with him when things at the orphanage settled.

Father Ralph was right. Those with evil intentions would stop at nothing to get to her.

Grace decided to search for Sofia. Some of the volunteers were with the nun and she had made it clear to them that it was important to get the children back to the safety of the orphanage—they needed to bathe and have something to eat. Although there was immense damage to the property and buildings and much repair work ahead, their continued prayers would always be at the front of their labour. This was the way of the people at The Cielo.

As evening descended, so did certain calm. Mama Sofia and her team prepared the children for bed. They were all asleep by the time the rooster that crowed each morning tucked its head under its wing.

Grace noticed Joseph was nowhere to be seen. She entered the lounge of the homestead, where she found Sofia seated on one of the sofas. Grace sat beside her. The intensity of the day weighed on their minds. They both sat quietly reflecting on the distressing events. Eventually Sofia got up from the couch to open one of the windows.

'You must be exhausted, Señorita.' Grace noticed that the nun's voice bore signs of breaking.

Sofia walked past Grace and into the kitchen to make some tea. Grace followed her.

'I thought my forced journey through the jungle was the worst I've ever had to endure. But the thought of the children being harmed today… well, there are no words for how I feel right now. I'm thankful, though, that none of them sustained serious injuries.' Grace looked optimistically at Sofia. 'Do you think Brutus' leg will be alright?'

'He's such an energetic one,' the nun replied, while handing a steaming cup to Grace. 'No injury will keep him from his future adventures—of that, I'm sure!' Sofia gave Grace her usual beaming smile, but Grace felt her heart sink.

'And you? How are you feeling? You've not had a moment's rest.'

Sofia's voice was soft when she replied, 'It's the Lord who gives me strength.'

Grace shared Cassia's vision with Sofia, how the child saw two angels protecting the children. Tears streamed down the nun's cheeks as Grace spoke, then she put her arms around the young woman. They stayed like that for a while before Grace asked Sofia how Joseph was coping. 'I noticed he was having a serious talk with an official. It didn't seem right to interrupt him. I was certain they were discussing something of importance around the accident. Joseph seemed terribly worried.'

Sofia dabbed her eye with the edge of her large sleeve. 'It appears, Señorita, that the sludge dams that broke over the orphanage weren't the result of an accident. The police believe from their brief investigation that the incident was the result of human tampering.'

Grace tried to calm herself. 'Who would do such a terrible thing? How could anyone carry out such evil?'

Sofia placed a comforting hand on Grace's arm, her voice was sober. 'The perpetrators were hiding in the hills for some days drilling holes in the foundation of the dam. Their intention was to weaken it enough for it to give way.'

The nun relaxed. 'Gracie, it is better for us to not be concerned with what might have happened. Rather, we should praise God for the miracle he has given us. Our children were saved from a terrible tragedy today, and little Cassia… well… she has been given the gift to see what God can do for those who put their trust in him.'

Grace was about to respond when the side door was

pushed open. It was Joseph and he looked a mess. She immediately hurried to him, and they embraced. They held onto each other for a while, as if to ease the strain that usually accompanies a situation of such dreadful consequence. Sofia walked over to the stove and began to brew more tea.

'Have you finished with the police, Josephie?' the nun gently inquired. She longed for things to be normal again. 'We will have to get to work first thing in the morning. There is much to be done.'

Joseph seemed oblivious to Sophia's questions. He motioned for them to sit—he had something say. Grace had enjoyed so many happy exchanges with her new family at the table where they sat. Now, however, she could not quell the dread she felt.

The priest chose his words carefully. 'I've not spoken to either of you about this. It's a matter I've been praying about. To be honest, I thought that by not speaking up, the issue would eventually dissolve. The time has come, however, for me to tell you what's been going on since we brought Grace to The Cielo.'

Joseph looked at Grace. His heart betrayed his thoughts. 'I've been receiving threatening calls for some time. I suspect they're from the militia. I don't know for sure. They're always anonymous.'

He got up from where he was sitting, and paced. 'The callers demand that I hand Grace over to them or suffer the consequences.'

Joseph searched her face. 'They said they have unfinished business with Antonio.' He shortened the space between them and then knelt in front of Grace. 'I'm so sorry, Señorita. I should've told you. Now I feel I have failed you all. I thought it better to keep you protected from the reality of the situation, but I'm afraid it has not worked out the way I intended.'

The priest folded his large hands over Grace's. They felt soft to him.

'In hindsight, I should've said something…' His voice gave way. 'I realise now that, in my own efforts to protect you, I was stealing all the power of deliverance from this matter. The truth is that I've placed The Cielo in terrible danger.'

Mama Sofia could not bear to hear Joseph speak this way. She wedged herself between Grace and the priest. 'Josephie, you are right. This situation was never yours to carry alone. We must look for a solution together, and we can only do this with the help of God.'

Joseph knew better than to wallow in self-pity with the old nun. He took Grace by the hand to invite her to join them in prayer.

Grace prayed with them, but she could not help feeling angered. Joseph was certainly not to be blamed for what had happened. She resolved to tell the priest her exact thoughts when they finished praying.

It all sounded right in her head but was so difficult to say. 'You're wrong, Joseph,' she finally blurted out. 'The one who has put everyone in danger is me. Who knows what evil these people are plotting next? The risk is far too great. I cannot—I will not—allow this to go on any longer!'

Stifling a sob, Grace gathered herself and ran up the stairwell that led to her room. She had a lot to think about. Although she hated to leave Joseph and Sofia standing there, it was up to her to figure out a way to save them all.

Joseph charged after Grace. He thumped his fist on the heavy door, pleading for her to open for him. Grace refused to give in. She knew Joseph would not persist for fear of waking the children. She waited till she heard his footsteps retreating, then she quietly wept into her pillow.

After she had calmed herself, Grace reached for her Bible. Placing it on her chest, she prayed. For the first time since she had opened her heart to be healed at The Cielo, Grace was afraid. Not even Joseph could help her now. Father Ralph was right... or rather, God had revealed to him what would happen. Grace felt completely powerless. She recalled the old priest's words that the Lord would make a way for them. They comforted her till she was able to fall asleep.

Grace woke the next morning to the roar of earth-moving equipment. She could hear people busying themselves with the disaster's aftermath. She made her way to the window. Looking out she noticed there were strangers among the people of The Cielo. Some men, young and old, had come to help; they were clearing the rubble with picks and shovels. Large trucks lined the edge of the area, ready to haul away huge amounts of debris. She could hear the children singing and watched them help where they could. Grace thought of how much they had taught her about faith and hope. It dawned on her that her reliance on God should be like that of the children. She saw Joseph in the distance with the other workers. He was hunched over some of the wreckage, working vigorously alongside them. Grace could see the path that led from the orphanage to the village. There was a faint column of people walking on it, and they sang as they made their way towards The Cielo. In their hands were baskets laden with food wrapped in flatbreads.

Although the sun was not that strong, Grace noticed that Joseph was already perspiring—his damp shirt clung to his back. She looked at his grim face and at the children who were helping. It was then that she realised how much she loved him.

She also knew that her battle was not theirs to fight. It was perhaps time for her to leave the orphanage in order to protect them all from further harm. She would have to depend on the Lord completely for her own safekeeping. She knelt at her bed and prayed, surrendering her life to the preeminence of God's will. Her heart and mind acknowledged that He alone knew all things hidden and revealed, the beginning and the end. She would have to trust Him implicitly for what lay ahead.

***

The next few days passed slowly. The clearing and reparations seemed endless. In between her English classes, Grace helped the children to reconstruct the vegetable garden that had been destroyed. This brought some comfort to her. Joseph had, however, distanced himself. Grace assumed that his detachment was as a result of his own feelings of failure—a man's soul-wrestling with God.

A solemn atmosphere pervaded the little haven as everyone became serious about putting the orphanage back together again. The threat of further harm from the offenders hung like an ominous cloud over the area. Grace still believed that leaving The Cielo was the right thing to do. She consoled herself with the fact that her decision would give her an opportunity to stand on her own and to grow in her new-found faith without being so dependent on Joseph. It was time to continue the journey God had planned for her life.

All too quickly, the time came for Grace to tell Joseph of her choice. It was, however, difficult to find the priest in one place for any length of time. She noticed that contributions had poured in to help repair what was damaged—even a new tractor, red and shiny, found its way to the orphanage. Sponsored equipment and an endless supply of building material had to be allocated correctly. A new outbuilding to store food for the animals was already underway. It was Joseph who worked tirelessly to fund and fix all that was broken. He rose before sun-up and was away till dark. Grace felt, however, that her decision could not wait any longer. She prayed for an opportunity to speak to the priest. God answered her prayer in a special way.

As expected, the usual routine of the children at the orphanage had been affected by the disaster. It became a common sight to find them playing amongst the old rubble or on a pile of hay that had been brought in by one of the neighbouring families. The grass bales were turned into trampolines on which the children tested their jumping skills. Mama Sofia said to leave them be—it was their way of saying goodbye to what was gone. The challenge, however, was for the adults to find the children when important chores had to be done and classes attended. Grace was amused with Sofia's constant frustration at trying to collect them for their duties. It was when she thought of not being able to enjoy the many special moments with the people at the orphanage that her heart ached the most. *Who would help them tend to the vegetable garden? Who would be patient with them as they tried to pronounce the vowels in the English language?*

On one occasion when Sofia and one of the volunteers called out for the children to wash before dinner, they noticed that young Cassia was missing. Grace was about to conclude her lesson with some of the older children. She looked from the window of her classroom and noticed small drops of rain begin to fall. They would have to make a dash for it if they were going to miss the pending downpour.

When Joseph entered the homestead looking for shelter from the rain, he heard of Cassia's disappearance—and immediately assured the nun that he knew of the child's whereabouts. A hen, which was raising baby chicks, had flown up to the loft of the newly built barn. The feathered family had become a pleasant distraction for the little girl. Cassia had been following the birds' activities all day—she could be found there, he was sure of it.

Joseph set out for the barn with the rain chasing his back. He called for the child till his throat hurt. As he entered the shed, he instinctively looked up. To his dismay, he saw that Cassia had climbed up and onto the highest beam of the barn's ceiling; he assumed the child had wanted to reach the hen and her chicks. Cassia was straddled over the newly erected strut which was meant to keep the roof secure.

Joseph watched as Cassia stretched her little hands towards the hen who had fashioned a neat nest between the grooves, where two of the smaller supporting beams met. The child made small clucking noises in an attempt to coax the bird from its nest. Joseph's heart softened. As he stood there watching her, fearless in her hope of reaching the bird, courage took hold of him, and he asked

God to forgive him for allowing his heart to harden. Joseph called out to the child again. 'Cassia, you are needed for dinner. Hold tight, I'm coming to get you.'

Cassia glanced at Joseph briefly but turned back to the mother hen. Joseph was surprised at her agility—she held onto the large beam with one hand, while using the other to entice the bird.

'I'm coming to get you,' he repeated.

It was clear Cassia had made her way up by climbing on a series of hay bales and ladders. These were still erected against the interior braces of the barn. Joseph could also see that it would be difficult for her to navigate her way back down again. Realising the same thing, she looked anxiously at him from her lofty position. Suddenly Cassia shook her head vigourously at Joseph.

'No, Josephie,' she insisted. Joseph smiled at Cassia's use of Sofia's name for him. 'I want Teacher Gracie to help me down.'

The child spoke assertively while balancing precariously on the long beam. Joseph looked desperately up at her, not knowing what to do. Then he noticed Cassia's expression change—she looked past him with the sweetest smile. The priest turned slightly, careful to keep his eyes on her, only to see Grace standing beside him.

Grace had brought one of the volunteers with her. She called out to Cassia, 'Hold tight! I'm on my way.'

Joseph watched in amusement as Grace bounded up the bales and ladders like one accustomed to living on elevated terrain. In a short time, Grace was straddled over the beam, safely behind the little girl. Grace told Cassia to fasten her arms around her neck. With her free arm she scooped up the rest of Cassia's small body and soon they were safely on the barn's floor. Grace snuggled Cassia, declaring what a little rascal she was, before handing the child over to the helper.

Joseph shook his head and smiled, his ego slightly bruised. He indicated to the young woman who had accompanied Grace that she should take Cassia back to the house for dinner.

Grace was about to follow the two of them when Joseph caught her by the hand.

'Gracie, we need to talk.'

Although it was the perfect time for them to speak, it had come too quickly. Sensing her hesitation, Joseph did not let go of her. He led her to one of the lower bales of hay.

'Señorita, I owe you an apology. It's not like me to avoid a matter as important as this. I feel as if my heart has betrayed how I've always known it to be.'

Joseph spoke in a firm, yet gentle voice. 'I know this whole affair has distressed you terribly. I've been praying earnestly for the best solution. Each time I see you, I feel I'm letting you down because I don't have an answer yet. I cannot bear to see you suffer, so I thought it best to throw myself into the work needed to restore The Cielo.'

The priest stopped speaking, searching Grace's face for a response.

Grace fought back her tears. She placed her hand on Joseph's arm. The gesture, although restraining, was filled with love. 'I must also apologise,' she said, 'for the evening following the disaster. My reaction to you baring your heart to me was unacceptable. For that I'm truly sorry.'

Grace let her hand slide to meet his. 'I've been

praying too.' Looking away, she continued, 'I believe I have a remedy to this awful situation. For the safety of everyone here, I must leave The Cielo.'

She had said it. Although her heart was breaking, Grace was also somewhat relieved.

'God already prepared us for this day. Father Ralph revealed the Lord's plan to us. I'm convinced of what must be done. The militia won't stop attacking the orphanage till they have me.'

She turned to face him again.

Joseph did not speak for a while. A war of emotions raged inside him. He fought the urge to take Grace in his arms and run away with her. But Joseph was bound in spirit and body to his family at The Cielo. He knew he would have to let her go.

Joseph stood up from his seat beside Grace. 'Then, this is what we'll do. As you have correctly stated, it was confirmed before we experienced any of this. For this reason alone, I'll stand by your decision.'

Joseph ran a hand through his hair, 'It would be selfish of me to persuade you otherwise.'

Before Grace could say anything, he continued, 'I have a good friend who can help you. He's many miles from here, but it'll be a safe place for you. In turn you'll be able to help him, just as you've been a blessing to us…' His voice trailed.

Grace could see that Joseph wanted to say more, but it was difficult for him. He took her face in his hands, then lowered his head to kiss her forehead. Without looking at her again, Joseph exited the barn hunching his body in the rain.

Grace looked on as Joseph made his way back to the homestead. She cried openly then. Her tears were not from regret. Instead, they spilled from her eyes like a soft balm, easing the sacrifice they were both making. A feather drifted down from the beam where Cassia had climbed. Grace noticed the mother hen tuck her wings securely around her chicks. She was reminded of a scripture she had read in the book of Psalms, *He shall cover you with His feathers, and under His wings you shall take refuge...*

Nothing was said of Grace's anticipated departure from The Cielo in the days that followed. Joseph had asked Sofia to help him keep the news from the children till it was time for Grace to leave. He had further entreated the nun that they should try their best to celebrate the good things God had prepared for the young woman. 'A celebration of his grace upon her life,' he had said. Joseph had reasoned that if the children could observe both him and Grace in a state of good cheer, their grief would not take long to heal. Sofia felt that Joseph was in reality talking about himself, which further saddened her.

Grace noticed that Sofia bustled more than usual around The Cielo. She patiently endured the nun's behaviour, for this was the way, Grace had learned, that Sofia processed her own pain. The nun was able to hide her aching heart behind an unbroken rhythm of busyness. Sofia did not allow herself to mention Grace's parting—the decision had been made by Grace and Joseph, even though she might not agree with it.

***

Sofia invited Grace to the terrace one morning to share a special breakfast with Joseph. It was the same spot where Joseph had shared with Grace the gospel of salvation through Jesus Christ. The outside air was cool as Grace stepped onto the patio. A red-and-white checkered cloth thrown over the quaint table flapped happily in the breeze. Grace noticed Joseph sitting there gazing into the distant hills. He turned to her when she greeted him, and although he was more reserved than usual, he could not hide how happy he was to see her.

Joseph pulled out a chair for Grace. 'I have some good news, Señorita.' There was a slight pause in his voice. 'I've spoken to my good friend, Mark Benton, who I mentioned earlier. He has a school in India. It is a learning centre for young girls who live in the mountains. Their families are poor, and they need someone who can teach them English.'

Joseph looked at Grace with hope in his eyes.

'Mark lost his wife some years ago in the city of Mumbai. They ran an establishment there to rescue young girls from the streets. Although he no longer lives in the city, he still works amongst the poor. Mark provides education for their daughters who are frequently abused. He also helps their fathers to improve their outdated farming methods.'

Joseph shifted in his chair to lean closer.

'I know this is a far place for you to go. I don't know how you feel about such a challenge, but I fear that nowhere on this continent will be safe for you right now.'

As she listened carefully to Joseph, Grace felt she had the answers to her prayers. God had prepared her for this time, and she knew she should take it. The people at the orphanage would be safe again.

Joseph's face was close to hers now. 'It's as if God gave you to us for this short time, Señorita. He has chosen to continue your journey, to take you to those who need you more than we do.'

His voice dropped to a whisper, and he touched her face. 'I will miss you, Grace.'

Grace placed her hand gently over his. 'Hush. I'm the one who has much to be grateful for. If you hadn't rescued me, I wouldn't be here. I wouldn't have known your love or the love of a God who is able to heal the brokenhearted.'

She wiped a stray tear with the back of her hand. 'I won't say goodbye. I don't know what the future holds, but I will see you again.'

Her tears fell freely now.

Grace and Joseph spent the rest of the morning together—two friends in pleasant conversation. They laughed and reminisced over the experiences they had shared at the haven. Perhaps they did so because they knew it would be their last, or perhaps it was because they understood that true love is an act higher than itself. Whatever the reason, Grace would keep forever the memories she had of Joseph and the dear people at the orphanage.

It was decided that the children would be told of Grace's departure the day before she left. A celebratory meal was planned by Mama Sofia. Joseph had made all the arrangements for Grace's passage to India. He told everyone on the eve of her departure why it was important for Grace to leave The Cielo.

For the younger ones, the priest used the illustration of a butterfly that had been recently freed from its cocoon. 'Teacher Gracie must fly to a different part of the world where she'll meet up with countless other butterflies from other countries.' He went on to explain that because she had learned so many special things at the orphanage, their teacher had to leave The Cielo to teach other children how to spin their own cocoons so that one day they too could learn how to fly.

Cassia sat on Grace's lap while Joseph spoke to them all. One of the older girls held her teacher's hand while Joseph concluded his speech. Joseph encouraged the children to pray for Grace. Sofia stifled a sob in the sleeves of her nun's habit. She managed to compose herself, though. It was not her wish to turn their last moments together into a sad occasion. Some of the older children went over to Grace to pray with her. Others needed to be close without saying anything.

***

In the early hours of the morning, Grace gathered her luggage. With Pedro's help she slipped out of the homestead to where Joseph was waiting. Pedro drove them down to the watercourse near the orphanage. The river was easily navigated by boat. Pedro would take Grace over to the other side where transport had been arranged for her to be lifted to Columbia's international airport. Before that, Joseph would say goodbye. Little tongues of water licked the side of the vessel while a breeze played with Grace's hair. She felt her heart ache for the man she was leaving behind.

The priest was quiet, wrestling with his own feelings. He had fallen in love with Grace. Everything Joseph stood for as a man could not let her go. More than anything, he longed to hold onto her. Throughout his years at the orphanage, Joseph had given of himself sacrificially. But this time was different—perhaps the most difficult thing he had ever done. Of one thing they were both certain, though. Far greater than the strength of their own desires was their willingness to submit to the will of God.

The two friends did not say goodbye. A lengthy embrace was all they could manage. As they held each other, not wanting the moment to pass, Grace noticed again the small tattoo etched under Joseph's collarbone. This time the inscription was quite clear: love—Life's highest gain.

Grace finally pulled away from Joseph and stepped into the little vessel. She turned to face the land she could barely see. As the boat slipped into the water, Joseph fell to his knees.

PART II

. . . better than both is he who has never existed, who has never seen the evil work that is done under the sun.
– Ecclesiastes 4:3

5
Red-Light District, Mumbai, India

Alisha sat patiently while she waited for the finishing touches to her appearance. Her madam, a panderer and old street woman, worked quickly to transform the young Indian woman's face for the night's festivities. If a client saw her girls looking less than attractive, it would be bad for business. Harita skilfully painted Alisha's features like an artist altering the landscape of a blank canvas—a dash of colour here, a subtle stroke there. She worked till the young woman resembled a beautiful figurine. It was a rule to make up one's face each night. The young street girls followed this principle faithfully for fear of Harita's wrath. They were daughters of the night, plying their trade when the sun had sanctioned rest for ordinary folk.

Harita loathed the word prostitute. She preferred to call her girls courtesans. This was more to preserve her own sense of self-importance than out of real concern for the girls in her charge. Facing Harita, Alisha's perfect composure beguiled the sea of emotions raging inside. She had learned the art of deception well: smile at the world through a glassy veneer—hide from them the truth of a fractured heart. What was left to see was only an empty shell, a vacant house that once held dreams of being inhabited by love and joy.

Annoyed with Alisha's constant daydreaming, Harita hurried the young courtesan from the girls' elevated quarters to join the others in the lively streets below. The Diwali fireworks display was underway. A plethora of brilliant colours lit up the dark Mumbai sky.

'Really, Al, you can at least put a smile on your face. After all, you don't have to work tonight. That should give you something to be happy about.' Alisha's only friend, Sabeehah, tried to cheer her up. Tonight, though, Alisha felt a thousand miles from everyone.

Harita called on the young women to stay together as they moved gracefully through the crowded streets. The woman was a force to be reckoned with. None of the girls dared to defy her. Alisha recalled an incident when instead of resting during the day, she had gone down to the river with Sabeehah. The people in the district believed that their waterways had special healing powers. The two of them had played in the churning water for hours, forgetting momentarily the misery of their lives. They had abandoned themselves to the sweet pleasantness that comes from time spent with friends. When night came, though, they were both so tired that they had failed to secure the clients they were expected to.

When Harita had heard of their disobedience, she was so mad at them that she kept them in a room hardly bigger than a closet for two whole days. It sent a clear message to all her girls. Harita meant business and she was willing to go to great lengths to let them know that they were her property.

'The night's still young. Perhaps you'll finally find your knight in shining armour after all.'

Sabeehah spoke as if she were performing on a stage, 'My darling Al, when will you realise it's all a fantasy. This *is* our destiny. We're the set-apart ones. We can't dream like the others.'

Sabeehah meant well, but Alisha was in no mood to talk. Sabeehah changed her approach. 'Let's go down to the temple. We need to pray to the gods.'

She hooked her arm in Alisha's and pulled her friend along. 'Here, I've brought with me some fruit and flowers.' The young woman held out her hands. 'The gods are the only ones we must please right now. If we do this right, someday they'll favour us in return.'

Alisha remained quiet. She had grown tired of all the empty promises their faith offered. Reluctantly she followed the party of street women as they made their way to the temple.

Tonight, seemed different to other nights, though. Alisha had a strange feeling that something extraordinary was about to happen.

What are these peculiar thoughts floating around my head like lilies on a moonlit pond? She quickly composed herself to avoid the glare Harita threw her. Alisha gathered the prettily-stitched wrap that draped her shoulders, as if to keep the familiar close.

They descended the stairs to the Hindu temple. Alisha arranged the exotic fruit and scented flowers in a neat display in front of one of the deity's bronzed feet. The simplicity of this customary gesture was in stark contrast to the ostentatious figure of the idol. The goddess had been created to provide solace and peace for those who were brokenhearted.

The other girls hung around the temple, chatting softly in groups of two and three. Alisha found a place to sit alone next to the effigy, and quietly reflected on her life. She had been a part of this trade for a long time. Taken from her family, who lived in the rural mountains of India, when she was just a girl, she had become someone she no longer recognised.

Alisha had long since learned to conceal her true self beneath the soft folds of her sari and behind the clinker of her cheap jewellery. The bracelets that adorned her arms passed her elbows and jingled as she arranged the flowers at the feet of the goddess. Their sound reminded her of her mother's old copper spoons which made melodic tunes when they came into contact with each other. The longing she had felt to see her parents and siblings again had faded like the ash from the incense that burned into the night air. Alisha still believed, however, that they would not stop searching for her. It was only that they did not know where to look. She consoled herself with this thought.

Alisha honoured the goddess Yellamma that night. By sacrificing to the deity in this way, the young woman was led to believe that the goddess would ease her family's financial burdens on her behalf. She comforted herself with the belief that although she had originally been brought to the red-light district of Mumbai by evil means, she was able to use the situation to ease her family's suffering.

From the moment of her kidnapping as an adolescent girl, Alisha had been prepared for a life as a *devadasi*, or temple courtesan. This meant she could never marry. Her life's work would be her devotion to the temple goddess—a union considered to be the same as a marriage. She would earn the title of "God's Female Servant".

Although India has outlawed most of these dishonourable practices, they continue to exist in the underbelly of Mumbai. Once, when Harita got word of officials snooping around her territory, she made the girls stop their work, and beg instead for money from the people who visited the temples. Much like Alisha and Sabeehah, the other courtesans were also born into a class of untouchables—a division in Indian society made up of impoverished families. They are considered the lowest in the caste system of Hindu society. The only hope of a better life for them, they believe, is secured in the cycle of rebirth. Through reincarnation these people hope to be born back into a higher class after their death. Few of them have heard of the gospel of Jesus Christ—the sacrifice of one who paid the price for all to be free. Alisha had once heard of the man called Jesus; the message about him had fascinated her.

Her thoughts drifted to the teacher who had taught at the school she had attended high up in the mountains when she was a young girl. The teacher's name was Mr Pradhi, though the girls and boys at her school called him Mr Prad. The teacher used to speak to the students between their lessons about a faith he referred to as Christianity. Each day, Mr Prad would set time aside to share the gospel with them, mostly when he had completed teaching his lessons in basic literacy. Mr Prad would read to them from a small book he kept in a secret place. He never shared the title of the book with them, and always kept it close to him when he read passages from it.

Alisha could tell from the short stories he shared that there was only one God. This God was great and mighty. He loved everyone equally, and he showed his love by saving them from the terrifying consequences of sin by sending his only Son to be punished in their place. Not only did this God perform this amazing deed for them, but he had also saved them from the beliefs and traditions that had kept them enslaved to poverty and a life of despair. Alisha recalled being astonished when Mr Prad had told them that the gift of God's Son was for free. They could receive him without price when they repented from their sins and believed in him.

Many of the students had scoffed at Mr Prad. The people in her village often reacted violently when it came to the incursions of other faiths upon their own. Alisha had listened quietly. She had kept Mr Prad's words in her heart for a long time.

Alisha continued to arrange the flowers around the idol's feet, then sat back in the folds of her sari. She remembered the day she was stolen from her family. It was a time of unspeakable terror.

***

Rural Tamil Nadu, Southern India

It rained on the frightful day of Alisha's abduction. She was just fourteen years old. The morning sun rose boldly above the rice paddies, caressing the crops in a dazzling display of white brilliance. As with all the days of her labour in the fields, the Indian girl got up early. She gathered her tools, neatly packed in a worn canvas bag, and headed out. The small rural school set on a hill overlooking the paddies was the only place of solace for her; learning to read and write was the only motivation she needed to get through the monotony of her work. Alisha loved to read. She imagined herself to be a famous writer one day.

Alisha stopped at the neatly thatched farm huts which were built with what soil and grass the fields provided. They were cozy, and smelled of wood fire and incense. She waited for her friends to walk with her down to the paddies. Sarika and the free-spirited Dharini joined her. They laughed openly at the failed attempts of their new teacher to keep their class in order.

'He's a royal prude,' Dharini offered in a high-pitched voice. She flicked her hair in mock sophistication and placed her hands firmly on her hips. The young girl had been given a fair share of bodily endowment. She believed this gift set her apart from others; her natural confidence, she reminded her friends, should not be mistaken for conceit. Sarika, who was always the cautious one, replied in a clipped voice, 'Well, I'd also need to be strict if I was your teacher, Dharini. Someone has to keep you in line.'

Always keen to have the last word, Dharini reacted playfully. 'Come now, Sarika, you really must be careful how you speak of me. I might assume you're Prad's pet!'

Sarika grew impatient. She stamped her foot before walking ahead of her friends in a huff. Her reaction only fueled Dharini's mischievous nature and she threw her head back to laugh mockingly. Alisha was used to her friends' lively banter. She often joined in, but this time she kept to herself. She was deep in thought about a matter that troubled her. How she longed to speak to her friends about the recurring dreams she had. They were, to her, like tormenting gnats on a hot summer night—the same dream visiting her mind, over and over again.

In the dream Alisha was standing in a field of rice. Its emerald stalks and golden ears reached her tiny waist. Suddenly, from a cloudless sky, rain began to fall. It made her shiver with cold. In the distance she saw a group of winged men dressed in long robes, wielding sharp sickles.

The dark angels glided towards her. Alisha was unable to cry out or run from them. They flew above her with their shadowy wings, and one of them lifted her onto the point of his sickle and carried her far from her beloved village. Eventually they reached a huge gaping hole in the ground spewing fire and smoke from its centre. The dark angel dropped Alisha into the opening of the burning chasm. Her dream ended.

There would be no sharing her dream today. Thanks to Dharini, Sarika had separated from them, and they were almost at the paddy fields. Alisha, however, could not shake her sense of foreboding. She wanted to tell her friends to run because evil was approaching. How could she, though? She would be treated as a fool. Was she not constantly teased by her friends for always having her head in the clouds?

The morning passed with usual uniformity as they removed the rice in bunches from their carpets of green, cut the bulbs free, and stacked the stalks onto wooden crates. Young men would later collect them to be transported to the sorting factory. The rest of the golden grain's journey was the responsibility of others more skilled than them.

Alisha's work was almost complete when she felt a still wind, like ghostly fingers, rake through the air. Hesitantly, she scanned the horizon for signs of an intrusion. These premonitions were overwhelming. They consumed her every thought. Then, to Alisha's surprise, droplets of water began to fall as if the heavens had pulled back a watery curtain. Tiny at first, the liquid beads grew bigger till they felt like shards of ice beating on her upturned face.

'Hello, Al.'

A young man stood in front of her with another one in tow. The voice was familiar. Alisha searched her memory. She knew the man. He was a relative—a distant cousin. *What is he doing here in the paddy fields? I haven't seen him in years.*

'It's, Ganesh. Don't you recognise me?'

'Of course… Ganesh,' Alisha ventured, wiping the rain from her face. 'It's just that you're all grown up now. How is Uncle Cheera… and your mother?'

Alisha struggled to dismiss the uneasy feeling that crept over her. She had always felt uncomfortable in her older cousin's presence. *How did he know I was here? Had he already been to my parents' hut, asking my whereabouts?*

The young man's response was guarded. He appeared restless. 'They're good, all good. Let's get out of the rain. I see a tree. We can take shelter.'

Ganesh placed his hand under Alisha's elbow. He urged her and Dharini to follow him to the nearby cover. His friend, a peculiar little man, did not leave his side.

'Join us at the village festivities tonight,' Ganesh casually offered. 'We can talk then, catch up on old times.'

Alisha instinctively felt this was not a good idea. She was about to oppose her cousin's proposal when an eager Dharini butted in, swiftly replying on behalf of her friend. 'Of course we'll be there, Al's cousin! We'll not miss it for the entire world. Not so, Al?'

Dharini raised an intimidating eyebrow. Before Alisha could respond, Dharini grabbed her by the arm and marched her decisively towards the dirt road that led to their humble homes.

***

On the well-worn road that led to the huts of the poor farmers, Alisha was persuaded by her friend to meet her fate at the festival that was to commemorate the birth of their gods. How was Dharini to know that her persuasion would cost them both their freedom. The young girls were unsuspecting of the heinous greed that dwells in the hearts of some. Alisha's parents had urged her to attend the festival with Dharini. 'This is the right thing to do,' they had said.

It was also decided that Alisha's brother would go along. Although he was younger than his sister, it would be appropriate to have a male accompany the girls. Innocent as they were, Alisha's family did not realise that doing the 'right thing' for the sake of convention often carries severe consequences. How could they have known that their daughters would be plucked from their meagre yet safe homes to become victims of human slavery. Alisha discovered later that her cousin was part of a syndicate who kidnapped young Indian girls to sell to brothels in the big cities.

Ganesh waited in secret for Alisha and Dharini. The moon had come up quickly that night, as if deliberately dislodging the sun from its private space. Its ominous face mocked the lively activities below. The festival was well underway when Alisha arrived with Dharini and her younger brother. The three youngsters gaped at the scene before them. This was the first time they had ventured so far from their huts on their own. Reluctantly, they stepped from the main street as the colourful procession floated by. Never had they seen such splendor. Some of the idols were hoisted carefully onto the shoulders of young men as the parade snaked its way down the narrow street. Dispersing small puffs of sand from their prancing feet, the people following the procession sang and danced around the statues in vibrant unanimity.

Eventually, the trio joined the dancers, enjoying the feeling of the leaves from the fruit trees strewn on the ground beneath their bare feet. Colourful flowers and the strong smell of incense filled the air with their heavy scent. This was a time when the humble folk of the rural plains of India took to the streets to celebrate the produce yielded from their planting and harvesting. It was their way of showing gratitude to the gods, no matter how inadequate their crops.

Alisha searched for Ganesh as they followed the masses. Still, she had a sinking feeling. Sensing Ameet's annoyance at his sister's behaviour, Dharini began to show some concern of her own.

'Where's your cousin, Alisha?' Dharini searched the multitude of worshippers for Ganesh and the odd little man who clung to him like a shadow. 'I thought he was to meet us here.'

Wondering whether Ganesh had forgotten their appointment, Alisha felt a light wind at the back of her neck. She caught sight of Ganesh and his friend making their way towards them. The young men appeared to have exited a building at the edge of the lane where the procession languished a little.

'Ah, there you are, cousin,' Ganesh addressed Alisha brusquely.

Alisha tried to avoid looking into Ganesh's shadowy face.

He spoke to the three of them. 'We've been searching all over for you. It's quite chaotic here, isn't it?'

Ganesh looked approvingly at Dharini. 'Good evening, Alisha's friend.'

He turned his attention to Alisha's brother. 'How you've grown, Ameet!' Alisha got the distinct impression that Ganesh was sidling up to his cousin. 'My aunt and uncle must be proud to have such a good-looking family.'

Ganesh placed his hand firmly behind Ameet's neck, easing the boy over to the little man. 'I want you to go with my good friend, Nirbhik. He will take you to where there's plenty of food and fun.'

Ganesh whispered the rest of his instructions into Ameet's ear, adding, 'I don't think your sister had that in mind for you.'

Chuckling, Ganesh poked Ameet playfully in the ribs and raised his voice again for all to hear. 'Don't worry, Cousin, you're in good hands. We'll meet up with you later.'

Alisha moved towards Nirbhik to protest, but Dharini was easily captivated by blatant charm, and pushed in front of her.

Giggling, she asked, 'And what have you in mind for us, Alisha's cousin?'

Ganesh did not like to be questioned. Alisha could sense he felt uncomfortable.

'Oh, not much, really,' he replied, feigning disinterest. 'Perhaps you would like to look at some jewellery a friend of mine makes. She doesn't live far from here. Actually, you will find her skill quite fascinating.'

Ganesh shifted on his feet. Then, with renewed interest he chimed, 'I'm sure she'll be willing to show you.'

The two girls accepted Ganesh's offer, and in that instant Alisha was separated from her brother forever. Reluctantly, Alisha followed Dharini, who was by now chatting continually to Alisha's cousin. Alisha thought her parents would not approve of Dharini's behaviour, and she began to panic.

Ganesh directed the girls to his friend's shanty. The commotion of the festival and colourful display of fireworks faded into the background. The path they were on narrowed. It took them to a quieter part of the town. A cold wind began to blow, lashing at their flimsy clothing. It was dark and the only light came from the dimly lit entrances of the quaint, tightly packed dwellings that lined the street. Alisha lagged behind Ganesh. He noticed her hesitancy and reached out to take her by the arm. His grip made her feel uncomfortable. She wanted to run from him, but found she froze instead. Alisha tried to signal Dharini but her words, like icicles on a cold window, stuck to her lips.

Dharini appeared quite oblivious to what was going on around them. She continued to chatter as if unaffected by the imminent danger the girls were in. Suddenly, from a dark lane that separated two of the shanty dwellings, the speed of which took the girls by surprise, a group of young men approached. Their faces were indistinguishable in the dim light. The men formed a tight circle around Alisha and Dharini. In an instant the two Indian girls were kidnapped from the festivities that venerated their gods.

***

Alisha felt her head tighten. She struggled to breathe. The words she wished for others to hear did not come. Questions flooded her mind instead. *What is happening to me? Where are Dharini and Ameet?*

A dissonance of sharp voices shook Alisha awake.

She opened her eyes and peeped at the scene in front of her as if she was watching a play on a stage. Men and women were talking loudly to each other. Their loose shirt sleeves flapped wildly as they engaged in some kind of verbal negotiation. Alisha's head throbbed. Her body went rigid. Involuntarily, she closed her eyes, reliving her earlier nightmare. She thought of Dharini again. *Was her friend with her?* Alisha had heard of such kidnappings, but the stories seemed imaginary.

She forced her eyes open when she heard the whimpering of other girls. Through half-shut eyes she watched as adult men and women pushed the girls around. When her vision cleared, Alisha noticed that they were being held in a box-like cage attached to a small house. There was no sign of Ganesh or the little man. The girls in the cage were tightly packed together. Some of them appeared to be drugged while others struggled to get free.

A scrawny-looking man with thick black hair made his way towards her. He had a bottle of dark liquid in his hand. Before he reached Alisha, an older woman sprang at him, filling the tight space between him and the terrified girl.

'She's mine, Sunil! I've already spoken with Ravi. This one's a beauty and a possible *devadasi*,' the woman barked at the man before dismissing him with a vigorous nod. 'She'll work the temple.'

This was Alisha's introduction to the woman who would become her madam—Harita. So began Alisha's life on the streets in India's Mumbai.

***

Harita kept a light burning all day and night at the entrance of her establishment. She did this to distract onlookers from the activities behind the narrow awning made of cheap fabric that fringed the doorway to her brothel. She was proud of her temple courtesans. Despite the fact that such practices were officially outlawed, Harita and others like her continued to make a living from it.

Although they lived in poor conditions above the streets, Harita's girls did not suffer the cruel subjections of the other prostitutes. Most of the street girls were underage. They were kept in cramped spaces when they were not working. The older madam preferred her girls to keep together in small groups on the streets. 'This way,' she had told them, 'you will be more alluring to potential customers.'

The sound of day-long traffic congestion and the loud honking of vehicles soaked the air with a heavy din.

Some of the girls had learned to shout out to their customers above the noise. Even the voices of hawkers and gangsters could be heard in the tragic mix. The customers were from all classes in Mumbai. They would walk down the streets negotiating a price with the madams of the girls in exchange for their services. This was a place where few people with good intentions ventured. This was Kamathipura, a region in the red-light district of Mumbai.

Alisha became attached to Harita at the outset of her abduction. It was a bond cemented by unrequited loyalty. Harita prided herself in not having to resort to drugs and alcohol to control her girls. She worked at maintaining a liaison of mother–daughter/mistress–slave with her girls. The panderer played a cunning game with her courtesans, keeping some of the money they earned, especially when she wished to extract some kind of favour from them.

Harita encouraged competition and invoked jealousy. Oblivious to the moral qualities that define human virtue, Harita was divisive. This was her way of teaching her daughters-of-the-night to become just like her.

***

Alisha sat at the feet of the idol that was supposed to relieve her family from their eternal cycle of suffering. She felt empty, defined by the momentary happiness she brought to the woman who owned her. Lamentably, Alisha was engaged in a battle she was destined to lose. Freedom was an idea only the street children understood. Mr Prad had spoken of a God who had offered his Son to be punished for the sins of the entire human race. This God could save humanity from its inclination towards self-destruction. Perhaps, she thought, this was a story like all others—a fairytale of flawless characters in an ideal world. Possibly, it was just a figment of Mr Prad's imagination. She bowed her head before the idol. As she sat there her thoughts drifted to the God of Mr Prad. Was it possible that he had the answers to a broken world?

***

Not all the girls kidnapped to be sold as sex slaves end up as prostitutes. Some of them manage to escape, but they have no way of returning home so they take to begging on the streets or joining gangs. Unsurprisingly, these girls eventually become victims of a system that will exploit their vulnerable positions.

One such girl was Esta.

The young Indian girl arrived in Mumbai's red-light district under similar circumstances to Alisha. Esta had, nonetheless, escaped from the evil intentions of her kidnappers almost moments after arriving in Kamathipura. Esta had always had an elusive quality about her. It was as if this gift was God-given. She was a Christian who held close to her heart the words of the English teacher she had met at her school in the mountains of Thane. Esta loved to hear the teachings of Jesus Christ. Only now, she no longer had the little book her teacher had given her—Esta had lost the small Bible during her abduction.

When she arrived in Kamathipura with her kidnappers, Esta had only one thought in mind—*run!*

She ran like a gazelle on that awful day when the axle of their heavily loaded truck broke. The other girls had huddled together for protection, but she had seized the moment and made a run for it. Esta was small and quick, and slipped from the hands of her abductors in the dark. The young girl did not stop despite the fact that she could barely see where she was going.

It was only when Esta collided with the burly frame of a flower vendor that her escape ended. Her eyes, wide and defiant, had looked up at the man. Pushing aside a strand of matted hair that clung stubbornly to her face, Esta had breathed heavily, not knowing what to do; she knew what she faced if she turned back. The man had mumbled something to her. He was a foreigner and his cheeks were puffy. Esta thought he looked strange, not like her people. The colour of his skin was pale and his tiny black eyes had looked down at her from behind narrow eyelids.

Just when Esta thought there was no getting away, the man's face broke into a broad smile. She was not sure whether to quickly slip past him or boot him in the shins.

She had witnessed her cousins do something similar with their stubborn livestock in the hills she called home. Distracted by the sweet smell that floated around the man, Esta hesitated. Then out of nowhere a second person appeared. The newcomer was an Indian girl about Esta's age. She seemed to understand Esta's dilemma. She also appeared to be friends with the man with the strange eyes.

She held out a colourful spray of fragrant flowers.

'Sweet child,' she said in Hindi, 'you look as if you're lost, or perhaps someone is chasing you?'

Esta was surprised at how grown up the young girl appeared.

'Don't fear, young one. You must have an angel watching over you, or perhaps fortune has smiled on you. Today you have run into the right person.'

The girl nudged the large man who seemed to have frozen. He smiled again. She introduced Esta to the sturdy stranger. 'This is Mr Shankar. He is a flower merchant. He saves girls like you from further quandary. You sell flowers for him, and he will give you food and water. For your efforts your new boss will also throw in a small allowance.

Although the girl spoke firmly to Esta, her smile remained. 'Mr Shankar is from Nepal and the traders do not like him very much. You see, sweet girl, he is very large and he has other strong friends like him who can protect you.'

She poked at the man who immediately broke into a hearty chortle.

'You may have noticed that Mr Shankar does not speak our language. If you want to accept his proposal, you must follow me.'

Esta said nothing, but willingly allowed the girl to take her by the hand. The girl chatted to her as they disappeared down an alleyway together. Mr Shankar heaved his large frame unhurriedly behind them. Esta had the distinct impression that she had just conceded to a one-sided business deal that had been orchestrated by God. Although the young Indian girl found herself in the care of strangers, she knew she was really in God's hands. Her new life in Kamathipura had just begun.

***

Esta enjoyed the sound of her own feet splashing in the dirty puddles as she weaved her small frame through the heavy traffic of Kamathipura's busiest street. She had been recruited by Mr Shankar and his loyal assistant to sell roses to pedestrians and motorists alike. Her new boss, who was quite kind, seemed to understand the conditions affecting those living on the grubby streets of the district. At least she got paid, albeit a small wage. The stipend did not include lodgings, but it was something to keep her alive and somewhat protected. Although she was still a slave in many ways, Esta felt free. God had not forgotten her. The peace she felt lifted her heart above the noisy bustle of Kamathipura.

It had rained all night, and finding shelter from the continuing downpour was challenging. Several street urchins and prostitutes crowded the narrow hallways of the dingy dwellings and shop entrances. Esta managed to find cover with a small band of boys. They huddled together around a mounted trash can beneath the awning of a vacant shop, which in a bizarre way was used as a symbol of solidarity. The bin generated a degree of warmth for the youngsters and protected them from the pelting rain. Esta was readily accepted by the little gang, who were careful to allow any stranger into their tight-knit circle. The boys realised that she was the one earning, and therefore good to have around.

The cheerful humour of the boys and the friendship she developed with them kept Esta motivated. Even though she detested their deviant behaviour she prayed for them and loved them in her own way. They reminded her of her brothers back home. Could it be that even the traditional promise of marriage to a boy in the mountains had prepared her for such a time as this?

The motorists and tourists appeared unusually grumpy that morning. Was it the rain, she wondered, or her own longing to be back with her grandmother and her old school in the mountains of Thane? Mr Shankar was a faithful master who honoured his part of their agreement. Esta came to know Shankar's trusty helper as Keshni. Keshni taught the younger girl all she needed to know about selling flowers in the streets of Kamathipura.

Esta learned special phrases from her, like 'Hello madam, you can buy these lovely flowers to light up your home' and 'These will make your wife happy.'

In short, Esta learned the art of constantly harassing tourists and locals. It was also here that she met the many street children of India. Most of them were not educated, but they were well-schooled in the art of hustling and thieving.

Nearly all of the flower trade in Mumbai is owned and run by Nepalese families who come to India to seek a living outside the harsh conditions of their own country. Each day the flowers are arranged at the dusty feet of poor Indian women and girls. Esta watched attentively as the flowers were garlanded into beautiful bouquets with the toes of their feet. She looked on with fascination as the big toe of a weaver girl's foot held some string in place while her fingers were used, with great skill, to weave the petals together. The girl's work continued like this till the whole creation resembled floral strings made from fragrant roses, blue lotus, and marigolds. The fragrances of the flowers and their vibrant colours of red, yellow and brilliant blue were enough to entice any passer.

Esta quickly learned to weave flowers. She attributed this fact to her days working at the stone quarry where she was abducted. She did, however, prefer to take to the streets and not sit in the sun like most of the other women and girls to sell her flowers. Her small body was well set for navigating the winding alleyways of Kamathipura. Mostly though, Esta was able to share the love of Jesus with others, knowing that she had a safe place to return to.

Mr Shankar grew used to the antics of his young vendor. The fact that she did not report to him every day gave him a sneaky suspicion that she was also about some other business. Soon Esta began to search and pray for an opportunity to meet other Christians. She believed there were those who were like her English teacher and the people at the school she had attended in the mountains. She just did not know where to find them.

***

One day, at a time when Esta had become quite accustomed to the demands of her new occupation, she happened to venture a little further from the confines of the familiar alleyways. She found herself in a dense maze of dimly lit passages and dark lanes. The labyrinth was lined with old buildings stacked against each other. This side of the district facilitated the seedier activities of Kamathipura.

Street women crowded the entrances to the dingy brothels. They called out to their customers constantly. Some were daring, others shy. Odours of rotting vegetables and human waste hung in the air as if the lid of a garbage bin had unexpectedly lifted. Lethargic canines lay around; some dug through the heaps of waste that had collected in mangy piles on the street corners.

Just when she seemed to have lost her way, Esta came across a large, older building. The edifice of the house was not like the others in the street. Its exterior was not bleached, nor was it painted in the typical powder-blue colour. The building was coated in a light terracotta shade. It had a hefty sign mounted on one of the walls which read "House of Joy". There was something about the place that attracted Esta.

From what she could see, the building was once used as a brothel. It had since been converted into a shelter for girls who worked the streets. As she drew nearer, Esta heard people singing. The melody wafted through the window of a room on the ground floor. She stood on the tips of her toes stretching her neck to take a peek inside. There, seated in a circle on some old chairs and jaded sofas, was a group of Indian women and girls. One of the girls looked similar to Mr Shankar. *Perhaps she is from his country*, Esta thought. An older Indian woman led them in song—her voice crackled along with a wracking cough.

Clearly, the song was about Jesus. Esta's heart skipped a beat, and she thanked the Lord that she had found sisters of her own faith at last. She stayed a while to listen to the words of the melody.

Soon the group stood and joined hands to pray. Esta did not know it then, but the Lord would use her as an instrument to bring girls from the streets of Kamathipura to the House of Joy.

***

Throughout the following months, Esta became friends with the people who lived and worked at the shelter. From time to time, she took refuge there. Other times she brought with her young girls from the streets who had taken ill or had been discarded by their pimps. Such was her special designation, it seemed. Esta would comb the highways and byways of Kamathipura in search of its casualties, to bring to the house.

The people at the shelter, most of whom had lived extraordinary lives themselves, had come to accept Esta's way. They admired her sacrifice for the things concerning God's kingdom. She became known to all at the house as Little Saamaree (Little Samaritan) of the Streets.

Life in the district was hard. Sanitation was poor for the people living there who had little monetary resources to purchase fresh food. Access to clean water was a formidable task. One of the challenges of those who loosely manage the Mumbai boroughs, like Kamathipura, is to keep the drinking water free of disease. The threat of an epidemic through waterborne infections constantly pervades the air that swaddles the labyrinth of lanes and squalid dwellings. The people give little thought to the consequences of such risks, often only addressing them when they enter one's home like a rabid dog that was once friendly.

When cholera struck Kamathipura it targeted a large section in the red-light district where proper water sanitation was the most concerning. Although the authorities stepped in quickly to combat the spread of the disease, their efforts were of no use. The plague had spread like a fire out of control. Countless people living in the small dwellings and brothels were affected.

Medical healthcare workers provided medicine and therapeutic solutions best they could. Mobile clinics could be seen parked in the streets of Kamathipura. The authorities administered different kinds of rehydration therapies and antibiotics as the symptoms presented themselves. Some parts of the district could not be reached, and these areas were placed under quarantine. Harita's brothel was in this vicinity. The authorities had isolated her block and her business had to be closed.

For days on end the disease did not abate. A deathly cloud hung over the area that had been prohibited entrance by the district authorities. There was no chatter or laughter to be heard wafting up and down the streets. Even the stray dogs had vacated the area. It was as if all life had come to a standstill. Some of Harita's girls had already succumbed to the symptoms of the disease. The old panderer was particularly concerned about one of them.

In all the years she had run her business, Harita had had numerous dealings with similar diseases wreaking havoc in Kamathipura, and somehow she had managed to pull through. This time, however, she was concerned for her trade. The situation was the most critical she had ever experienced. Harita wondered whether they would all come out of it alive.

Alisha, her best girl, was not well. The young woman

always brought in an attractive amount of revenue, but she had not worked for a while. Harita noticed that Alisha was weakening as the disease took hold of her.

She moved Alisha to one of the spare rooms on the ground floor of the brothel, away from the rest of the girls. Harita had previously used the room as an office during times of prosperity. The authorities stayed away from her. They hoped that the disease would starve itself and finally come to an end in her section of the district. Harita felt she had no other option but to enlist the help of a traditional Indian doctor. She hoped that he could bring Alisha back from the brink of death.

Alisha, doubled over in pain, was placed by Harita in solitary confinement. She was frightened and alone, and her symptoms were growing worse. Alisha felt as if her life was slipping from her. The traditional healer administered all kinds of liquid remedies to try to help her, but none of them had worked. She began to show advanced signs of the disease. Her eyes had taken on a sunken look and her skin was cold, wrinkled from its decreased elasticity. Alisha cried out to the only gods she knew—the ones she frequently paid homage to. Still, she continued to suffer.

One morning everything changed. The Indian healer told Harita he could no longer do anything for the young woman. 'Her condition,' he had said, 'is too advanced.' They could only hope that she did not suffer too much as death approached.

Alisha lay on her bed, pale and immobile. Her deep breaths were the only sounds that came from the small room. Then, in a desperate bid, she called out to God.

'God of Mr Prad,' she rasped, 'if you are real, help me. I promise to serve you in return. Only, save me.'

As Alisha called out that morning, she did not know that the God of Mr Prad is always listening—even to the cries of those who have not yet called him Father.

***

The young girl sold into slavery and who sold flowers for the Nepalese vendor had, at the time that Alisha prayed, taken flowers to some families in the cordoned-off area. Esta did not allow the infectious disease to prevent her from praying for the sick. She happened to walk past the brothel where Alisha was lying when she heard a woman gasping for air. She stopped at the window and listened. The woman was asking God to heal her. Esta pulled her small body onto her toes and looked into the room.

Leaning through the peeling frame, she saw a beautiful Indian woman lying on a bed—but she appeared to be very ill. Esta prayed for her. It was a simple prayer. She asked God to touch the woman and to make her well again. As she stood at the open window, a most blessed thought came to her to get help from her new friends at the House of Joy. *I must get to them quickly. Surely the prayers of many will bring the dying woman back to life.*

The people at the shelter were busy that morning. They were tending to the sick brought to them on stretchers and makeshift beds. Some had been rolled up in old blankets and dumped on their doorstep. The people in the area had noticed that those living at the establishment had not succumbed to the disease. Instead, they had made themselves available to everyone who needed help.

When Esta walked into the house, she noticed steam rising from large pots of boiling water. With well-organised precision, the caregivers were determined to destroy any germs attempting to invade their sacred haven. Some of the women were washing clothing and bedding. The younger girls were preparing an aromatic broth. There was also a group praying for the sick.

An old lady who managed the establishment was the first to notice Esta. She went to greet the young girl, always happy to see her. The woman called for some of the girls to leave what they were doing and greet their sister. Although not bound by blood, they were all sisters of a common faith in Christ. The term was used both respectfully and generously by all the people at the house. Explaining how she had heard her cry out to their God to save her, Esta shared her experience of the dying woman.

'Little Saamaree, you must slow down or we'll not be able to understand you.' The old woman spoke gently to Esta as she placed a thin arm across the girl's shoulders.

This was indeed difficult for the Little Samaritan. Although she tried to appear calm, Esta was excited. 'Jesus healed many people from fevers and diseases. I have read about this in the Holy Bible the English teacher gave me. He healed a girl I once knew where I worked as a slave at a stone quarry.'

Esta slowed a little to catch her breath before continuing, more purposeful this time. 'I know you're helping those who've come to you, but I have a good plan that will not interrupt your work here. There was a man in the Bible called Paul who looked after churches. He prayed over the clothing and scarves of those who were sick or belonging to the people taking care of them. When the dying touched these items, they were miraculously healed.'

Esta's simple faith began to stir the hearts of those

who were listening.

'We can do the same for this poor woman. Surely God will also heal her.'

The old woman was overcome. She marvelled at Esta's faith. It was true she could not spare anyone to go with the young girl. The reminder, however, of what the apostle did all that time ago was indeed a wonderful plan. God still performs miracles for his children. He never grows tired of blessing them. She knew that he was using the child for his special purposes. It would be wise to act on it.

The woman unravelled her scarf from its comfortable position around her neck. She gave it to Esta. Some of the other women and girls gathered to form a circle of prayer. Together, they prayed with Esta for the healing of the dying woman. Before they looked again, the girl was gone. She had the scarf in her hand and was running towards the forbidden area of Kamathipura.

When she arrived at the brothel, Esta cautiously climbed through the half-opened window and stepped into Alisha's room. The room was dingy and did not smell good. The woman still breathed. Taking the scarf, she gently placed it over her motionless frame. Before she left, Esta whispered these words, 'Who has the Son, has life.'

***

In the still hours of the morning a soft breeze blew down the alleyways of Kamathipura. It carried with it a sense of hope for the suffering. Alisha, who was still weak, felt the faint warmth of that celestial wind steal its way into her room. She felt it caress her cheek like the breath of a person close by. It warmed her body and pushed its way into her. She felt no pain, only its warmth. The young woman remained like that for a while. Then her heavy breathing seemed to ease as a deep sleep enveloped her.

The next morning the main road that had been quarantined was alive with the chirping of birds and the joyous chatter of people. Even the mongrel dogs which had vacated the area began to make their way back. The sun shone brighter and there was a crisp, clean smell in the air.

Alisha woke to the singing of the feathered creatures that perched on the low-lying cables above her room. For the first time since she had been struck by the terrible disease, she was able to help herself out of bed. She lifted her head and raised her hands. She had life in her body. The God of Mr Prad had heard her silent cry. He had come to save her.

'Thank you. Thank you,' she whispered as she tried to speak again.

She made her way to the window, shuffling her feet across the floor. Her vision was blurred. Alisha pushed her head through the opening and breathed in the sweet air. She thought of her miraculous healing. Still, she was unable to see clearly. It was as if the edges of her vision were folding so that the pictures that came into her view were vague.

The door to Alisha's room suddenly opened and in walked Harita.

'Alisha, my child! You're awake. I've been worried sick.' Harita's only concern was to get her girls ready for business again.

She threw her arms dramatically above her head and cried out as if there were others in the room to hear.

'I see the remedies have finally worked! The gods must be favouring you this time, daughter.'

How wrong you are, Alisha thought. Nothing the Indian doctor had given her had worked. It was only when she had cried out to the God of Mr Prad that she had been healed. Alisha tried to protest, but she was weak and the words would not come. Slowly, she walked towards her madam—though she struggled to see.

Noticing that something was amiss, Harita stepped back from Alisha.

'What's the matter? Your eyes, they have a strange colour about them.'

Harita moved further from the young woman as if something worse than cholera had descended on the brothel. Feeling cautioned to not alarm Alisha further, the old panderer finally said, 'You must rest. I'll call for the doctor again. Perhaps the disease has affected your eyes. He'll know what to do—I'll send for him at once.'

Alisha heard the panic in Harita's voice. She reached for her, but the woman moved away each time.

Finally, Alisha gathered her strength. 'No,' her voice was thick and desperate, 'don't send for the man. I don't want him to come near me. Someone else is taking care of me now.'

Harita was confused and wondered whether Alisha had a man in her life. Perhaps he would be interested in buying Alisha from her. Her mind raced.

As if reading her thoughts, Alisha continued, 'It's not what you think, Madam. I speak of God. The God of Jesus Christ has given me my life back. He will take care of me from now on. Even if I lose my sight completely, my eyes have been opened to the greatest mercy of all.' Alisha's voice softened. 'I am a changed person. I see only God's love for me now.'

Harita was silent, unsure of whether to stay or flee. Alisha sensed Harita's uneasiness. Nevertheless, she continued to witness to the woman as if her new life was all that mattered.

***

It is a wondrous thing how a newly converted soul is completely consumed by the love of God; the believer feels compelled to share their profound joy with others.

'Harita, you may not be able to see him, but he's right here with you and me. He's knocking at the door of your heart.'

Despite her failing eyesight, Alisha's body seemed to glow with a radiant light. Harita had never experienced anything like this before. For one who was seldom without words, she struggled to speak. It was at that moment that Harita realised she had lost Alisha forever. Harita did not know of this strange god. Whoever he was, he was about to destroy everything in her life. She began to shake with fear. She had too much to lose. Alisha would have to go, and she would have to go quickly.

Ignoring the joyous shouts coming from the streets of the people who had been restored, Harita's heart hardened. She quickly devised a plan. It was her cunningness that had always helped her survive—not some mysterious god. Alisha would still work for her, but as she was near blind and would be of no real use, Harita would make her beg on the streets of Kamathipura for money. People always took pity on the blind. Although the young woman would not bring in the same profits, it would be better than nothing. *After all,* Harita thought, *I still own you, Daughter.*

Harita rose early the next morning to put her plan into action. She had not slept well and her dreams had troubled her. Nothing would deter her from her decision, though. She moved quickly to wake Alisha. Gathering some of the young woman's things, she draped one of her own wraps across Alisha's shoulders.

Bewildered, Alisha reluctantly allowed Harita to lead her out of the building. Her voice trembled, 'Where are you taking me, Harita? You appear to be excited about something, but you're not saying what it is.'

Feigning concern, Harita replied, 'Keep this wrap around you and use this stick I bought for you to lean on. It'll help you detect any obstacles in your way.'

Harita took Alisha gently by the arm and steered her into the street. They stepped into the sun together. Although Alisha could not see the glint of its brightness, she could feel the sun's warmth. The gnawing feeling in her stomach did not subside, however. Harita, more determined than ever, led Alisha down the street.

As they walked, Harita tried to console her. 'I'm taking you to a place where you can rest and work at the same time. You'll come to no harm. We'll all benefit from it in the end. I only ask that you trust me.'

Harita was persistent. 'You won't be able to please my customers anymore. Nobody wants a blind girl—surely you must know that.'

Alisha was quiet. She clung to the woman who had been a mother to her for so long. Harita led Alisha to a large open area near the temple where the young woman had once been a *devadasi*. The place was crescent-shaped and covered with concrete. There was a tall fountain in the centre where myna birds and docile monkeys came to drink. Most of the district's beggars, old and young, sat there cross-legged, begging for alms and food from tourists and visitors to the temple.

Alisha prayed as fear gripped her, 'God, you saved me from death before, but I know that here, I will surely die.'

She could hear the familiar voices of the other prostitutes who had once been her friends. They congregated near the temple, sneering at her. A strange odour of rotting fruit and scavenger animals hung in the air. Finding a spot to settle her, Harita spread the veils of Alisha's sari, completely covering her. Even the luscious, black locks that crowned the Indian woman's head were hidden by the folds of the fabric. Only her milky eyes could be seen through the slit Harita had created between the top of Alisha's head and the bridge of her nose. Alisha began to tremor. She felt helpless and abandoned.

Tears slid from Alisha's eyes. She was unable to dab at them for fear of disturbing Harita's arrangement. Her tears seemed to annoy Harita. The older woman became impatient. 'Now, now, Daughter—don't cry. This is the only way we'll all eat. I'll fetch you before sundown.'

Harita stepped back from the young woman who was once her cherished possession. 'I want you to put your hands out as if you're scooping water. Tell the passersby you're a poor, blind woman—they will give you their small change.'

Alisha tried hard to shut out Harita's words. She tilted her head to hear the piercing cry of a raven fighting over some scraps that had been tossed to the creatures at the fountain. They were merely fighting to survive, and so was she. It suddenly dawned on her that she did not belong to Harita anymore. She was now a daughter of the only true God.

Harita turned to leave when she noticed Alisha's withdrawal from her. She did not like the fact that Alisha dared to defy her. *Except*, she thought, *how much defiance can a blind woman have?*

For several days Alisha sat in the hot sun like the rest of the beggars. There were not many who gave their coins to her, and what she did collect was immediately taken by Harita. Alisha spoke to God every day and she prayed for the other beggars around her.

There came a day, however, when the young woman heard the patter of small feet. They seemed to touch the concrete with a melody of their own. More feet joined the first pair. They drew closer. Alisha lifted her knees slightly off the ground as if to protect herself from what she could not see. Then, a gentle voice addressed her.

'Don't be afraid, Precious One. We've come to bring you good news.'

The voice was young and kind. 'The Saviour you've come to accept and love has sent us to fetch you. We'll take you to a place where you no longer have to beg. It's a house where you'll find shelter and care.' Alisha grabbed hold of the hand that touched her shoulder.

Then an older woman spoke. 'A new and better life is waiting for you, Daughter.'

The strangers helped Alisha to her feet. Her heart filled with joy. They held her close as they led her away from the squalor and shame that had for a short while been her only companions. This was the day Alisha met Little Saamaree, the girl who had prayed for her healing and who eventually introduced Alisha to the family at the House of Joy.

6
Northern Somalia

North of the Somali border is a place of stark yet alluring beauty. White sands and tawny uprooted tree trunks bereft of their once succulent plumes speckle the coastline. Feeble waves lap lazily against the shore, exhausted from the wars on the living. A Somali girl by the name of Aayana, meaning eternal flower, is on her hands and knees. She is crawling across the broken seashells that cling to the exposed rocks. Aayana is desperate to get food for her troop. She cannot return to their camp empty-handed—food is needed for strength to fight.

Aayana scrounged amongst the rocks, plucking mussels and barnacles with her cold fingers. Only the salt from the foam brought her some comfort. As she rummaged for marine provisions amongst the jagged stones, she noticed a large shell of luminous colours. The shell was wedged between the slippery rocks. Prizing the creature from its rocky prison, Aayana turned it over in her hands. She admired its unusual appearance. She thought of the frailty of life. The most priceless things are often hidden in plain sight. While she crouched, contemplating the fate of the life inside the shell, she noticed in the distance a male dressed in military gear. He made his way towards her. The man's distinctive beret covered his brow, an AK rifle swung casually over his shoulder.

As the young soldier drew nearer, Aayana realised it was her good friend Sam. He stood over her and groused affectionately.

'What is it with you, Aayana? You're like an owl in the night. Turning your head, yet not attacking; hunting, yet not taking. I fear there will come a day when suddenly you will set to flight, and we will not find you. You'll be to us like a ghost in the wind.'

The young man admired the girl. Aayana's inner beauty, her aquiline features, and tall frame were more special to him than she could imagine.

Aayana did not respond. Sam became annoyed. 'Rise! We must return to the others before sundown. You know Papa won't be happy if you're not back in time to cook the food you've found.'

The thought of punishment from their troop leader brought Aayana quickly to her feet. She rose to her full height, almost reaching Sam's. Long-limbed with ebony skin, Aayana moved with feline grace across the sand. Her charcoal eyes surveyed the stretch of palm trees a few metres up from the beach. It would be a long walk back to the base camp. She began to sing a song she had heard at the relief camp just outside her village she had visited as a younger girl. Those had been better times, when she had learned of the one called Jesus. She had received him as her Lord and Saviour, and her heart had since carried in it an inexpressible peace. Aayana's ethereal voice could be heard echoing across the beach, redolent with hope.

Sam tried to quiet her. He was afraid for her life. 'What is this song you sing?' he whispered. 'Your songs cut deep into my heart. I feel that God's speaking to me through them. You've shown me the way of peace,

Aayana… I long for the same. It's like an invisible cloak you wear across your shoulders.'

Sam stopped talking but continued to think about the girl who walked beside him.

Aayana gave no indication that she was listening to Sam. She continued to sing as they made their way back to the base camp.

Sam did not want her to know, just yet, of his feelings for her. It was too soon to reveal the secret he kept. He was a patient young man who had been through much. He had joined the Resistance Army as a child when he lost his family. The vigilante group he served as a soldier had provided him with a sense of belonging. He had been with them for more than seven years. Now, as a young man, he could think for himself and follow the desires of his own heart. He secretly hoped that the lovely Aayana would someday feel the same about him.

Aayana did not make it back to the base camp on time, nor did she give to Papa enough of the food she was obliged to honour. Sam stood motionless, his anger concealed as he was forced with the others to watch Aayana's punishment. Papa warned them that Aayana was "the wayward one". She was too stubborn and independent. If it had not been for Sam, who placated the troop leader each time Aayana stepped out of line, the Somali girl would have been left to fend for herself, alone in the plains.

Papa liked Sam. The young soldier was compliant and did what he was told. The warlord gave Sam a cautious nod. Lately, though, he thought that the young man had been behaving strangely. There was something stirring between the soldier and Aayana. Papa did not like it. *I had better keep an eye on the two of them,* he mused. These kinds of alliances were not good for their mission, and besides, he had hoped that the girl would be his someday.

***

Small fires were ignited by the vigilante soldiers as the sun slouched behind the low hills. Papa knew it would be a long night. This night was to be set aside to make a sacrifice in honour of the voodoo idols that would give them strength and power to continue their mission of war and plunder across the Somali expanse. Papa lit a cheap cigar and stared warily at the peculiar shadows emerging in the darkening sky.

Aayana gathered herself after the harsh lashing from the warlord. Her body throbbed with pain. *Where had Sam been?* she wondered. Although she had suffered many times at the hands of their leader, she could always count on Sam to help her back to the sparsely thatched shelter in the woods. Here, the female soldiers were meant to wash and sleep. As she made her way up the mound, hunched over and sobbing, Aayana noticed the indistinct outline of a male leaning against a tree. She knew it was Sam. *Why is he here and not at the base camp?* It was forbidden for the men to go near the girls' shelter when they were preparing for the celebrations of the spirits.

Sam moved from out of the shadows. 'Forgive me, Aayana.' The young soldier was desperate. 'I wanted to help you but I couldn't look at you. Another beating...'

Sam fell to his knees, his eyes fixed on Aayana's bent frame. He touched her back gently, hoping to console her in some way. Then he let out a groan like that of an animal caught in a snare too long. It was a cry for freedom from the predicament they were all in.

'Come away with me, Aayana. Let's leave at once.' Sam's voice was hoarse and it trembled with fear.

Aayana did not say anything. Instead, her heart swelled with compassion as she looked at Sam. She knew she could not leave. Although she was mad to not go with him, something restrained her. A greater sense of purpose seemed to be tugging at her.

Aayana helped Sam to his feet. They clung to each other as they made their way to the thick bush behind the tree. She tried to calm him. The consequences for desertion were grave, but Aayana felt courage take hold of her. Although she was afraid for the young soldier, she felt it was time for him to break free from the band of marauders he had been subjected to for so long. Aayana said a silent prayer for Sam. Surely God would help him escape.

Taking Sam by the shoulders she looked at him. 'Listen to me. It's you who must fly now. This is your only chance and you must take it.'

She paused. 'I'll not go with you this time.'

Aayana's voice was resolute. Realising her determination and knowing how stubborn she could be, Sam pulled from her. Like one deranged, he staggered into the sea of dense foliage. Aayana watched as his movements became more of a plunder. He pushed through the thick bushes into the dark space where the owls witness how creatures of fear become victims of prey.

***

Sam did not look back. The Somali girl pressed her weight against the tree to support her tired frame. She watched till she could see him no longer. The night was the blackest she had ever known it to be. Sacrifices would be offered to the idols, and Sam was gone. But Aayana was filled with peace. She fell to her knees and began to pray. She had come to believe that God's love will carry you even in the darkest hour.

Papa would eventually discover that Sam had deserted them, and Aayana knew that some of the child soldiers would have to pay. She would most certainly be one of them. It was a sacrifice she was willing to make for Sam's freedom.

The smell of fires burning around the camp drew Aayana's attention back to the evening's festivities and the ominous celebrations that lay ahead. Their commander was not only a soldier but also a man of a priestly class. He was fluent in the ancient practices of ancestral worship. It was Papa's desire that the vigilante group should prosper and find success in their crusades to rid his people of all Western influences and Christianity. To help him with his mission, the warlord held regular voodoo rituals.

Papa was born into a family who believed in attaining spirituality through pagan rites and promoting such activities within their community. Together with his soldiers, he habitually sought assistance from the non-visible realms.

Aayana stayed near her hut that night. She hid in the shadows, refusing to join in the rites that were underway. Papa would not miss her just yet. He was already in a trance-like state, caught up in the ceremony. The hard thumping sounds from the wooden bush drums rose above the camp. The noise made Aayana tremble. The mood around the camp was charged with fear and excitement. The young men danced perfunctorily around the fire, their bodies quivering as they invoked the spirits and ghosts of the past.

The shadow that arched over the camp was foreboding. Aayana longed to be wherever Sam had gone. That was impossible now. Instead, she chose the tall tree next to her shelter to escape from it all. She climbed slowly up its colossal trunk in search of a safe branch to sit in. Finally, she settled in the fork of two strong limbs. She leaned her body against the thick trunk of the tree and straddled her legs over the thinner branches. Closing her eyes, she began to think of her village and her family in an attempt to block out the chilling activities below.

***

Climbing trees of this height was not unusual for Aayana. She had practiced this sort of stealth since she was a child. Aayana's large-sized family was not unusual for the people of her clan—there were many brothers and sisters to take care of. Whenever she needed a break from her noisy siblings, Aayana would find solace in the branches of the tallest tree in the village. One particular tree had become her secret hideaway. Here Aayana learned to balance her body in such a way that she could fall asleep on the branches quite comfortably without falling off.

The villagers were always in awe of her courage. They called her "Aar", which translated means "lioness". The people would say of her, 'There goes Aar-Aayana, the brave girl who climbs tall trees.'

The tree, a tall acacia which spread its branches like

an elaborate spider's web from close to the ground, grew near Aayana's homestead. The only time she refused to climb its branches was when it flowered, when the wind came and shook copious amounts of pods from its grayish-white limbs.

Aayana recalled the activities she observed from her lofty place. She had witnessed the men in her clan praying several times a day in the area near the corral designated for prayers. They were Muslims of the Sunni sect who prayed facing a place many miles across the world.

Aayana's father was a leader of their faith. The people of her village feared and respected him. Aayana had always been different from her siblings. From an early age she exhausted her parents with her many questions about religion and life. It appeared quite senseless to her that the elders of her clan prayed facing this mysterious village. How could a place so far away help them in their hardship? Their sorrows did not lessen despite their continuous petitioning. Ongoing wars still ravaged her people. A pervasive sense of loss continuously ran through the villages of the Somali coastline, like a ghostly stream—never visible, always there, taking with it their souls.

She recalled, from her lofty perch, the day white men came to her village to drill for water and install a pump to be used by everyone. The men had said, 'Clean, flowing water will improve sanitation and reduce waterborne diseases.' It had lasted for a while, but soon the pump broke and no one came to repair it. Bit by bit it was dismantled and the parts were used for other things. She remembered the tears that stained her dark cheeks when the device could no longer pump clean water. But still, Aayana would return to her tree to find solitude and protection from the strong winds that blew from the semi-arid plains of Guban. It would touch her face with its sharpness, reminding her that in the movement of air was a whisper of hope.

From that special tree, Aayana would watch her younger brother playing below. Ishaar wasn't much younger than her. In fact, they were only a year apart. She loved that she was older and therefore responsible to watch over him. Some of her other siblings had died, taken callously by diseases such as malaria and tuberculosis that still prevail in parts of Africa. It gave her great comfort that she had a special connection with Ishaar. Sometimes, Aayana imagined that it was only the two of them in the world. Although her mother admired Aayana's sisterly attentiveness, she would scold her for daydreaming. Theirs was a household where all members had to serve each other equally if they were to survive. There was no doubt, however, that Ishaar was the family sweetheart, loved and spoiled by all.

One day, Ishaar had gone missing from their village. He was found later by some hunter-herders in a hole that had been constructed to trap a wild animal. The boy's return was celebrated with great joy and a festivity similar to the one given when a baby was born or when a woman got married and all the storehouses of their poor village were unfettered. Animals were slaughtered and hundreds of *muufo* flatbreads were baked from ground corn and cooked on the outdoor wood fires. Everyone from near and far was welcome to attend. So it was with Ishaar's return—it was as if he had been born all over again.

Aayana remembered the frightful day of Ishaar's

disappearance. She had been given strict orders from her mother and elder brother to not go looking for him; this was the responsibility of the elders and older men of the village. Aayana had disobeyed, but only because she would do anything to find her most beloved brother. She had searched for Ishaar on her own, scouring the dirt roads he loved to frequent with his stick and wire hoop. Aayana remembered hearing his laughter wafting up and down the trails that weaved a maze around their village. Frantically, she had pressed through the density of a clump of trees calling for Ishaar. All at once, a wind rose. It pushed its way towards her. Aayana remembered hearing a comforting voice console her, 'Aayana, do not be afraid. Your brother is safe and will soon be found.'

When Aayana returned to her village, Ishaar was waiting for her. Except for a few scratches, the boy was unharmed. Her heart had filled with pride as she listened to Ishaar gallantly retell his story to the villagers. While Ishaar was given a good soaping down in an outdoor basin by her grandmother, Aayana endured her mother's punishment. She had not protested like she usually did. She would do anything for Ishaar, even if it meant suffering for his sake. What she did wonder about, however, was where the voice in the wind had come from. It had come looking for her with the hope she needed in her time of distress.

***

Aayana was raised in a port village near the North of Somalia. Her parents were poor with many mouths in the household to feed. They were descendants of the *habash*—nomadic herders who had migrated to the

Horn of Africa. Her clan was of a lower class. Although her people still kept livestock, they had settled in small villages along the plains of the great rivers whose waters, like the endless irrigation of a heavy rain cloud, sustained their existence. Here, on the river's banks, they were able to farm corn, millet and vegetables. Animals were raised for milk and meat. The people prepared their produce in cozy, dome-like huts, some of which were made of wooden poles covered with hides for easy dismantling when hard times hit.

War and famine frequently visited Aayana's people like vultures to a carcass. Aayana learned quickly because she felt deeply. It was a great sorrow to her that her clansmen were often displaced as a result of relentless wars on their land.

It was the smell of her mother's cooking and the attentive way in which she served the family that drew Aayana down from her tree each day. She loved to watch her *hooyo* arrange the cooking utensils in preparation for their meals. Aayana helped her mother keep the storage boxes dust-free. Together they stocked the water bags and arranged for the woven mats to be placed neatly on the floor for the family to sit and eat. Aayana's family generally did not eat three meals a day. They were only faintly nourished every few days, so of course money for an education was out of the question.

The children in large poor Somali families are loved as equally as they are disciplined, and are mostly educated by their mothers. Aayana's brothers had been given the opportunity to attend Arab schools. The spread of the Islamic faith in their part of the world was as pervasive as it was subtle. Education was not available to girls—an injustice Aayana carried from young for she longed to read and write.

***

Three marked incidents ended Aayana's trips to her hideaway above the clouds of dust. The first was the death of Aayana's father, a devout Muslim man and elder.

Like all religious leaders in the Somali villages, Hanad was revered. The villagers believed that men like him had the power to bless and curse the land and the people. However, after returning from a nomadic trip with a group of young herders one summer, Hanad became fatally ill. It was thought that he had contracted malaria. After months of no improvement, Hanad finally drew his last breath.

Aayana was deeply saddened by the passing of her father. The funeral had been just as bountiful in provision as with other celebrations, though instead of joy and laughter there had been much sorrow.

Aayana's mother had not taken her husband's death well. After she had completed the traditional four months of mourning in seclusion near their settlement, she finally rejoined the family. The woman was, however, never quite the same again—she seemed to have gone to the place of her husband. Aayana's grandmother had taken charge of the family. Because of the new responsibilities, Aayana found less time to hide in her tree.

The second incident that stopped Aayana from visiting her tree was when a relief organisation set up camp near Aayana's village. The man in charge went by the name of Mister Mark. The man was a foreigner who had taken an interest in helping the girls from Aayana's village to read and write.

Mister Mark had encouraged the villagers to allow their daughters to attend lessons at the camp in the afternoons. There they were taught basic life skills and how to speak English. Aayana had begged her mother to allow her to join the classes but, as with everything else, the older woman was disinterested. It was Aayana's grandmother who finally made the decision that only once Aayana's chores were done could she attend the school.

Most of the classes at the camp were held in the open under the trees. The young women and girls were diligent in their attendance. Mister Mark showed himself to be a dedicated and generous tutor from the outset. Aayana had sensed at their first meeting that there was something different about him. Beneath his large frame and shaggy hair, the colour of ripened corn, Mister Mark appeared to be concealing a deep sorrow. More than that, Aayana had been struck by the man's love for her people. His inner strength testified of something greater than he. Perhaps he had had help from someone during a dark trial of his own.

***

Aayana recalled the first week of her trips to the relief camp. Her grandmother had arranged for her to be taken to and from the site in a cart drawn by mules. Gingerly, the Somali girl had wedged herself between the goats and chickens to get a comfortable seat. Thankfully, the animals had not minded. It was as if they had sensed that Aayana was on some important mission. Her excitement at the prospect of learning to read was far greater than her temporary discomfort.

Arriving for her classes on that first day, Aayana had

noticed that the camp was abuzz with activity. Men and women had scurried around the open spaces arranging bags of food and provisions into neat piles. They were purposefully rationing and counting the items to meet the needs of the various villages they were helping. Amid serious verbal exchanges over steaming cups of dark water, they had also laughed. Aayana had been struck by the energy that pervaded the camp. Although some of her peers appeared nervous, she had been quite drawn in.

Mister Mark had waited for the girls to arrive. He had led them to the area where they would be taught throughout the duration of the relief workers' stay. Their class was set up in a makeshift tent near the entrance of the camp. A female interpreter had accompanied him. The woman also helped to make the girls as comfortable as possible. Mister Mark had started the programme by asking this woman to sing a song to the students. Although Aayana had not understood all the words, she had felt that the song was special. It was as if the woman had sung to someone she loved with all her heart. Her teacher had then read from a small book. Although he had read in English, the interpreter did a good job of translating for him.

'Before we start our lessons today, I'd like to share a story with you. You all like a good story, don't you?' Mister Mark had made the girls feel welcome.

Aayana had listened attentively. The interpreter never missed a beat—she had tried to imitate the good teacher's humour and enthusiasm best she could. The story Mister Mark had shared was about a woman who had lived in ancient times. She was visited by an angel of God. The angel had told the woman that she would give birth to a male child. This child would become the Saviour of the entire world. He would also die on a wooden cross to deliver all of humanity from their sins.

Mister Mark had gone on to explain how wicked rulers of that ancient land had sought to kill the child. God, however, had prevented them from doing so. He had sent wise men to take gifts of gold, frankincense, and myrrh to the infant's secret place of birth to honour him. The teacher had added with enthusiasm that Somalia was a unique place. It was a land that had played a role in that baby king's birth. Ancient people were attracted to her special trees which produced the aromatic gum resins, myrrh, and frankincense. The fragrances were deemed to be of great value and were sold all over Africa.

Aayana had felt important. After all, her country had played a vital role in providing gifts for God's Son. She recalled finding the story extraordinary. It was unlike any she had ever heard, and she sensed the story was mysteriously connected to the voice she had heard in the forest. The great God of the universe had come searching for her in her time of need. He had given to her, at that moment, an indescribable peace in her heart—her own religion had never done this for her.

Mister Mark had concluded the story by saying that God loved the Somali people. Aayana had felt her spirit lift. It was as if many years of sorrow and loss were taken from her—much like the time her father had freed their mule from its burden. The animal was allowed to roam freely in the field to graze. It would raise its head to face the sun.

***

Throughout her time learning at the relief camp, Aayana,

like a sponge, had soaked up the incredible stories Mister Mark had read from his special book. There had been a new story each day. Aayana had learned that the name of the baby king was Jesus. She learned about his life on earth and how he had shown compassion to those who were sick and hurting. He had healed them and had given freedom to those who were oppressed. Aayana also learned that Jesus had been condemned to death by some wicked people. He had died on a wooden cross so that if she believed in him, she would not be condemned to a life outside of Heaven.

Aayana had been especially drawn to the tale Mister Mark had shared about a woman who poured some expensive perfume over Jesus. The woman had washed his feet with her long hair. Aayana had thought that if she had had hair like that, she would have done the same. Mister Mark had said to her, quite perceptively, that it was not in the outward show, but in the spirit in which it was presented, that made the act so important. This woman had been willing to give of her very best for Jesus, knowing that he had given his all for her. Mister Mark had added, 'God wants our whole heart all the time.'

Aayana had been filled with certainty when her teacher spoke of the things of God. She had silently said to herself that she believed the stories to be true.

The young Somali girl had learned to read quickly. She had been eager to read from the book Mister Mark shared from each day. One day she plucked up the courage to ask her teacher if she could have one.

'So, our dear Aayana wants one of these books?' Mark had smiled gently at her. He had gone on to say that he would secure her such a book as soon as he was able to. Mark had also shared his concerns with her that the book would not be well received by her family and the people of her village. They had not yet heard of the man called Jesus, the One who brought a new way of living to all people. This might cause them to turn on her. He would, however, make sure she always had it to read when she came to the camp for her lessons.

Aayana recalled these times of reading as the happiest moments in her life. She had taken every opportunity to devour its pages when she was there, and had many questions about the book. One time, tilting her head slightly to make sure she could see Mark's face, she had asked him a question in her best English.

'Why did some men want to kill God's Son?'

She had held a hand over her eyes to protect them from the sun's glare. 'They shouldn't be afraid of Jesus. He helps everyone and he shows people how to live right. He leads them to the God of Heaven. Why did they not listen to him?'

Mark had been touched by the girl's honesty. 'My dear Aayana, it's been true throughout the ages that most people will not let go of their traditions and beliefs to embrace something new. Light must shine for them to see that their hearts are filled with darkness. This is why we must share the light of the message of Jesus Christ to all people—at every opportunity we are given.'

Mark had spoken to Aayana like someone who had found this truth himself. 'These men you refer to were known as the Jewish elders of their village during Jesus' life here on earth.'

He had wiped his forehead with the back of his hand as the heat of the day bore down on them. Shielding his eyes, he had called for the interpreter to help him.

Mark had explained to the Somali girl in the simplest way, 'Aayana these men were following the way of what is known as the Old Covenant that God had made between himself and his people.' He had added that they had also inhabited tents much like those of the Somalis. Aayana had frowned. Mark continued, 'A covenant is something of great value. It's an agreement that joins two people, or groups of people, to each other forever. People make covenants all the time. They make agreements that'll benefit both parties as long as everyone sticks to the rules of the agreement.'

Aayana had nodded and offered an example of her own, just to make sure. 'I think this covenant is like the time my father agreed to allow the herdsmen to live in the corral near our village. In return they had to take our goats and camels out every day to graze with their own. They had both done something good for each other.'

Mark had been amazed at Aayana's insight. He had gone on to explain to her the reason why the Old Covenant had not worked. 'Sadly, the people couldn't keep their part of the agreement. They worshipped gods which God had forbidden. In short, they were disobedient to the laws God had given them.'

Mark had paused to make sure Aayana understood him. 'Most people aren't able to stay faithful to anything. This is because of the sin that entered God's beautiful world at the very beginning of time.' He became more serious. 'Nevertheless, Aayana, God loves the world. His love is so matchless that we'll never be able to understand it. He made a new way for everyone to find their way back to him. He also promised that he would remove our pain and feelings of shame.'

Aayana had clung to the words of her teacher. She

was hungry to know more about the king who had come to save the world.

Before Mark concluded their time together, he had said to her, 'This New Covenant is the way of God's Son. It's no longer about what we can do for God—we fail every time we try.' He had chuckled softly. 'It's about what he has done for us. He'll make us turn from our sins and give our hearts back to him.'

***

So it was that Aayana learned about the unconditional love of God. She began to grow in her newfound faith. It was a little at first, then stronger each passing day. No one in the village knew what the future held, but the girl they called Aar-Aayana carried with her a certain peace wherever she went.

Aayana's siblings were the first to witness her change. Her kindness surprised them. People in the far-off villages began to speak of her transformation. Those who visited her village came to hear more about her conversion. Even Aayana's mother, who had been struggling for a long time over the loss of her husband, sought her daughter's company. She sat listening to Aayana as the Somali girl sang songs about her Saviour while doing her daily chores. This was a special time for Aayana and her family. The ravages of their struggles began to heal.

The way of the Lord, however, is seldom as we perceive it to be. For Aayana, her journey with him had only just begun.

***

The third event that prevented Aayana from visiting her favourite tree was the one that had changed her young life forever. It was the day Aayana was kidnapped and recruited by the vigilante soldiers who had come to plunder her village. They had taken the children to train as soldiers to fight alongside them. Just like the harsh winds that carved a path across the mountains surrounding the villages, that day was forever etched in Aayana's mind.

Wars on the inland territories and coastal shores of Africa sanction the recruitment of soldiers for military purposes. Young people of the calm settlements nestled along the shore areas of Somalia fall victim to the insurgents sweeping through the villages. The warlords steal the children and use them in their attempts to dominate the surrounding territories. This heinous practice challenges the conscience and universal consideration that a human being under the age of eighteen is called a child—a child who deserves to be valued as one who needs protection and care. Little thought is given to the fact that the exploitation and abuse of children in wars is one of the most atrocious crimes in our modern times.

It was a time forever imprinted in the memory of Aayana's clan. Some of the villagers had managed to escape. They had made their way to the refugee camp where Mark and the other volunteers were somewhat protected from the onslaught. The camp was barricaded, only allowing a certain number of people in. The whole area was sealed off as the situation in the villages grew worse. Aayana and her family lived to the north, which was quite a distance from the relief camp. They were sadly not among the fortunate ones who had managed to escape the terror.

Heavy dust storms had blown that frightful day,

sweeping with great intensity across the Guban plains. The rebel soldiers had arrived in large numbers, their faces covered with scarves and their eyes shielded by dark sunglasses, and they had taken the village by force. Their intention was to turn the settlement into a training camp.

Aayana had been sharing some *muufo* bread with Ishaar when she heard the sound of horses' hooves and the heaviness of many legs trudging through the dry sand. She had looked across from where she was sitting and witnessed a dark horde of descending soldiers. Her first reaction had been to grab hold of her brother and run, but instead she was overcome with fear. Most of the villagers had fled to their huts. Ishaar had dropped the flatbread he was eating, and had run past Aayana calling for his mother and grandmother. In a matter of moments, Aayana had witnessed the once tranquil life of their village turn into mayhem.

The warlord in charge had barked out orders for his men to round up the people and bring them to the central area of the village. His men had executed his orders swiftly. Aayana and her family were gathered with the others. She had clung to her grandmother and mother. Trembling but keeping close, the women had determined to not let go of each other. Perhaps they had felt that if they did this, they would appear less vulnerable. Whatever their reason, their actions made no impact on the rebel leader. Instead, his soldiers appeared to have gained confidence each passing moment.

The villagers had fixed their eyes on the man in charge of their fate. A stoic figure, he sat unmoved on his heavily breathing horse. An AK rifle was slung over his shoulder, and his beret was pushed further over his face than usual. He had instructed his men to separate the girls from the boys. He felt he had better control over his captives this way.

The leader had continued his verbal barrage, alternating between giving orders to his men and to the people. He had told them that he would use their village to help his men recuperate and to train new recruits. Specific children would be chosen to supplement the ranks of his armed troop. The rest of the villagers would be used for the general purposes of the soldiers—to cook and clean and to obey his orders as the need arose. The people had tried to conceal their fear, stifling cries against the clothing of their families. They had turned to each other for comfort as their children were taken from them.

Aayana had stood in the middle of the female group, holding her head high. She was a strong girl, and since she had found her new faith she carried a certain confidence—the lioness in her began to rise.

Aayana had thought of Mister Mark and the people at the refugee camp while she stood there. *Surely they have heard of the incursion by now. How will my teacher get help to us?* While she had pondered these questions, Aayana suddenly broke free from the girls' group and ran towards her mother and grandmother. They were crouched in the sand with some of the other villagers.

She had called out to them, 'Hooyo, Ayeeyo! Let us run. We must search for Mister Mark. Surely, he'll rescue us!'

The warlord and his soldiers had been taken by surprise at the audacity of the girl. Her display of courage was, however, thwarted and Aayana had found herself pushed to the ground by one of the men.

Her decision to disobey his orders had infuriated

the warlord. He dismounted his horse and made his way towards her, his boots crunching firmly on the sand.

'What do we have here?' He had spoken scathingly to Aayana in her native language for all to hear. 'We have here a plucky one. A girl who dares to defy me!'

The man had turned to the villagers. 'What she does not realise…' Pausing to clean his teeth with a short blade of grass, and checking his nails for cleanliness, he had repeated, 'What she does not realise is that this act of courage has in fact sealed her fate.' The man's tone had been unusually casual, as if he was quite familiar with the fear it evoked. He seemed to relish the authority he had over the destiny of another human being. He lifted the rifle from its straddled position.

Aayana's family's pleas to spare her life could be heard above the warlord's commanding voice. The Somali girl had looked up at him. Her eyes had been ablaze with a fire that for a moment took the man by surprise. Then, a sudden gust of wind, stronger than the one that constantly blew over the village, distracted the leader. He had turned to see his favourite soldier at his side. The young man's name was Sam. He was one of the commander's most trusted men. Sam had placed his hand calmly on the arm of his leader, but the warlord had only become more annoyed.

He had turned sharply. 'What are you doing?! I have no time for games. You're disturbing an important message I must send out to these people through this girl.'

Undeterred, Sam had replied, 'Let's not be unwise, my lord. Such a brave and beautiful girl can only be an advantage to us. How many villages have we plundered and not found one so bold? See how she's even prepared to offer her life for her people.'

The leader had contemplated Sam's words. Finally, he threw his rifle over his shoulder and addressed the young man. His eyes had remained fixed on Aayana.

'You are a shrewd man, Sam, I'll give you that. What you're suggesting is that we keep the girl alive to show the rest of these people that we can be forgiving. In exchange for our kindness, they must give us their loyalty.'

The warlord had looked at Sam with a glint in his eye. The soldier was not like him. He was impulsive and often attracted trouble because of it. This time he would listen to Sam. There was indeed more to be gained by keeping the girl alive. It had made perfect sense.

Aayana had hunched her body over the sand. She had silently thanked God for sparing her life. When she looked up again, she caught the eyes of the young man looking down at her. He had returned her gaze before marching off, compassion veiling his sharp features. Eventually Aayana was scooped from the ground by one of the other men. She was taken to a group of youngsters who had been deliberately set apart from the others.

***

The weeks following the invasion had been insufferable. It was as if a cloud of terror had settled over the whole area. It had once been a place filled with the laughter of curious youngsters and noisy livestock. No longer was it a haven of chattering women and strong men. In an instant it had been taken from them by the soldiers who had come to destroy their village and steal their children.

Aayana and the other chosen ones had supplemented the warlord's ranks. They were required to attend classes erected under trees or in some of the private dwellings secured by the warlord and his men. Here they were indoctrinated with the words of the Quran. One of the first things they had learned was that they would be rewarded in paradise if they were willing to die in combat. There had been teachers among the soldiers whose sole purpose was to inculcate the younger ones with this ideology.

The soldiers would threaten their family members if the learners did not submit to them. They believed that they should recruit as many girls and boys as possible because a young mind is easy to instruct. The warlord and his men pushed the idea that it was easier to turn children into hardened assassins—an apprentice ruled by fear and alternating kindness would soon become like clay in your hands, and you could mould them into whatever you wished. The victim would eventually become the victimiser.

Every day, Aayana prayed for the safekeeping of her family. At one point she felt that she had been abandoned by God, but she kept praying. Aayana believed that he would eventually deliver them.

She had worked diligently. She told herself that she would work as unto the Lord. Aayana had even asked that God would make a way for her to share the gospel of Jesus Christ with the soldiers.

Once, when Aayana had attended an indoctrination class, the usual teacher did not turn up. The young soldier who had been instrumental in saving her life had come to teach them instead. Somali girls are required to place the veils of their dresses across their faces. This was the order of the religion they were being instructed in. At first, Sam had spoken hurriedly, as if he was annoyed at being there. Then, noticing Aayana under her headdress, he changed his pace and delivered his message more carefully. He had presented the students with an illustration that would reaffirm the honourability found in making a sacrifice for one's faith while young.

'Some beautiful flowers were once crushed underfoot by a herd of camels used to fight in men's wars,' he had said. 'Although the plants died before they were in full bloom, their life was given back to them because they provided nutrients to the soil into which they were pressed. Someday many other flowers will grow from this ground.'

All at once Sam stopped speaking, and had walked slowly over to Aayana. With the tip of his finger, he moved the veil covering her face, and stared into her dark eyes.

Looking down at her Sam had continued, his voice a whisper, 'And they will someday become magnificent blooms, these trodden ones.'

Sam had let go of Aayana's veil. Lowering his head, he left the room.

Unbeknown to the young soldier and at that precise moment, Aayana had silently prayed to God for Sam's salvation.

***

There came a time when Aayana noticed a shift in the mood around her village. The warlord appeared agitated. He had become short-tempered. On one particular day, he seemed to lose his temper over the smallest things.

Behaving like one possessed, he had ordered his men to rally for a meeting. Aayana had later learned that the leader and his troop had been recalled to their headquarters in the Northern territory, closer to the coast where much of the piracy occurred. The soldiers had gathered the children, making no distinction between boys and girls. Stretching to her full height, which gave her a distinct advantage over the other youngsters, Aayana had searched for a glimpse of her mother and brothers. She was unable to see any of her family. Her heart had pounded in her chest.

A brief moment of chaos had followed as children and adolescents were bundled together. Most of them had cried at the prospect of being taken from their families. One of the older soldiers, a burly man, had tied the young captives loosely together with a rope. He had funnelled them into a line and ordered them to keep it straight. Aayana pulled back from the twine, tears streaming down her face. She had no idea where they were taking her. And, what about the other children? Some of them were younger than she was.

While all of this was happening, Aayana had been drawn somewhere else—to the foot of the cross of Christ. She had given him her pain and those of her people. Here she found the strength she would need in the months that lay ahead.

The youngsters were led out of the village by the soldiers. The cries of their families echoed eerily in the wake of the encroaching darkness. Their victims' pleas for mercy had gone unheeded. The only voice that could be heard, like a lion roaring into the night, was that of the warlord's, declaring 'I will give them back to you!' But he added, for only his men to hear, 'When I am finished with them.'

Papa had laughed mockingly. He motioned for his troop to step up their pace. The villagers were well-schooled in this common practice—wounded and maimed children who had fought as soldiers would almost always be sent back to their families.

7

They had marched for days towards the northern territory. Aayana noticed the younger children become increasingly weak; they had been given little to eat and drink. It had also been difficult to stay attached to your own group. If it hadn't been for the ropes that kept them together, Aayana would have succumbed to the weight of the children trying to stay on their feet.

Their journey seemed to never end. To make matters worse, other children were added to the original groups of captives along the way. Aayana had wondered what had happened to the children who disappeared from the first groups. One minute they had been there, struggling to keep up with the march, and the next they were gone. A terrified thought had crossed her mind, *Have they become prey to the wild animals who constantly stalked them?* She had seen their hungry eyes at night, glowing like coals of fire.

The northern borders were nowhere in sight. Aayana had wondered whether it was all a big lie. Perhaps they had been taken on this treacherous journey by the warlord and his soldiers only to perish on the plains.

Aayana had felt Sam near her, even though he had been careful to keep his distance. There had been times when she felt she was given a little extra than the rest—to drink and to eat. Although she had not been able to determine who the provider was, Aayana had felt Sam was responsible for the benevolent acts. Was the protection she had received from Sam part of God's plan to keep her strong? During the course of their forced march, Aayana had been given strength to help the other children survive the grueling journey, especially the younger ones. She had found that she was able to keep going when most of the others could barely put one foot in front of the other.

Although Aayana was able to maintain her physical strength, her true feelings were buried (common to those in times of war) beneath the layers of countless attempts to preserve her whole being. Gradually, over time, just like the sand that burns into their feet, the children of war begin to wilt. Aayana had watched helplessly as they all suffered.

Some of the youngsters who had been specifically trained to raid the villages along the way were taught to use heavy artillery and to loot. They had become hardened till their hearts were impenetrable. For them, Aayana had prayed each day that the evil one would not have the power to destroy their souls. There were others who had become so weakened that they had attempted to break free from their group. Hoping that they had not been noticed, they were nonetheless always recaptured. Because the area was so bleak, it was easy to spot a youngster making their way out to the hills on their own. Their fate was certain. Aayana found herself helping the injured children who had tried to escape. She had comforted the wounded and prayed for them.

Clearly stronger than the others, Aayana knew that Sam had something to do with the fact that she was not used for fighting. He had become her guardian angel. The Somali girl was used, instead, to help the younger girls around the camp who cooked the food and fetched water, cleaned weapons and made fires. They even helped to assemble landmines. Knowing the consequences of such violence released tears of anguish from her eyes.

A strange mix of loyalty and fear pervaded the camps. Sadly, some of the older girls fell pregnant. Aayana's heart broke at the thought of an infant being delivered into their brutal world. She did her best to not anger the warlord. The other soldiers had left her alone. Perhaps it was because of Sam's watchful eye. The more he cared for her the more she was able to take care of the others.

Aayana recalled the morning she finally found the courage to speak to Sam. The sun had risen with its usual gallantry and the birds in the sparse trees had sung their first songs. Aayana had woken from where she had slept under the stars and begun to search for the dry wood she used for making the breakfast fires. She had quietly gone about her work with no intention of disturbing anyone, yet keeping within the confines of the camp. One could never be too careful. There were always suspicious eyes about—soldiers looking for Papa's approval. Aayana had hunched her body close to the ground. Humming one of the melodies she had learned at the relief camp near her village had been her favourite thing to do while she searched for wood. To her surprise, a young man had quietly joined her and helped her to gather the thin dry branches that were plentiful.

It was Sam, the young soldier. Aayana's heart had beat within its slim cavity. He had noticed that she was uncomfortable with him being so close to her and had quickly apologised before he spoke. 'Don't be afraid. I mean you no harm. The villagers call you Aar-Aayana, don't they?'

Aayana had kept quiet, working briskly and keeping her head low.

'It's okay to speak, unless you don't want to. That's also fine.' Sam had tried to lighten their one-sided conversation. 'I hope you've noticed that I've been looking out for you—that I can be trusted.' He had spoken just loud enough for Aayana to hear him. His voice had been kind, unlike the way he spoke to the other soldiers.

'There is something different about you, Aayana. I noticed this right from the start when I saw you lying in the sand. You have… a quiet confidence. It is as if an invisible presence is with you. I would like to know more about it. When the time is right.'

His voice had trailed, and Aayana had remained quiet. When he finished helping her, he made his way back to the camp.

This had been how Aayana came to know Sam. Each morning he would come alongside to help her collect wood. They would also gather a kind of weed to brew for the soldiers—a drink the men believed would give them power. Sam would stay just enough to talk to her, and not cast any suspicion around their rendezvous.

One morning, while collecting wood, Sam had asked Aayana, 'How do you get your strength? It's clear you are the strongest of all the young villagers we have captured.' Still, there had been no response from the Somali girl.

Sam had heard Aayana speak to herself, softly under her breath, while she gathered a woodpile. It had been as if she was reciting a passage of some kind. He had thought he had heard her say that she would not look to the hills for help. *How peculiar,* he had thought. There were no hills, just dry flat land for miles on end.

Sam had been careful to keep a respectable distance between himself and Aayana. He had made sure that they got back to camp before Papa woke. Aayana slowly began to trust him.

On one occasion, Sam had shared his life story with her. 'I never chose to be a soldier. I was also kidnapped as a youngster by Papa and his troop. His army was growing into quite a formidable force back then. I've not known much of a normal life but what I do know is that I've been forced to be what I am.'

Sam had stopped what he was doing, and looked up from the ground. 'I hate it all. I long for a normal life, but I'm afraid.' There had been a small tremor in the young soldier's voice.

For the first time since Sam had been helping her, Aayana looked up from her work and searched Sam's face. When she finally spoke, her eyes filled with compassion.

'The things we want the most are what create a certain fear in us. It's a fear that we may never get what we desire. I've learned that there's One who'll give to us what we long for. We all want to be free.'

Aayana had not waited for Sam to respond. Quickly she made her way back to camp, looking back just once to see Sam staring longingly at her. Aayana turned her face to the soldiers who had begun to stir. The first rays of the early morning had crept upon them like the tears that slipped from the young man's face. He had not bothered to wipe them away.

This was the way Sam heard about the gospel of Jesus Christ. At first, he had only listened to the Somali girl. Then, slowly, he began to spill from his soul the pain that he had concealed for most of his life. Aayana had been there beside him. She had comforted Sam and had prayed that the love of God would fill his heart and heal him.

The soldiers and their captives had continued with their journey to the northern provinces, raiding many coastal villages on their way. Papa's plan had been to leave the child soldiers with the militia at their headquarters. He would then continue with his pillaging of the small Somali communities. Just like their inland counterparts, the coastal villages also suffered at the hands of the insurgents. The warlord aimed to eventually make his way back to the southern borders closer to where Aayana's village was located.

The temperatures in the north had been insufferable. The pressing heat at the boundary of the desert had borne down on them as it touched the plains that fringed the vast ocean to the east. Still, they had trudged on. Throughout the Somali conflict many revolutionary movements, including the military, were led by warlords who controlled huge areas of Somali land. The people faced relentless terror at the hands of faction and rogue groups, led by men of self-possessed power and authority. Aayana understood that she had been captured by the leader of a smaller rebel group who harboured an insatiable desire to capture as many areas as he could.

This conquer-and-control philosophy by rogue warlords is what led thousands of Somalis to be displaced. An ongoing famine in the land further worsened matters. Continuous invasions and a shortage of food weakened Aayana's people. Another variance to the wars which developed along the coastlands was the recruitment of child pirates. Children were kidnapped from their villages. They were trained to terrorise the seas and to kidnap for ransom.

Aayana feared the worst for her brothers, who would be soft targets after the recent plunder of her village. She had thought of them daily and had offered petitions to God for their safekeeping. Aayana had prayed that they would find Christ as their Saviour and that their suffering would be eased. She had heard Mister Mark speak of organisations that worked to educate children who had been used in the armed conflicts of Somalia. She had prayed that her brothers would find such relief and that someday, although it seemed impossible, she would see Mister Mark again.

When they had finally reached their destination, Papa immediately separated the youngsters who would remain at his headquarters from those who would continue with him. The group had been exhausted and Sam had entreated the leader to allow them to rest a bit. Papa had reluctantly given into the young soldier's request. It had been no surprise to Aayana that she had been selected to continue with the troops along the coast. She believed that Papa thought her an asset. Although she had experienced great difficulty under the people she served, Aayana had worked sacrificially—always hoping and praying that they would survive another day. It was with great sadness that Aayana left many of her friends behind. She had cared for the younger boys and girls as if they had been her own brothers and sisters, doubting she would ever see them again. The group had moved on. A ray of hope flickered in Aayana as they turned south. She had the distinct impression that she was homeward bound.

***

It all seemed so long ago now, Aayana's kidnapping and the long march with the vigilante soldiers. Months under these conditions had passed. Aayana had no record of what time of the year it was. Sam was gone and here she was, nestled in the boughs of a tree. She missed her family. She felt sad that each time she tried to recall their faces, her mind retrieved only a blur. Aayana began to doze. Her thoughts drifted to happier times and the love she had shared with her parents and siblings.

A loud shout from someone standing at the foot of the tree jolted Aayana awake. It was Papa, staring at her threateningly. The warlord ordered her to come down. Aayana had hoped that while the voodoo celebrations were underway her absence had gone unnoticed—it had not been long since Sam had escaped. She shuddered to think what might happen to him if he were to be found by Papa. The voice coming from the base of the tree was relentless. Aayana wondered whether Papa had become suspicious of Sam's absence. Pulling herself together, she scrambled down, praying under her breath, 'Father, please watch over Sam. Let the only thing that confronts him be your salvation.'

Aayana landed at Papa's feet. She pulled herself to her full height. The warlord looked at her through half-opened eyes, his stance menacing. Papa's eyes were swollen, and his breath smelled of *chibuku* beer and strong tobacco. He quickly filled the small space between them.

'So, this is where the lioness is hiding.' Papa's words were calculated—he spoke with a slur. 'Or would you prefer me to call you the queen of Africa? After all, you do seem to think you are a cut above us. And where is Sam? For some reason you both think you have no need to join our celebrations.'

The warlord folded his arms across his chest as if to say to Aayana that there would be no getting out of this one. Aayana had learned during their long march that with Papa it was better to face him squarely. This tends to throw him off guard and gives his opponent the upper hand—if only for a short while.

Aayana lifted her eyes and looked directly at him before answering, 'Yes, I have been hiding, and no, Sam is not here.' She added, quite fearlessly, 'I do believe I'm the queen of Africa!' Aayana lifted her veil from her face to show him the fire in her eyes.

Papa was surprised at her defiance. He laughed out loud. 'Aayana, Aayana, what am I to do with you?'

Papa shook his head. 'Follow me. There is a matter I wish to discuss with you, perhaps you can help me find a solution.'

Aayana had no choice but to allow Papa to lead her. He had become her enemy. She thought about her dilemma as she followed him back to the base camp. *It's easier, Lord, to love those who love you in return, but to love those who hate you… it is impossible. Only through the strength that you give me will I be able to carry out your command to love my enemies.*

They trudged through the low bushes. A sense of something sinister enveloped Aayana. She held her hands tightly at her sides, taking care to keep her balance, not wanting Papa to see how she was trembling.

Papa led Aayana towards a group of tents arranged in a half-circle near the center of the camp. These were the housings of the higher-ranking soldiers.

'Hayaan, get up. I must speak with you.' Papa pushed at the small opening of one of the tents. The man called Hayaan scrambled out while he pulled a shirt over his chest. He quickly positioned his body in the required military stance. Standing upright, he waited for further instructions from his leader. Papa told the man to relax, that he only needed to clarify some things with Hayaan in the presence of Aayana.

'I'd like to give our African queen a chance to tell us her version of a perplexing tale I've recently been made aware of.' He added, somewhat dryly, 'Somalis must never be seen as unfair or dishonest.'

Aayana felt her heart pound in her chest. She tried to remain calm.

The warlord grew agitated when he noticed the soldier hesitate. 'You must speak up. If you have something important to tell me, now is the time.'

Papa looked impatiently at the hedge of low-lying bushes which, like a net, secured their camp from intruders. The morning's first rays made him squint. He had already made up his mind about the incident but was willing to endure any discussion to deceive his people into thinking he was fair. It was important to him that his soldiers respected him.

The man called Hayaan was crafty. He enjoyed being the eyes and ears of his leader. Hayaan pushed his chest out. 'It's not been a short time that I've observed the close friendship between Aayana and Sam. Sam looks out for her and Aayana gives him more attention than she does the other soldiers.'

Hayaan shifted on his feet. 'You see this tall tree Aayana likes to climb?' He pointed towards Aayana's hideaway. 'I venture to say that this tree, if it could speak, will defend my charge that Sam's no longer with us. He has deserted you, my lord.' Hesitating, Hayaan added,

'And Aayana helped him to escape.'

The soldier concluded his indictment. 'I'm sure Sam is long gone. He'll not return to us.' The man flashed a mean, yellow-toothed smile at Aayana.

Papa did not react immediately. He was as cunning as the desert foxes that roamed the plains, waiting for the right time to strike. He looked at Aayana with contempt. The Somali girl's resolve crumbled till she gave way to a torrent of tears. Her reaction only annoyed the warlord further.

'You've betrayed me, Aayana!'

Aayana wiped her eyes. She felt like a trapped bird—unable to break free.

While Papa waited for a response from her, Hayaan interrupted him. 'It may be wiser to turn her over to the council and let them decide her fate. You don't want them to assume that a mere girl has betrayed the loyalty of the whole troop *and* outsmarted you.' Hayaan kept a respectful distance. 'Let them decide. Your hands will be clean. Surely, they will not let an act of betrayal go unpunished.'

Papa contemplated the words of the soldier. Then, spitting some of the tobacco he was chewing onto the ground, he turned abruptly to Aayana. 'Come with me.'

Aayana was afraid of what awaited her. The difficulties she experienced growing up in her village had been simpler to overcome because there was always someone she could turn to for support. Now, she was completely alone. She had to lean on God while she was at her weakest.

They made their way to where the council usually assembled. Aayana's thoughts drifted to her visits at the relief camp. She thought of the times Mister Mark had shared from the Bible. He had read from the books of the Old Testament—of the great stories of faith. One particular narrative had caught her attention. It was the story of the Hebrew leader, Joshua. Mister Mark had spoken to them with compassion in his voice. It was as if he knew that they were all about to go through a difficult time. He had read the words of God to Joshua, *"I will not leave you nor forsake you. Be strong and of good courage..."*

Aayana had let her heart soak up the encouraging words of her teacher. Now, she allowed them to resurface, holding onto them as Hayaan ordered her to walk faster.

Aayana felt the sun on her back as she stood before the warlord and his council. In the end, it was decided that Aayana would be punished with thirty lashes.

When it was over, Aayana could no longer feel the sun's warmth or hear the birds chirping their silken songs. Her eyes remained closed. Papa's retribution was, however, not complete. He would do what was customarily practiced by the vigilantes. Rallying his soldiers together, he indicated that they should pack up and continue south towards Aayana's village. They would take her with them to leave her there. It was of no consequence to him what further became of the Somali girl. He would not see her again.

Aayana began to move, slowly at first. Some of the older child soldiers helped her up. They gave her some water to drink and cleaned her wounds best they could. Aayana was astonished that the children who were taking care of her were the very ones she had helped during their terrible march together.

***

They journeyed south. The council was in agreement that Aayana would be given back to her already broken family. This was the way of the rogue soldiers. Give back to the families their maimed children so they would have the burden of caring for them. This practice strengthens, in turn, the control of the warlords over the villages. Papa would be the salt in Aayana's wounds. It would remind her family of his power over them.

After many days the troop arrived at Aayana's village. They dropped her near the water well. The morning had already lifted its covers to the sun whose heat bore down on Aayana. Only at noon, when the villagers were certain that the soldiers had left, did they call for Aayana's mother and the rest of her family. The Somali girl was weak and thirsty. In her semi-conscious state, she thought of the deep suffering war brings. She thought too of Jesus. He had suffered a worse death on the cross, all because of his love for humanity.

When they heard the startling news, Aayana's mother and grandmother hurried over to where their child lay in the dust. With the help of Aayana's uncle, they gently lifted the young woman. Their pleas for her life to be spared hung eerily over the village. Together they lowered Aayana onto the back of a cart. It was drawn by one of the mules that had taken Aayana to the relief camp before she was kidnapped. When they arrived at the little settlement, her younger brother, who was by now quite tall and muscular, ran out to her. Aayana could hear him call her name over and over. The sorrow in his voice was clear, yet comforting.

Aayana tried to open her eyes. Some of the elders in the village heard of the Somali girl's return and the condition she was in. Having lost some of their own children to the marauders, the men went over to the homestead to see where they could help. Although the vigilante soldiers had long gone, a cloud of suspicion and concern of further attacks still hung over the people. One of the elders brought with him a traditional healer. Although Aayana's religion strictly forbade them from doing so, her family welcomed the soothsayer along with his curative rituals.

Aayana vaguely heard him as he stamped his feet, chanting words she did not understand. The man began to throw all kinds of inanimate objects around her. The Somali girl was, however, soaring elsewhere. She felt herself being lifted through a shaft of bright light high above the earth. The place where she was taken was where the angels worship the Holy One; where God intervenes on behalf of his children—a place some call Heaven.

The healer threw the last of his objects to the ground and let out a howl, as if he were a creature of the night. His body shook fiercely, indicating that Aayana was no longer with them.

Suddenly Aayana's grandmother broke away from the mourners. She cried out to the man, 'Away with you, away with you. Aayana will live and not die!'

The old woman drove the man from the hut. He ran wildly as if an invisible force was chasing him.

She ordered her family to take Aayana to the main dwelling. There they placed the girl on a bed made of animal hides.

Placing her own body over her granddaughter's, the woman prayed in a loud beseeching voice, 'Oh God, the God of Aayana, I have known for a long time that you are her true Father. If Aayana were given the chance, she would offer her own life to save her family. Bring her back to us to finish her work on earth.'

The old woman continued to pray for a while, pleading for Aayana's life while the rest of the onlookers were too frightened to intervene.

***

In that moment when heart connects with Heaven and sorrow yields to love, Aayana felt the earth growing smaller beneath her. The light around her was pure and cleansing. It embraced her with its brilliance. She felt herself being carried through a grassy meadow. Its radiant stalks were like comforting arms around her. A river ran through the field and a small herd of deer drank from its clear water. Aayana was brought to a valley—dry and desolate. She saw only the stumps of trees there. Many of them dotted the vast area. Then, as if she was deliberately being lowered, Aayana saw women with their young children standing next to the tree stumps. They wore clothing from a place that was foreign to her. Their upturned faces, framed by dark locks, were fixed with sorrow. They seemed to call to her for help.

Aayana looked up to see the sky open. A voice like that of rushing water finally spoke to her. It was powerful, yet compassionate. 'Aayana, do not forget what you have seen here.'

She turned towards the voice. 'Lord, what would you have me do?'

Although the voice did not speak again, Aayana knew that God would make the meaning of her vision clear to her when the time was right.

Another voice was calling out to her. This time it was familiar. It was Aayana's grandmother asking the

Lord to return her granddaughter to her. Aayana felt herself moving back to the place of her birth.

Holding her granddaughter's body in her arms, the old woman felt Aayana jolt back to life. There was a great shout from the people who had been mourning for her. They cried out over and over again, 'Aayana's God has brought her back to life!'

Some of them began to dance around the hut. Others clung to each other. A great miracle was witnessed the day Aayana was returned to her people.

***

Aayana slowly regained her strength. Her deep wounds began to heal. For days she would fall into such a deep sleep that her family wondered whether she would ever wake. They took turns listening to her breathing to make sure she was still alive. During her time of recovery, Aayana dreamed often. She dreamt of strange places—of women and girls who were not at all like her people. She saw herself working alongside them, helping to rescue them from a deep abyss of suffering.

When she finally woke, Aayana thought she saw her grandmother enter her place of rest with a man who had long hair the colour of ripened corn. The man smiled down at her. His smile did not sit quite straight in his face. The man was familiar. Aayana tried to lift her head to get a better look at him. *Could it be Mister Mark from the relief camp?* she wondered. Aayana did not get her answer immediately. She was right, though. Mister Mark had come looking for her.

While her younger brother fed her the next morning, Aayana heard voices near the entrance of the hut. Her sleeping quarters were separated from the living area with a partition that had been woven from goat hair and soft grass. Her grandmother pulled back the screen and entered the room. There was a man close behind her—the one from the previous day.

Although his eyes were warm and friendly, the man had a concerned look on his face. Aayana eyed him carefully from the rim of her bowl. Yes, it was Mister Mark. Her face lit up for the first time in weeks. How thrilled she was to see her teacher again. It was indeed a miracle that he had come to find her. Gently instructing (in Somali language) Aayana's brother to leave the room, the old lady signalled for Mark to sit on the edge of Aayana's makeshift bed. The divan was strengthened by grass mats, to give Aayana as much support as possible.

Aayana looked sheepishly at Mark, her eyes soft. Mark was the first to speak. 'I came to look for you the moment I heard what had happened. It took me some time to get here though.' He chuckled. 'The elders of the village are understandably hesitant about allowing strangers back into the village.'

Mark's face grew serious. 'I'm so sorry for everything that has happened to you. I've thought of you often and I've prayed many times for your protection. The day you and the other children were taken away was one of the saddest days of my life.'

Mark gently took Aayana's hand in his own while her heart filled with happiness. Although she did not have the strength to respond, Aayana offered him her best smile. She closed her eyes briefly as if to savour the moment.

'Your grandmother shared with me how God brought you back to them. There is one thing I'm most certain of Aayana. God is alive and he does answer our prayers.'

Mark added before he got up, 'Hold on, sweet girl.' Aayana smiled and closed her eyes as he quietly left the room.

***

The next weeks found Mark regularly visiting Aayana and her family. The Somali girl was growing stronger each day. Ishaar did not leave her side, helping her wherever he could. Aayana began to walk a little, first with cautious steps around the room, and then to other areas of the homestead. Her grandmother also remained close throughout her courageous attempts. Aayana noticed that although her mother was concerned for her well-being and seemed pleased to have her daughter back, unlike the others, she remained distant. This troubled Aayana greatly.

One morning, Aayana woke to feel the warm air blowing from the plains. She was restless, so she decided to pray for her *hooyo*. Looking for a comfortable position, her hand touched something that had been placed under her straw headrest. She removed it from its snug position and discovered that it was a Bible. Aayana recognised it as the one Mister Mark had used when he had shared the gospel of Christ with the girls at the relief camp. Her eyes welled with tears of joy. For the first time in a long while, Aayana let her happiness be heard.

Ishaar, who was outside unloading a cart of dry wood, thought his sister was in some kind of trouble. He immediately ran to her. 'Aayana what is it?' The boy was quite breathless.

Aayana stretched out her arms to pull her brother closer, almost toppling him over. What a relief it was for him that his sister was unharmed. He smiled at the realisation that she was at least regaining her usual strength. How wonderful it felt for Ishaar to have his sister back.

'Easy, Aayana. I think your muscles have grown twice their size since you've come back to us.'

Aayana laughed with her brother. God has designed such moments for painful memories to find a resting place in the souls of his children. She showed Ishaar what she had discovered under her headrest. 'I'm so excited. Mister Mark has given me the most wonderful book. It contains the holy scriptures of the God of Jesus Christ. It's written in English, but I'll try my best to read it to you.'

When he heard it was the book for those who followed Christ, Ishaar drew back. 'Ah, but that book is for Christians, Sister. It's not for people of our faith. You'll have to be careful with it, or the elders will drive you from our village. I couldn't cope with losing you again.'

Ishaar brushed a stray tear from his cheek. Trying to be brave, he quipped, 'What do I care anyway? Our faith hasn't saved our family from all the pain and sorrow we've suffered. It's only you and my family that I care about.'

Aayana took her brother's hands in hers. She showed him the same compassion she had given to those she had helped during her captivity.

'I was not saved by a religion, Ishaar. I was rescued by a Person. Brother, you're tired and crushed because you don't have someone you can depend on each day for comfort and peace. I'll pray that your eyes open, so that you'll understand that what Christ has done for us is all that matters.'

Ishaar closed his eyes and hung his head as he listened to his sister. She gently placed her hand under his chin so that his gaze met hers. His cheeks were wet and his lips trembled, 'I want what you have, Aayana. I've seen the miracles of this God you talk about... how he kept you strong even when you were at death's door. Pray for me, Sister, that I might know him also.'

Aayana prayed a simple prayer with Ishaar. A bright light had filled the room. Aayana noticed her grandmother and mother kneeling beside each other at the foot of her bed. There were others there too. Some of them were her neighbours. And Mister Mark was there, praying for the people. Aayana's heart swelled with gratitude. It was a glorious time, that out of so much sorrow, peace and joy had finally come. Aayana's whole household acknowledged Christ as their Saviour that day.

***

Over the course of some months, Mark read to Aayana's family from the Bible. Aayana helped with the translation. It was a special time of spiritual growth for them all. The bond of love and the power of prayer united the believers while their numbers grew.

On one occasion Mark shared with Aayana and her family that he had lost his wife some years ago in a distant country called India. The tragedy occurred while they were working together to rescue women and girls who had been sold into slavery. His sorrow had been so great that he had decided to leave India for good. He had taken a position with a nonprofit organisation to set up a relief camp in war-torn Somalia. Even though it had been difficult for him, Mark had hoped to find some solace for his broken heart. He told them that lately he felt that his work in India was not yet finished, and that it was time for him to return to the place he was first called to. His time in Somalia had sadly come to an end.

Mark would always keep the people of Somalia in his heart and in his prayers. He mentioned to them that he would also be leaving for an area in rural India to set up an outreach farm. He would show the people there, those who lived in the mountains, better ways to feed their families. He would also provide for their daughters an education—which was desperately needed.

The rest of Mark's conversation with Aayana's people centered round his upcoming departure as well as his sorrow over having to leave the good people of Somalia behind. Mark passed a photograph around for everyone to see. It showed his wife, the shelter they had set up in India, and the girls they had helped. The picture was taken in front of a large building. A fading sign which rested above the door frame read, "House of Joy".

Although Aayana's family struggled to understand him, they seemed to get the general idea of where he was going. They nodded in agreement, their eyes large and curious. Mark felt his heart soften. To expect sympathy from these humble folk would be a travesty of conscience when they had been through so much suffering of their own. Still, the family seemed to understand his loss.

Finally, when he finished, the man they had all grown so fond of walked over to Aayana to retrieve the photograph from her. Mark noticed that Aayana was fascinated with the picture's subjects. She looked up at him with a radiant smile.

'Mister Mark, these are the same people I saw in my dream. The women and girls with pale skin and black hair are just like the ones in my dream.'

Aayana could not contain her excitement. She stood up and threw her arms around her teacher—just as any daughter would to thank her father for a wonderful gift.

'A great voice spoke to me from the clouds. The voice in my dream told me to not forget what I'd seen. Our Lord was speaking to me about the suffering of these people.'

Mark responded in a way that surprised them all. 'Well, that settles it, then. You're coming to India with me.' Aayana squealed with delight. She did a small leap in the air. A new day had finally dawned for the young woman from Somalia.

PART III

How then shall they call on Him in whom they have not believed? And how shall they believe in Him of whom they have not heard? And how shall they hear without a preacher?
Romans 10:14

8
India

Nothing could have prepared Grace for India. The country's communal rhythm moved her at the outset. India welcomes the ones entering her bosom for the first time, but her gigantic spirit consumes those who for generations are unable to rise above the shackles of their ancestry. The country was founded on the Indus Valley Civilisation, an immense dome of historic trade routes and vast empires permeated with commercial and religious wealth.

Grace's guide navigated her through the less affluent areas of Mumbai in a motorcycle taxi, down the narrow streets of the urban villages towards her destination.

Aagman excelled at taking care of his passenger. He made sure that Grace was not exploited by the street urchins and beggars who occupied the ramshackle houses and shadowy boulevards. Barking his imperatives at them in Hindi to 'Move out of the way and let the English lady through!' amused Grace.

As they raced on, Grace was overcome by the stark contrast of a country garlanded with beauty, yet with many of her people living in squalor. A shaman sat cross-legged against a wall that was plastered with powdered paint. Seemingly in a trance, the man blew ambivalently on a *pungi*, a stray canine licked his feet, and a woman, frail and preoccupied, thumped her washing against some stones in a futile attempt to rid her garments of their dirt. Like a pebble thrown into a large body of water that sends hundreds of concentric circles towards its edges, the homes and makeshift dwellings that lined the potholed streets reverberated centuries of poverty and shame.

A variety of odours from vegetables and spices like cardamom, chilli, garlic, and ginger overwhelmed Grace as they sped on. This was India and Grace was captivated. Her heart thumped deep in her chest; her blood rushed like the wild Ganges through her veins. She listened to Aagman chanting in Hindi the words of an unknown Indian poet. He sang about the mighty river, of her love and refuge, and of her sacred place of rest from disease and suffering. As she listened to him, Grace wept for the poor of India. She contemplated the myths and beliefs surrounding the great Ganges. The river was a natural wonder and an integral part of the Indian people—their culture and their religion.

The Ganges flows like a gigantic force from its source in the Himalayas through India and Bangladesh, where it eventually empties its soul into the Bay of Bengal. Even though the watery passage is one of the world's most polluted rivers, it is believed to contain good bacteria that devour bad micro-organisms infecting its waters.

The river is sacred to the Hindu people. It is worshipped like a god and is revered as a life source to millions. Multitudes arrive daily from near and far to cleanse themselves in her waters. The Ganges is believed to provide hope to the hopeless. Each day worshippers of the vast tributary pay their respects to their ancestors by floating hollow clay pots lit with oil and scattering flowers on the river's surface. It is the place where the

Indian people take the ashes of their deceased ones to bear, across the waters, their spirits in the cusp of her watery bosom. Her waters are constantly moving and flowing—therefore she must purify. Nothing is more holy to the devotees than to plunge into her. The people believe the river has the power to remit them of their sins—not just those of today but also those of an entire lifetime.

Grace could see that Aagman was proud of his land and his people. The man spoke in perfect English of his love of the Ganges, 'The beautiful sight of our great river when the sun casts her last rays across the slate of darkening water will take your breath away.' Grace closed her eyes. Her heart opened as she said a prayer for the Hindu man. Aagman seemed to appreciate her quiet respect for him.

How tiresome, Grace thought as they travelled on, *that the poor are compelled to go back to the river many times over to be cleansed of their sins.* She contemplated the consequences of waterborne diseases, and their threat to children and pregnant women.

Grace was reminded of the words of Jesus where he said in the gospel of Matthew, ... *Those who are well have no need of a physician, but those who are sick. But go and learn what this means: "I desire mercy and not sacrifice." For I did not come to call the righteous, but sinners, to repentance.'*

Joseph had once said of the poor, 'There are times, Señorita, when you must not share the good news of Christ's love with great persuasiveness. Instead, you must *be* the good news to them. Be a shining light, a living example. The way they see you is the way they will experience Christ. Like the parable of the Good

Samaritan, only once you have poured the oil of healing onto their bodies will their hearts be ready to receive the gospel.'

Joseph had concluded his conversation with her in his usual perceptive way. 'We are his eyes, his ears, his touch.'

Grace knew who the True River was. He had washed her clean and had filled her with his peace. Here were a people tired of their struggles and unrelenting poverty. Sadly, the Ganges brought them only temporary solace. They were never completely cleansed from their sin and shame.

God was everywhere though, even in the Ganges. He created it all. However, it is to him the people must turn and not to his creation. Grace was drawn to the truth of her own experience. Of one thing she was sure—the fire that God had put in her could never be doused; the song he had given to her could not be silenced. His love would flow from her like that of a mighty river, providing water for the thirsty and bread for the hungry.

***

Aagman parked his taxi near an area that housed various kinds of human-drawn vehicles. Grace was immediately attracted to a colourfully adorned rickshaw with its somewhat frayed yet fragrant carnations. The flowers were draped casually around the vehicle's metal framework. She climbed into the back seat as the Indian man pulled the carriage with his strong arms, hoisting his legs intermittently. They zigzagged through the streets towards the great Mumbai railway station with Grace clinging to the sides of the rickshaw.

The second part of their journey would be less comfortable as transport to the rural areas would be more crowded. What lay before her, she was uncertain—but for the grace of God, she might have turned back. Grace thought of Joseph and wondered whether he ever thought of her. How she longed to see him again, to feel his heart beat close to hers. The warmth of his presence had always stilled her fears. How blessed she felt that God had granted her such a special one.

As they neared the station, Grace's thoughts took her back to the times spent with Mama Sofia and the rest of the children at The Cielo. She remembered the wise words of Father Ralph. Although they were oceans apart, they were in her heart; the love and compassion they had shown her would be her constant companions.

The train ride took Grace towards the outskirts of the Mumbai district, closer to the hills. She was able to find a seat while Aagman stood opposite her. He held onto the thin, vertical railings as the locomotive lurched and swayed. The train was jam-packed with locals. Most of them were travelling to unknown places to sell their wares. Grace ducked as a man balancing a large basin of freshly chopped chicken heads pushed passed her. The smell of old vegetables, spices, grains, and musty cloths hung heavily in the air. She squeezed her head through a small opening in the window of the train to stop herself from gagging.

A breathtaking sight greeted her. The scenery and inhabitants of the Indian countryside were magnificent. In rural areas, agriculture is the chief source of livelihood along with fishing, cottage industries and pottery.

Grace found herself occupying yet another mode of bucolic transport after she exited the train with Aagman.

This time it was an old vehicle—half jeep, half sedan. The makeshift carrier was driven by a friendly man.

For the first time in her journey, Grace felt her stomach knot. She thought of the challenges that lay ahead. She was to be an English teacher to a group of girls who were not only strangers, but who were also from a completely different background to hers. These were girls whose young lives were under constant threat of early marriage, debt slavery, and other heinous forms of human trafficking. They could scarcely speak her language, let alone relate to her culture. Grace prayed. She reminded the Lord that her life was in his hands to do as he pleased. She thanked him again for the opportunity to be a blessing to the girls she would meet.

Grace wondered how much further the uncomfortable ride would be when she noticed the road taper. The curb looked as if it had had some form of human attention. It flanked a gravel road that led to a large clearing where the corrugated roofs of some old buildings came into view. A tiny billboard pushed into the grassy verge of the road boasted a fading picture of Gandhi. Grace guessed they had arrived at the place that would capture her heart for a while.

The vehicle ploughed on till it came to a stop in front of a wide iron fence. Layers of paint showed beneath its fading exterior. To the side a large sign read "Pathshala School for Girls". Grace loved that she could extract the word "path" from the name of the school. Here she would lead those less fortunate than herself to the sanctified place she had found in Christ.

An older woman dressed in an elaborately patterned sari, her dark hair streaked with grey and pulled into a chignon, made her way to the gate. She greeted Grace and her companions dressed in an elaborately patterned sari. She wore a receiving smile, and was in the company of a younger man who seemed just as eager to meet them. Grace assumed this was the gentleman Joseph had told her about. The man opened the gate to let the group in. The older woman welcomed Grace, bombarding her good-naturedly with many questions about her journey.

Although Grace was tired, she tried her best to be polite. The younger man introduced himself to Grace as Mark. After embracing her, he made a point of letting her know that he was a good friend of Joseph's, and that he was grateful she was willing to take the position of English teacher at their school. Mark quickly ran through some of the formalities that would make Grace's stay comfortable. Grace sensed that Mark was not one to be bothered with too much detail. She thought him handsome in a rugged way, and he had a relaxed air about him, which made Grace feel immediately at home. Together they walked up to the main house.

Grace had arrived at the Pathshala a few weeks before the school holidays ended. It was decided that she would not stay at the school but would travel each day to and from the outreach farm where Mark lived with the other volunteers.

The older Indian woman, introduced to Grace as Aayshirya, was the school's headmistress. Although Grace got the distinct impression that Aayshirya managed the school with an evident sternness, she sensed that beneath the woman's visage was a wise and kind heart.

The new acquaintances sipped tea together on the veranda of the main house. The school buildings were just smaller versions of the main building. Grace relaxed with her new companions. She learned during their conversation that the girls who attended the school were poor, their families barely able to feed their children let alone provide an education for their daughters. Some of the children were forced to work in the stone quarry of a mountain that loomed above the school and farm. They were used to pay off family debt, forfeiting the chance of formal learning. If ever such an opportunity arose, it would go to the eldest boy first. The families were therefore grateful for the Pathshala.

A relentless cycle of debt alleviation exists in these parts of rural India. This social problem is sadly exploited by people who wish to become rich on the backs of the poor. The girls from these families are also in danger of being sold as sex slaves in the nearby red-light district of Mumbai. Because they are always in a state of financial need, their unsuspecting parents readily give their daughters over to people with evil motives.

The families are told that their daughters will work as housemaids in the homes of the wealthy, and money sent to support the girl's family back home. This is more often than not the case, and most of the girls are forced into prostitution instead. The benefits of providing a good education for these girls are consequently immeasurable.

Grace learned from her new friends that the state assisted their work by providing the girls with one meal a day. The parcel consisted mostly of cooked rice. Other donations were used to provide the students with satchels and stationery, and to cover the enormous costs related to maintaining the school and its paltry facilities. Grace noticed as she surveyed the classrooms from where she sat that they needed a good paint; at least some repair work was already underway. The grounds were sparsely covered with grass—most of it was exposed and sandy.

A tarpaulin strung between two trees provided some shelter for the girls when they needed a break from the unbearable heat.

Preoccupied with her thoughts, Grace was startled when Aayshirya appeared at her side. The older woman seemed to read Grace's mind. 'Walk a little with me. I'll show you around and you can ask me all the questions you like.'

Grace blushed. Then she smiled. 'I'll take you up on that. I've so many questions, I fear they may be more than the answers you can provide. I want to know everything about the young people here.'

Aayshirya assured Grace of her support. She responded congenially, 'You'll see that I'm fond of words, Grace. There's little that keeps me from talking, especially when I'm with such pretty company.'

They ambled down a well-worn path that led to the school buildings. Grace exhaled a sigh and smiled contentedly. Aayshirya eyed her young companion. 'You seem to be happy about the decision you made to come here.'

'India is beautiful. It's as if God reserved his best ideas to create this special land. His most careful and perceptive thoughts were, I believe, used to fashion the people here.' Grace smiled respectfully before she added, 'Do you think this is why they worship his creation the way they do?'

'Our land certainly surpasses her rivals. You are right, though. The people pay homage to the gods of the water and life systems, but they do not worship the One who is the true giver of life. The creation they worship is unable to relieve them of poverty, nor give them the hope they need for a better future.'

Aayshirya placed her hand in the crook of Grace's arm before she continued. 'Most of our people do not know what it is to have the King of the universe, the Creator of all living things, dwell in their hearts.'

The two walked on, quietly enjoying each other's company. Aayshirya addressed Grace's living arrangements. 'Your new home is not far from here, but there's still plenty of time to get you settled. We have a saying that goes something like this, "The day is not done till the myna birds sleep". As you can hear, they are not quite there yet!'

Aayshirya laughed heartily. She steered Grace back to the main house. Their brief trip around the school grounds left Grace anxious to see the vacant buildings filled with the laughter and chatter of the girls when the holidays ended.

Aayshirya and Grace joined the rest of their companions, who were still engaged in light conversation. Grace was immediately intrigued by the stark difference between Mark and Joseph. The priest was quiet in his convictions, his honesty born from a deep compassion for humanity. Mark struck her as an outgoing, pragmatic man who took life by the horns. There were, however, similarities between the two which Grace found quite remarkable. Both displayed an indomitable spirit of service to God that was resolute and unshakable. They shared a passion and love for his children, no matter their repugnance or fragility.

Mark had embraced Grace in a bear-like hug when they were first introduced. She had felt an immediate fondness for the man. His face was hidden in months of unshaven hair, and his smile was as broad and lopsided as the Ganges. A long mop of fair and wavy hair framed his face. Mark sported the gentlest blue eyes with a roguish sparkle. He was a man one immediately loved. Grace came to learn that Mark was held with the fondest regard by the people who worked at the Pathshala.

The people's love for him was not the only thing Grace learned about Mark. The man had lost his wife to a fatal illness some years back. The living conditions in the poor communities of India were known to be harsh and unrelenting. Mark and his wife had lived and worked in Mumbai to rescue young Indian women and girls from various forms of slavery. They believed that while it was important to educate their daughters, the families and their sons who earned a meagre living from the land needed their help just as much. The boys farmed alongside their fathers in the fields. Better living conditions meant improved choices and the resistance of the temptation to sell their children, especially their daughters.

The couple were also convinced that the spiritual welfare of those they had rescued was just as important as their physical healing. Together they had put their trust in a merciful and loving God who did not expect ritual and sacrifice, but rather true fellowship with him. Even though the challenges were not removed, Mark and his wife, Joy, had found that their relationship with God only deepened when they served others. Mark's story of sacrificial love would become a constant inspiration to Grace in the months that followed.

***

When she arrived at the outreach station, Grace immediately felt at home. The place sat snuggly at the foot of an elevated natural structure which was more of a mountain than a hill. She had taken a long journey to get here, and in her bones felt the ache of a weary traveller. A hot shower was what she needed. Mark was a good host, and he signalled to one of the volunteers to help Grace get settled. Her room was sparse, yet neat. It had a bed, soft bedding, a floor mat, and a wall mirror. A large Bible sat on top of an old cabinet.

There was no electricity to the farm. Grace was fascinated, however, by the nifty ideas that made the place sustainable. The people who lived and worked there had certainly honed their skills by tapping energy from every conceivable source. Grace was led to a shower cubicle that had a brass pipe coiled above it. The mechanism helped to keep the water hot. A plethora of solar panels fastened to the roof captured the sun's heat during the day, providing power to the house at night.

Dozens of little furrows from the water wastage points led to all kinds of garden projects. Strawberries sprouted from old used gutters. Beans, radish, and cabbage grew amongst the many pathways to and from the main buildings. The farm itself was surrounded by poorly cultivated farmlands. Mark and his volunteers worked relentlessly to help the local farmers improve their dated farming methods.

Once she had washed, Grace took a stroll around the main homestead. She stepped out of her bungalow and scanned the mountain that overshadowed the farm. Grace placed her hands over her eyes to avoid the sun's glare, and looked up to see a solitary bird of prey screech at her. The bird spread its wings as if to obstruct her view, but she could make out from the stony outcrops and deep fissures that the stone quarry her friends had mentioned was located further up.

While she stood there gazing at the rocky horizon, Mark appeared and stood beside her. 'Are you happy with your room? I realise it's quite plain. Nonetheless, I hope you'll feel comfortable.'

Grace turned to Mark, desperately trying to conceal the sudden longing for her family in Colombia. She thought of them constantly but did her best to keep her mind on her new life in India. 'I'm quite comfortable. I can't thank you enough for receiving me with such generosity.'

Mark looked at Grace through his fair lashes. He immediately felt admiration for the slender yet strong woman beside him. The picture Grace painted as she stood there was, in fact, quite breathtaking for him. Aware of Mark's gaze, Grace self-consciously asked him to lead her back to her bungalow.

On the way, Grace remarked, 'What you're doing here, your work amongst the people of rural India, is truly amazing.'

'A great poet once said—I think it was Keats—"A proverb is no proverb to you till your life has illustrated it". The maxim I try to live by is found in Proverbs, ...*he who has mercy on the poor, happy is he.*'

Mark's response resonated with Grace. She almost lost her footing as they neared the house, but Mark took hold of her arm to steady her. She smiled warmly at him and nodded, 'A truth we'll all do well to remember.'

From then on, Grace relaxed with her new friend. Mark's careful attention to her well-being reminded her of her first days at The Cielo, and the special way in which Joseph would guide her up the stairwell to her room while she recovered—now oceans away. She thought of them—Joseph, Sofia, and the children. *Will I ever see them again?* As if reading her mind, Mark asked Grace to join him in his study. There was a letter waiting for her from Joseph.

Grace had not heard from the priest since her departure. She had wondered whether his lack of contact had something to do with the safety of the people at The Cielo. Nevertheless, the mention of Joseph's name caused her heart to race. Mark left the study to give Grace a few moments to read the letter alone.

My dear Gracie

I must confess I have sat down to write to you more times than I care to remember. Why I would find it so difficult I cannot say. I have a suspicion that it has to do with a certain fear of mine—that in writing to you I will somehow betray my deepest feelings, and that once I have begun to pen them, I'll not be able to stop. So it is that I've decided that it would be better for me to write to you as a dear friend who misses you terribly, one who longs to have a glimpse of your lovely face and a taste of your sweet spirit.

How are you? We think of you often and wonder how our beloved Gracie is doing. The children miss you exceedingly. They wear me down in a wonderful way with their many questions as to when you will be returning to us. I do not grow tired of their enquiries as I am convinced that God will return you to us if it is his will that you come back to the orphanage someday. I am, however, comforted more than you can ever imagine that you have been obedient to the will of God and that many lives will be changed through your sacrifice.

Now for some good news—our dear little Cassia has begun to speak in great volumes to all the family here. In fact, she has become a budding spokesperson of sorts. She is certainly making up for her years of silence. The boys cover their ears at times, showing their good-natured tolerance of her incessant talking. It appears her newfound instrument must be heard and enjoyed by all. I am eternally grateful to our Saviour for bringing you into her life. Through your kindness and natural instincts, you were able to restore Cassia's trust in maternal love. How often it is that in seeking to rescue ourselves, we are often used to help others. Needless to say, Senorita, Cassia asks after you frequently. I have, if you will permit me, told her that I would ask you to write to her of your travels and the interesting people you have met. I cannot say what the future holds, as our lives are in the Master's way. I can only pray that you continue to experience his grace and strength, and that you will be able to deliver the same hope to the people he has assigned to cross your path. His staff comfort you always.

Yours in longing,
Joseph

After she read the letter, Grace sat for a while in Mark's warm study. She wrestled with the awful ache in her heart. Grace did not know it then, but her life was about to take an extraordinary turn—that of the Master's way.

***

Grace spent the following day working with the people at the farm. School had not opened yet and she was beginning to enjoy her new home. During her first days there, Grace encountered a remarkable young woman. The girl emerged from the fields just before lunch was served, tall and dark-skinned, appearing to be of African origins. Grace was immediately struck by the ethereal glow of the girl's slender frame. Grace greeted her with her usual warmth, and the girl dipped her head in response, moving away from Grace's immediate space, preferring to keep some distance. Grace kept an eye out for the girl, who moved around the farm like a panther sashaying its way through the shadows of a jungle. Grace was intrigued and wanted to know more about her.

On one occasion, Mark, who had come up to the main homestead to have lunch, thought it was time to introduce Grace to Aayana. Grace would soon be teaching at the Pathshala, so it would be a good time for the two of them to get acquainted. Mark had set out to do just that when he noticed Grace curiously observing the Somali girl from her seat in the sun. He caught Aayana just before she entered the dining area, and introduced her to Grace.

'Grace, this is Aayana. She's of Somali heritage, and a precious addition to our family here. Aayana has quite a testimony of what the Lord did for her and her clan back in Africa.'

Grace smiled at the girl. Although Aayana looked her way, she avoided Grace's eyes. Mark continued, unperturbed, 'Aayana speaks some English, Grace. But she's been awfully shy with the people around here. Perhaps you'll have better luck than I at getting her to open up.

Mark's words were well-intended, and Grace embraced the challenge to befriend the young woman. 'It's lovely to meet you, Aayana. What a beautiful name you have. What does it mean?'

Aayana looked at Grace, her face surprisingly engaging. In her best English she answered, 'My name means "flower that never dies".' The Somali girl stammered slightly, showing her perfect white teeth which according to her culture is a sign of respect.

Grace was impressed by her courage. She repeated Aayana's words, 'Eternal flower, how lovely. I only speak one other language, Aayana. It's a language from the place of my birth—a country in a continent on the other side of the world. I've spoken it since I was a child.'

Grace held a hand over her eyes to avoid the sun's glare and to give the young woman her full attention. 'You're doing well to speak English the way you do.'

Grace turned to Mark, and with an affectionate chuckle she added, 'You're a brilliant teacher, Mister Mark.'

With that, Mark laughed. He invited the women to follow him into the dining hall. The loud gong of a brass bell stationed outside the homestead sounded. It alerted the folk who were working in the fields that lunch was about to be served. A delicious fare of Indian breads and aromatic meats accompanied by freshly julienned vegetables soaked in chilli vinegar awaited them.

When the people at the outreach farm gathered to share a meal, Grace thought with great longing of Joseph and the dear people at The Cielo. There were many similarities between the two ministerial works, but for now, Grace was beginning to feel content with where God had placed her.

Grace quickly learned to follow the set schedule which was placed on a bulletin board outside the dining hall each week. The roster provided the names of the people who were arranged in teams to perform their various duties. There was also a set time to rise each morning.

Much like the orphanage in Colombia, the people would gather together in the dining hall before breakfast to share the Word of God and to sing songs of thanksgiving. Most of their prayers included petitions to God to return to them the daughters and sisters who had been sold into slavery. They prayed also for those who had been ensnared by other vices on the streets of the great cities of India.

Grace particularly enjoyed her time spent in the kitchen of the sprawling house. She found herself rising earlier than the others when it was her week to prepare food for the family. She helped to light the fires of the wood stoves to cook the *dalia*, a kind of Indian porridge, and to prepare the flatbreads that had to be baked till they were golden and crisp. The grainy breads were placed in tall batches on the long wooden tables lining the kitchen walls. Their fresh smell filled the kitchen. It was an even greater treat when Grace saw Aayana's name next to hers for kitchen duty.

While they prepared the family's meals together, Grace learned that Aayana was quite bright. Grace enjoyed her gentle yet direct personality. She helped Aayana to pronounce the names of the variety of vegetables they had to prepare together. Getting Aayana to sound out the English alphabet with the corresponding letters and consonant blends was not an easy task. Grace helped the Somali girl to divide longer words into syllables, like to–ma–to and horse–ra–dish. They laughed together as Aayana struggled along. Aayana explained that she could not stop her tongue from sticking to the roof of her mouth, so that "radish" was pronounced as "wadish".

One morning, as Grace was cleaning bundles of fresh spinach, she noticed a small striped caterpillar crawling along one of the leaves. Grace went to grab the creature from its place of comfort with the intention of crushing it underfoot when she felt a steady hand on her arm. She turned to see Aayana calmly lift the worm from its snug position. Aayana placed the caterpillar gently between her fingers, and opened the kitchen door that led to a quaint herb garden, the enclosure was protected by a wire fence. She bent low to place the worm in a small bed of nasturtium flowers. Noticing the compassionate look on her friend's face helped Grace to understand Aayana better. This was a young woman who had endured much hardship.

Aayana calmly shared her reasons for rescuing the caterpillar. 'I know you may think my actions strange. Putting this tiny worm out here places it in even greater danger. There are many hunters lying in wait for such a little animal.'

Aayana wiped her brow with the back of her hand before she went on. 'The reason I like to rescue God's creatures, big or small, has to do with my clan.' She gave Grace a shy smile. 'We're a tribal people. Every day we must face the harsh elements of our land. Sometimes it's the drought, other times it is disease that brings sudden death. Still, we remain strong. We celebrate the life we have, whether we live or die. It's important for us to do our work outside, together with nature, or we'll cease to exist.'

Aayana hesitated, but Grace encouraged the girl to go on.

'Only when a foreign intruder who's not part of our cycle of life comes to pluck our sons and daughters from us, is the spirit of my people crushed. We lose the strength that makes us who we are. The constant wars made my family powerless till Mister Mark introduced us all to the love of Jesus Christ. Now we have peace. God calmed the war that raged inside us.'

Grace moved towards her new friend and embraced her warmly. Now she understood. Her heart beat with empathy for Aayana and her people. She silently asked herself, *Does evil have no end? Still, let your love burn stronger in us, O God.* Although Grace did not know the full extent of Aayana's war and that of her people, she felt it had become hers also.

Aayana also spoke of her friendship with Sam. Aayana longed to know what had become of the young soldier. Grace in turn shared with the Somali girl her love for the priest she had to leave behind in the land of her birth—and of the special people who lived at The Cielo. And so, during a time of regular conversations, a special bond of friendship developed between the two women.

The weeks before school started passed quickly. Grace mastered more of the Hindi language. Mark encouraged her, however, to speak English to the people at the farm. Much of Grace's free time was spent with Aayana and Mark. Grace was looking forward to school. She missed teaching and was eager to meet the girls who would be quite different from the youngsters she had tutored at The Cielo. She could not, however, shake off the apprehension she felt when she looked at the grey mountain that loomed ominously above the farm and the Pathshala.

Perhaps, Grace mused, this was due to the fact that Mark had told her that the men at the quarry recruited debt slaves to work there. The products carved from the cut stone ranged from tombstones to building materials regularly shipped off to the Americas and Europe.

Mark had said to her, 'The idea of low-cost labour on the backs of poor and underaged workers gives the manufacturers of the stone products a considerable advantage in the western marketplace. These people are able to undersell their rivals from the countries who forbid the practice of child labour.

Unbeknown to Grace, the very hills that garrisoned them also housed an unspoken evil waiting for a vulnerable moment to pluck from the Pathshala their most precious ones.

9
Pathshala

Grace rose early to catch the school bus Aayshirya had arranged for her. 'You'll get to know the girls better this way.' Adding with assiduous charm, Aayshirya had said, 'I'll never require of you what I have not enjoyed myself.'

Aayshirya is quite right, Grace contemplated as she boarded the bus. She greeted the zealous driver in her best Hindi. The man, in a shrill voice, ordered the girls to make sure their teacher had a comfortable seat. Grace thanked him for his goodwill. He quickly replied in broken English, 'No problem. Hari take care of you. No problem.'

What a journey it was becoming. Grace reflected on the amazing people she had met along the way. Joseph had once said to her, 'All were created by one Creator, and all are loved by him.' The hefty bus, typifying an old schooling system, came to a halt outside the school. After saying her goodbyes to Hari, Grace was whisked along by a small sea of talkative girls towards the school interior. It was only when she found her feet that she got a clearer picture of her surroundings. Things appeared different to the day she was escorted around the school by Aayshirya. This, she supposed, was due to the energy of the girls—they certainly transformed the place. The broken panes and splintered lintels seemed to lift their dreary countenance.

In the whirlwind of skirts and glossy dark braids brushing against her frame, Grace encountered a petite girl who could not have been older than thirteen. The girl was notably smaller than her peers and seemed to stray purposefully from their high spirits. Grace gently broke away from the group who had good-naturedly buttonholed her with their questions about her life and travels. She made her way to the shy child and put out her hand to introduce herself.

'Hi, my name is Grace. I'll be teaching you English.' The girl looked up at her new teacher through a veil of thick lashes, her serious expression beguiling her tender age.

Grace felt her heart fill with compassion. 'And what should I call you?'

The girl looked shyly at Grace before she replied. 'Esta, Teacher. I'm called, Esta.'

Grace continued to gently question the young girl in the hope of pushing past any cultural barriers. She could at least speak some English.

'Which part of Thane are you from?'

The girl's face lit up. 'My family are from the villages not far from here. We're farmers. That's what we do here—we farm a lot.'

There was a special brightness about the girl when she spoke of her family.

The school bell rang in the distance. Grace got up from her seat beside Esta to join the group of young students. They made their way towards a spacious classroom which was used as a meeting hall. Aayshirya was pleased to see Grace with them.

'It's good to see you, Gracie. I see you're already making new friends. The girls are most eager to begin their classes with you.'

Aayshirya invited Grace to join the rest of the staff at the back of the hall. It was lined with old chairs of various styles and sizes—functional and comfy. In front of the teachers stood a somewhat skew lectern, frequently used by Aayshirya to address the girls at the start of the school week.

Aayshirya introduced Grace, then concluded by saying, 'So you see, girls, you'll be in perfectly good hands.'

Holding out her hand, Aayshirya invited Grace to join her. Grace smiled warmly at the girls. Up till then, the headmistress had addressed her pupils in English. Now Aayshirya continued in Hindi. It was important that the girls fully understood what she was about to say next. 'Teacher Grace is a special gift sent to us by our Heavenly Father. She is a Christian, just like the people here at the Pathshala.'

Aayshirya stressed her words. Grace noticed how the girls' faces lit up. A whisper of delight rippled through the hall.

Aayshirya opened with a prayer and a story from the Bible about a woman called Ruth. She read of a great famine that had taken place in the land of Ruth's birth. It was at a time when there were judges chosen by God to rule over Israel. The girls were immediately engrossed with the story. Grace got the distinct impression that Aayshirya twinned stories of the Old Testament with the life stories of the poor people of India. The headmistress explained that the young woman called Ruth was the daughter-in-law of an older woman called Naomi. Naomi had lost her two sons to a dreadful war. One of the woman's sons had been married to Ruth. As Aayshirya shared from the Bible, Grace felt a measure of sorrow. She realised that this was the plight of many women across the world. She marvelled at the way Aayshirya, who had lost her own husband to battle, brought the story to life. Her accent and animated gestures kept the girls transfixed.

Aayshirya went on to explain how Naomi had told her daughters-in-law to go back to their families—she alone could not take care of them. One of the daughters, Orpah, kissed Naomi and went on her way. Ruth on the other hand refused to leave Naomi. She clung to her mother-in-law. 'I'll stay at your side and serve you. I'll also follow your God.'

Aayshirya raised her shoulders and moved her head from side to side. She chuckled a little before crossing over to Hindi. 'In India a mother-in-law and a daughter-in-law do not always get along so well. Perhaps you have also witnessed such mild skirmishes in your country, Teacher Grace?'

Aayshirya winked at Grace. A ripple of giggles broke out. 'Let's get on with our story, shall we?'

Aayshirya continued in English. She explained to her students how Ruth had travelled with Naomi, staying as close to her as a myna bird with her chicks. The two women had been afraid of being assaulted by bandits who lived in the hills, preying on vulnerable travellers. They had continued their journey till they arrived in a town called Bethlehem at a time when the barley harvest had just begun.

Enlightening her students with some interesting details about the food plant, Aayshirya explained how it was a part of a family of grains cultivated to feed people, and that it was still used in this way. Grace loved the way Aayshirya effortlessly turned parts of the story into a lesson for the girls.

The headmistress went on to say that when the two women arrived in Bethlehem, Naomi had taken them to a relative of her late husband who was a man of great wealth in the region. This man's name was Boaz. Ruth had offered to work as a gleaner in the fields that belonged to Boaz. This meant that the young woman was only allowed to glean the chaff of the barley that was of little value. Ruth had done this day in and day out so that she and Naomi could survive. It had been a lowly position.

Aayshirya grew serious. 'Daughters of India, this is what a young woman was willing to do to help her mother-in-law.'

There was a quiet hush. Aayshirya explained how Boaz had come to inspect his fields one day. While there, he heard of Ruth's great sacrifice. Aayshirya softened her voice. 'It was Ruth's willingness to surrender everything she had for Naomi that caused her to find favour and grace in the eyes of Boaz.'

There was a glint in Aayshirya's eyes as she went on. 'In fact, the story of Ruth is also a great love story.' Aayshirya cocked her head to one side and lifted her eyes to her enraptured audience.

One of the girls with a cheeky countenance and shiny braids tied together just above her ears, called out mischievously, 'Mother, do they get married? I hope this boss-man falls in love with Ruth.'

The girl pulled her knees up to touch her chin while a flutter of giggles broke out. The rest of the students playfully tugged at each other. Aayshirya quickly quieted them with a raised hand. 'Sara, firstly the gentleman's name is Bo–az.' Aayshirya pronounced his name carefully, assuming they had all missed it. There was another wave of silly laughs. 'Secondly, my dear child, you will not be able to hear the rest of the story if you keep interrupting me.'

Feigning sternness with a perceptive smile, Aayshirya encouraged the others to settle down. Once again Grace was impressed with the way the headmistress handled the students. She balanced control with kindness. Aayshirya had told Grace about the young Indian girl called Sara when they had first met. Aayshirya had never been able to have children of her own. Her husband had died during the Kargil conflict between India and Pakistan in the late nineties. Some years ago, a woman from the nearby village had brought a baby in a grass basket to the school. Unable to take care of the child herself, the woman had left the infant on the doorstep of Aayshirya's office. Aayshirya had raised the child as her own.

Although strong-willed, Sara had brought much delight to Aayshirya. The girl was also loved by the people who worked at the Pathshala.

'Sara is,' Aayshirya said, 'like a lily on a pond, kept there with much resolve. Everyone can see its splendor, but they don't see the effort needed to keep it afloat.'

Aayshirya had named her adopted daughter "Sara". She believed that just as God had blessed Sarah of old with a child even though she was beyond the age of childbearing, so too had God blessed Aayshirya with a child of her own.

Aayshirya drew the Bible story to a close. 'Boaz took Ruth as his wife. He protected her from all the other young men. He sealed his devotion to Ruth with an ancient customary practice… Boaz removed his shoe to give to his neighbour. In this way, Boaz, who was the owner of the land, declared to his witnesses that he would take care of Ruth and Naomi for the rest of their lives.'

Somewhat tenderly, Aayshirya added, 'Boaz sacrificed something precious to seal his love for the women.'

The headmistress concluded the story by saying, 'This narrative, dear girls, is one of the most beautiful illustrations of the grace of our Lord.' She clasped her hands together to demonstrate the privilege she felt to share with them that the genealogy of Christ was ensconced in the love story of Ruth and Boaz. 'Their story is also an example of God's love for us. By sacrificing that which was most precious to him, his only Son, God demonstrated how much he loved us.'

Aayshirya asked the girls to join her in a prayer.

While Grace sat listening to the words of the headmistress, she remembered the story Joseph had shared with her when she first arrived at The Cielo. It was the simple yet poignant tale of a father in search of a bride for his son. Although the woman he eventually found was flawed, she had cried out to the man to save her from a life destined for the gutter. Grace felt sad at the thought of not having Joseph near her. Aayshirya's message, however, reminded her that she was the daughter of a Father who does not look upon one's culture or position in society to lavish his favour; instead, he searches for the heart willing to let him in.

Grace fell into line with the girls, and they were dismissed by Aayshirya to their various classes. The older woman placed a firm arm around Grace's waist as she was about to leave. 'Gracie, you're a great blessing to us. God's going to use you here at the Pathshala in ways you can't imagine. Thank you that you came from so very far to be with us.'

Aayshirya squeezed Grace's hand. Grace knew that God had brought her here. For how long, she did not know. She followed the girls to their classrooms. Although the buildings and rooms for learning were less than sophisticated, Grace felt that her students were probably getting a better education than most. They were learning not only about life, but also about living in the kingdom of God. This included a measure of laying down one's own life.

***

The classes at the Pathshala were not without their challenges. Grace focused on getting to know her students and a culture unlike her own. The girls were charming and astute—and they kept her amused with their fondness for animated stories. Grace used illustrations from scripture to highlight the principles of redemption and forgiveness—much like Jesus presented the stories of the Kingdom of God through parables. One morning, Grace found herself teaching a younger group of girls. The young girl Grace had met on her first day at the Pathshala was also in her class. Grace had given the girls a lesson in grammar which included some aspects of poetic language. She asked the girls if they could come up with a metaphor using the word "shackled". Esta, who had been quiet during class, raised her hand. Her English was slow, and Grace was impressed with the girl's courage.

Esta smiled before she offered her example, 'The poor of India are shackled.'

Grace applauded Esta. She encouraged the girl to

continue with her questions even though they did not have a direct bearing on the lesson at hand.

'Why do the poor have to suffer the way they do? We've lived like this for generations, yet we cannot break free from the effects of our caste system.' Esta threw back the glossy braid that had fallen over her shoulder. 'These are the only shackles our people know, Teacher Grace. The chains of a life without hope.'

Although Grace felt unqualified to answer the young girl, she knew that these were the shared questions of the poor in India. *Why should they be made to suffer the harmful cycles of poverty preserved by their traditions?* Grace silently prayed for wisdom. She remembered Joseph's personal story—how his was similar to that of the chronicle told in the Bible of a Hebrew man whose name was also Joseph. The young man was sold into slavery by his own brothers. To answer Esta, Grace shared with the girls the tale of Joseph from the Bible. They listened closely.

'The young man was taken from his father and his family through an awful act of jealousy and betrayal at the hands of his own brothers. Joseph was unsuspecting of their evil motives. There was nothing he could do to defend himself. If Joseph was guilty of anything, it was that he loved his whole family unconditionally.'

Grace looked across the sea of girls with the impression that they could all identify with the story of Joseph. Many of them had had an experience of a family member or friend sold into slavery in one form or another.

'Joseph's brothers took advantage of his love. Because they were deeply jealous of him, they tried to take his life by throwing him into a deep well.' Grace paused. 'There are times when we find ourselves in a similar situation to Joseph. We feel abandoned and alone. However, God is always secretly at work. He's fighting for us even though we cannot see it.'

A slight breeze entered the classroom through one of the open windows. Grace was relieved as the heat was intolerable.

'It appeared that for the young Hebrew man all hope was lost. One of Joseph's brothers, Judah, was overcome with the guilt of what they had done. He convinced his brothers to sell Joseph to a company of wandering traders who were taking aromatic spices to Egypt. When Joseph arrived in Egypt, he was sold as a slave. He had to work in the courts of the king's palace. However, betrayal at the hands of others did not stop there. One day, Joseph was falsely accused of being overfriendly with the wife of his new master, a man called Potiphar. Potiphar was an officer of the king. Joseph had worked hard and was devoted to Potiphar. The officer had no choice but to throw Joseph in prison. Because of his faith in God, and despite the way he was treated, Joseph clung to the hope that the God of the Hebrews would rescue him from the terrible situation was in.'

Grace asked her students, 'How should we react, dear ones, when things grow worse despite our unwavering faith in God?'

The girls looked at each other with wide eyes, but Esta kept her eyes fixed on Grace as her teacher continued. 'Much of what I've experienced in my own life is like the story of Joseph. I was surrounded by people who didn't treat me kindly. But God is more than able to save us from every dark pit. He rescued me, just like he eventually saved the young Hebrew man from prison. He is able to take the evil some people do, and turn it for the good of his children.'

Grace paused before she continued. 'God brought the solution to Joseph's terrible situation while he was in prison. Often, in times of great need, God gives us our most glorious triumph.'

She chuckled intuitively. 'Joseph found himself sharing his cell with a baker and a butler who had also worked for the king in his palace. One of the men was to be hanged for an alleged crime. Neither of the men knew who it was going to be. In time, both servants had separate dreams, which they shared with Joseph. God had given Joseph a special gift to interpret dreams.'

This was a subject close to Grace's heart. 'God has given us all special gifts. He gives them to us in ways that make us uniquely different. They are also given to us so that we can help the one who will benefit from them the most.'

'Through his interpretation of their dreams, Joseph correctly foretold which one of the servants would be hanged and which one would go free. That is exactly what happened. The head butler of the great Pharaoh was released from prison, and the chief baker was executed. Joseph asked of the freed man, who was of course elated, to remember him when he thanked the Pharaoh. The butler, however, was so caught up with the good news of his release that he forgot to do as Joseph had asked.'

Grace thought she saw small tears in Esta's eyes. She encouraged the girls to look away from their own difficult situations and to look to God for their freedom. 'Still, Joseph remained in prison for a long time afterwards. Why this was, I can't say. Joseph's story, nevertheless, reminds me of the *Dalits* of India... the ones you may know as the untouchables.'

Grace knew that some of the girls in her English class had been born into this social order. 'These are the people the world has mostly forgotten. Daughters of India, God has not forgotten them. He formed each and every one of us perfectly in the wombs of our mothers. In fact, he knew us before we were born.'

Grace paused. Her voice filled with compassion. 'It is for the weak and poor in spirit that the true God of this world came.'

The girls were quiet as Grace continued. 'One day, the Pharaoh had a troubling dream. It distressed him so that he searched in all the corners of the kingdom for someone who could interpret it. Surely, he thought, there would be one wise enough to tell him its meaning. It was only then that the chief butler remembered Joseph. He recalled how the young Hebrew man had accurately interpreted the outcome of his own dream. The butler shared his story with the Pharaoh, who demanded the immediate release of Joseph from prison. Joseph was summoned to the royal palace where he was asked to interpret the king's tormenting dreams. He knew that God was the real interpreter and that he, Joseph, was only his mouthpiece. He explained to Pharaoh what he believed God wanted to say.'

To keep her students' attention, Grace increased the tempo of her voice. 'Joseph told the king that his dreams meant that the land of Egypt would produce good food for seven years, after which there would be a drought for another seven. The king's dreams came to pass, just as God had revealed them to Joseph. Pharaoh needed someone to oversee the project to store grain from the years of plenty so that there would be enough for the years of famine. The king gave Joseph the responsibility to oversee this project for the people of Egypt. In fact, Joseph was made a prince in Pharaoh's courts.'

Grace smiled warmly at the group of girls. 'God used the situation that was meant for Joseph's harm, to unite him with his family. When his brothers came to Egypt looking for food during the time of the great famine, Joseph, who had forgiven them, was also able to provide for them.'

Grace concluded her story. God had helped her to share with her students the Biblical narrative of a young man whose life paralleled those of the young girls—their hardship and betrayal and, for some, the freedom they needed for their own families.

Looking directly at Esta, Grace finally said, 'No matter our circumstances or positions in life, God will always make a way for those who have the courage to put their trust in him.'

Esta felt her heart fill with joy. Although she was still young, Grace sensed that God had given the girl the gift of compassion for her own people.

***

Grace enjoyed her time getting to know the young girls at the Pathshala. Her trips to and from the outreach farm were enlightening. She learned about the poor of India along the way—their simplicity and the challenges they have to face in the modern world. Grace did not have much time to think about the family at The Cielo, but she always remembered them in her prayers.

Grace's busyness was in fact a masked blessing. It concealed the yearning she had for Colombia. She missed Joseph, but she consoled herself with the fact that they had both surrendered to the will of God in their lives—service that required sacrifice.

On the other hand, Grace's friendship with Mark blossomed. God had given her friends to ease the longing in her heart. Mark would visit the Pathshala whenever he could—when he was able to grab a moment outside his busy schedule or when he had to pass by to get supplies from the local village. During his visits to the school, he would bring with him treats made by the women at the outreach farm—a basket filled with fried bread that had been stuffed with fragrant vegetables cooked in aromatic spices.

Aayshirya would smile at Grace and say, 'Mark has been visiting much these days. I'm not one to complain though. The food he brings with him is rather tasty.'

With a mischievous smile, Aayshirya would touch Grace's arm affectionately, as if to say she was not displeased with Mark's interest in the English teacher.

Grace would openly blush.

On one occasion, Mark brought with him several corrugated sheets to repair the roofing on some of the older buildings. After he had completed his work and Grace's classes were done for the day, Mark asked Grace to join him on a walk down to the river that ambled near the school.

He led her down a path that took them to the edge of one of the river's banks and to a mound covered with soft grass. As she followed him, Grace admired her friend's easy confidence. She hadn't noticed it before, but the relaxed manner in which Mark tied his shoulder-length hair from his face and for the few stray strands that had tugged free, Mark now seemed altogether attractive to her. Grace realised, however, that her heart did not race as it had with Joseph.

They found a cool area under some shady trees. Grace could tell that Mark knew the place well. Perhaps he had spent time there, processing alone the grief he had experienced after losing his wife. The view from their high position was breathtaking. Strong light spilled in endless streams from a cloudless sky. It squeezed its rays through the flexible branches of the trees. Birds and tiny fauna used the pools of water that had settled between the rocks to have an afternoon bathe. Mark sat close to Grace. He admired the wisps of golden hair that touched the sides of her cheeks before they gently fell over her shoulders. Her deep blue eyes and long lashes caught his breath. For a brief moment he felt like a schoolboy again—too shy to speak.

It was Grace who broke their silence. 'You seem to know this place well.'

Mark looked at her for a while before he responded. 'Joy was taken from me in India. I don't think I've told you the full story, though. She died during a time when we were having great success at rescuing girls sold into the sex trade of Mumbai.'

Grace knew a bit of Mark's story from what Joseph and others had told her. She sensed that he carried a deep sense of loss in his life. His laidback manner and natural bravado helped to hide his pain. Joy was the love of his life, and he still missed her.

'How was she taken from you… if I may ask?'

Mark shifted his gaze from Grace to the little creatures that had gathered around the pools of water. 'Living amongst the poor in India is fraught with challenges. This is how it has always been—hardship on every corner. Joy became ill at the shelter we had set up.

We worked in one of the busiest areas of Mumbai known as Kamathipura.'

He tugged at a piece of grass and set it free from the soil. Placing the sweet end of the blade between his teeth, Mark continued, 'After that, I got out. I couldn't go on anymore. I was constantly questioning God while I tried to repair myself. My personal pain and ensuing anger eventually became the sole focus of my existence. I began to lose compassion for the impoverished people around me. In the end I was broken and angry at God.'

Grace chose her words carefully. 'But… God was always there. He never left your side, did he? You're still doing amazing work for him here in rural India. It seems he restored your heart and replaced it with a greater capacity to love. Perhaps more than you could've ever imagined possible.'

Grace looked away from Mark, enjoying the gentle rhythm of the river that stretched for miles as it pressed on between its banks towards the sea. *This courageous man beside me, gently rolling his teeth on a sugary blade, is much like this strong river,* she thought, *unassuming in its way, yet depositing life wherever it flows.*

She turned to Mark again. 'How did you end up in Somalia before you returned to India?'

'Well, it is indeed a true saying that though you may run from God, you can never hide from him.' Mark gave Grace a roguish smile. The twinkle in his eye was from a man who knew the proverb well, because he had lived it. 'In Psalms, the prophet and king in his darkest hour wrote, *Where can I go from Your Spirit? Or where can I flee from Your presence? If I ascend into heaven, You are there; If I make my bed in hell, behold, You are there.* It's all about him—God and his kingdom. It consists of broken people, the orphans and widows—sheep who need his care. I eventually realised that if God has called you for such a mission, don't assume he'll call another. Despite my desperate situation, I was only harming myself. I thought it wiser to do something of value with my life again. Of course, the Lord was secretly tugging at my heart to return to him. I took a job with a nonprofit organisation. We were employed to transport aid to war-torn countries in Africa—really just my way of getting away from it all. I was punishing myself for something I felt I was responsible for. I beat myself mercilessly with thoughts and feelings of guilt… perhaps I had not taken sufficient care of my wife; perhaps I had possibly not heard the voice of God to go to Mumbai in the first place. I finally resolved to head for the villages of Somalia with a group of aid workers.'

Mark exhaled a soft chuckle. He looked at Grace with gentle eyes. Shrugging, he admitted, 'Of course God had other plans for me. As broken as I was in that refugee camp, he began to heal me. God knows how to put a man back together again.'

Grace was humbled by Mark's story. It made her think of Joseph and the people at The Cielo. She thought of how God had not only rescued her but had also knit back the stitches that had unravelled in the fabric of her own life.

'Was there a specific turning point for you?'

'Turning back to the Lord happened as I served the people who visited the camp each day. God, of course, knows me better than I know myself. As I engaged with those who were suffering, my heart began to soften again.'

Mark smiled. 'I wept at my own selfishness. Yes, I'd lost the one love of my life, but Joy was with him in a glorious paradise. The village people were losing their loved ones to war and disease every day. Eventually all I wanted to do was to share the love of God and his Good News with them. None of the food we had brought with us, even the medical aid, though important, could truly relieve their endless pain.'

Grace was quiet for a moment. She had witnessed something similar elsewhere. 'I've read in the book of Malachi how the Lord said, ...*he will turn the hearts of the fathers to the children, and the hearts of the children to their fathers.* The prophet mentions in the scriptures the great day of the Lord, where God will send his Son to turn the hearts of his children back to him. His children live in all the nations of the world. He will come to us with healing in his wings. Your testimony illustrates this perfectly.'

Grace took hold of Mark's hand. They sat, quietly holding onto each other. She had not eaten a morsel of the food Mark had brought with him. It seemed right, though, that food at that moment was of little consequence. Grace watched the river as it made its way to the ocean, feeling surprisingly satisfied.

***

Grace was pleased with the progress her students were making. Their mastery of the English language and their spiritual growth was a blessing. Grace grew closer to Esta each passing day. The young girl, in turn, felt that her new teacher inspired her to learn. Most of the students' learning material was derived from school textbooks and the Bible. Grace found that Esta was bright—that she had a natural love for languages. The girl fascinated Grace with her keen observations. She once told Grace that she believed every natural law of God should be confirmed by his Word. This challenged Grace to search through the scriptures herself. She would say to Esta, 'Give me a day or two and I'll get back to you on that.'

Consequently, it was not uncommon for Grace to be found sitting up in bed at night studying the scriptures with the aid of a kerosene lamp. Grace enjoyed the challenge, however, and was surprised to find most of the answers to Esta's questions. All the same, Grace asked Mark for a Bible to give to Esta as she thought it would be better if she searched the scriptures herself. When she handed Esta the small Bible, the girl threw her arms around her teacher, and confidently gushed, 'You see, God does know all things!'

Many months passed at the Pathshala. The time spent giving of herself to the people there, although unhurried, was rewarding for Grace. In reality she had become unaware of the changes happening in the world outside. When Grace knelt at her bed to pray each night, she remembered Joseph. Only then did she feel a certain sadness. She tried not to dwell on her sorrow, though. At times, however, she wondered whether God had brought someone else into Joseph's life. As the tall trees cast long shadows against the walls of her room, Grace fell asleep with the hope that Joseph was still in love with her.

One morning Grace woke to see that clouds had gathered in the sky with the promise of rain. As she readied herself for her customary trip to the Pathshala on the school bus, an anxious feeling crept over her. Brushing it aside, Grace chided herself with the fact that she would have to get used to the monsoon climate of India. She had learned, though, that oftentimes such feelings were a burden the Lord sent her way to pray about.

As she climbed onto the bus that morning, Grace was unaware of the events about to occur over the next few days that would alter her life dramatically. After greeting Hari, Grace immediately noticed that Esta was not in her usual seat. The young girl had never missed a day of school—she was so eager to learn. Grace walked up the aisle and greeted the other girls. She asked them if they knew of Esta's whereabouts. No one knew where Esta was that morning. Grace thought to ask the driver.

'I'm so sorry, Esta was not at her pickup-point.' Hari held the large wheel of the bus tightly as the vehicle pitched its way along the bumpy road.

Unsatisfied with Hari's answer, Grace questioned the man further. 'It's just that she loves school so much, I was wondering whether she might be ill?' It wasn't easy conversing with Hari through the small rearview mirror suspended above the wide windscreen of the bus.

But Grace felt that Hari was hiding something from her.

'Please, it's important that I know if she has come to any harm. I understand that you may not be in a position to speak, Hari. Give me a nod if you feel that Esta is in danger.'

Grace waited patiently. She looked into the small mirror. Hari slowly nodded while he kept his eyes on the road. Grace felt her heart sink. Her stomach knotted into a tight ball. The driver had just confirmed her earlier premonitions.

Hari, who was usually quite cheery on their trips to the Pathshala, grew unusually quiet. Grace turned to look at the girls who were chatting softly. She had a sneaky suspicion that they also knew something of Esta's whereabouts but were too afraid to speak—perhaps out of fear for their own safety. Grace knew that the daughters of poor families in rural India were under constant threat of being kidnapped. The girls had devised ways to protect themselves, one of which was to observe a strict code of silence.

After she exited the school bus, Grace walked briskly to Aayshirya's office to tell her about Esta's strange absence. When Aayshirya heard of it, her skin paled. She asked Grace to close the door. Drawing Grace to one side she said, 'From what you've told me, I fear our daughter may have been sold into a practice here called chattel slavery. Occasionally, we lose girls because their families sell them to people who own the stone quarries. They do this to pay off the debt they owe to the owners of these mines. I've been concerned for Esta for some time. She is a high-risk child. Esta's the only girl in a large family of poor farmers who live up in the mountains.'

Grace closed her eyes. She couldn't cope with the possibility of Esta being trafficked. 'How would she be able to withstand the trauma of being taken from her family and sold as a slave?'

Aayshirya's voice was grave. 'I agree with you. Esta is one of our more diligent students. We'll have to wait and see. Perhaps she's not at school for some other reason. We must keep praying for our girls. Too many mouths to feed and generational debt makes them vulnerable to traffickers.'

***

Some weeks passed. Despite Grace's best efforts to find Esta, there was still no sign of the young girl. Mark had alerted the families who lived in the area. It seemed, however, as if an anxious hush had settled over the whole area. No one spoke of the incident or of Esta's possible whereabouts. It was as if the young Indian girl had disappeared into thin air. Grace noticed that Aayshirya and Mark were quite accustomed to such tragedies.

The people at the Pathshala went about their daily work with more zeal than usual, hoping that the pain they felt at losing one of their daughters would heal. The safety of the remaining girls was also uppermost in their minds. Further threat to their security was an ominous reality. Daily they prayed for Esta. They thanked God for his comfort in their grief—pressing on without her.

Grace and Mark continued to meet with Aayshirya in her small office to pray. One morning Mark voiced his own concerns for the first time. According to his sources, there had recently been a surge in the kidnapping of girls from the mountains to be sold as slaves in the sex industry of India's larger cities. The possibility of a worse fate for young Esta seemed too much to bear. The three friends joined hands. With united spirits and the persuasion that a threefold chord is not easily broken, they lifted their voices to God for the missing girl. When they were finished, they stepped out of Aayshirya's office to go about their day. A sudden explosion in the distance stopped the trio in their tracks. The deafening noise shook the whole complex. Grace clung to Mark as the three friends looked towards the source of the blast. It seemed to come from the mountain that loomed ominously above them.

10
Thane, Northern Mumbai, India

A slow sun crept above the mist rising from the lakes that covered the Indian district of Thane. The first rays, like silken fingers, danced across the eyelids of the sleepy inhabitants. They finally settled on a child who had not succumbed to the velvety darkness that had cloaked the village the night before. The young girl, still restless from the news she had received, responded to the celestial caller. Her head pulsated with a cacophony of voices— her uncles, her older brothers, and her grandmother.

Today was the day they would take her away. She had to get up. Perhaps by some miracle she would escape her fate. The more she tried to lift her small frame, though, the more she felt shackled to the invisible arms and legs of her straw bed.

'Esta. Esta!'

The fatigued voice of her grandmother brought the girl to her senses. 'Get up my child. It's time to go. You mustn't keep your new master waiting.'

Esta flung herself at the feet of the old woman. Her grandmother had been the only mother she knew.

'Don't let them take me away, *Dadi Ma*. I can't leave you! Who will help you with the children? You know my brothers are like magpie birds. They must steal from others because they're too lazy to build their own nests. It will be hard for you to manage without me. What about school? The English teacher says I'm smart, that I learn a foreign tongue quickly.'

The girl cried out in desperation, 'You mustn't let them take me, *Dadi Ma*!'

For a brief moment the old woman wrapped the tearstained face of her only granddaughter in the frayed hems of her sari. She exhaled a deep sob. There was no turning back. It had been more of a curse than a blessing to have more grandsons than granddaughters. The boys skulked around all day, as useless as a thin wrap on a cold morning. Just as sure as the rains forced their way from the monsoonal heavens each season, she had known that one day she would have to give Esta up to save them all. That day had come all too soon. Today would be the day she would lose her granddaughter to the chains of debt slavery.

The old woman tried her best to console the frightened girl. 'What your father has done to this family is an evil act, my child. It's a wicked deed that even the space of many years will not have the power to heal. My sorrow's great. I've no choice. You're the only one who can save us from a future so utterly dreadful, I fear we may already have offended the gods and sealed our fate.'

The *dadi ma* stroked her granddaughter's hair with her bony hands. 'I can only hope and pray that what was meant to bring you harm will someday be used for good. Didn't you tell me before two sun-ups this week that the English teacher spoke of a man called Jesus? That he is the one who gave his life to the world so that we might live with him in paradise? This is a great sacrifice she speaks of, this English one. You mustn't give up my child. Perhaps there will come a day when you too will be granted such a gift.'

Spittle and tears slipped down the old woman's cheeks and onto her lap. She did not turn to look as Esta's uncle entered the shack to take the weeping child from her. Instead, she began to slowly fold and unfold the hems of her shabby sari. It was a gesture that reflected her family's years of affliction and shame.

Esta was flung onto the back of a ramshackle wagon. In an attempt to keep from sliding through the gaping holes of the surprisingly fast-paced cart, she clutched at the straw that softened her landing. To her astonishment, the dry grass suddenly came alive. Scrawny arms and dark eyes poked and peered at her like seeds germinating in a hothouse. She quickly buried herself in the straw when she realised she was not alone in her bid to survive. Esta clutched the small Bible the English teacher had given her. Besides the bundle of food her grandmother had prepared, her Bible was the only item she had with her. Alone and afraid, it would be a difficult ride to the stone quarry.

As the cart ascended, Esta searched for comforting thoughts. Like butterflies wafting over a summer field, her mind drifted to a time when things were better. Although a life of poverty was all the Indian girl had known, there was also the wealth of family love. Her younger brothers were sweet and innocent, much like the deer that wandered the hilly outcrops of her beloved Thane.

Esta remembered a time when she was to be betrothed to a boy. The real ceremony would only take place when they were both old enough to marry. Her grandmother, her brothers, and her father (who was barely sober that day) had taken Esta down to the Ulhas River to meet with the boy's parents. They lived on the river's banks along with their large family. Esta recalled how they had all laughed together and how the children had playfully tugged at her long braids. She loved her hair. It was the one thing everyone said, even those she hardly knew, she had inherited from her mother.

Esta loved the good-humoured perkiness of the family she would be joined to someday. There was Ahur, the cousin of her betrothed. Stout and jovial, the boy was the family clown. Ahur frequently brought tears of joy to the eyes of the audience he enthralled with his antics. They would laugh so hard that their sides ached as much as the time they had all overindulged at the Mango Festival. Then there was Brendu, the tall and lean brother of Ahur. As the summer in Thane is as different to her winter, you would not have found more dissimilar siblings in the entire district. There was the hilarious time when a giant rooster chased Ahur around the chicken coop till the poor boy could not breathe. Brendu had stepped in to prevent the already disgraced Ahur from further embarrassment. Booting the rooster with his foot, Brendu brought the bird's terrifying reign to an end. The rooster was quickly scooped by the other children who were delighted to have an easy meal at their disposal.

When the ceremony of her future betrothal ended, Esta recalled sitting at the back of a wagon with her husband-to-be. The cart had been different to the one she currently occupied. It had been decorated with sweet-smelling carnations and bright marigolds. The two children had held hands as the sun swayed over the tea hills, their smiles as broad as the emerald valley below. If their carefree youthfulness had taught them anything, it was to live for today. They knew not what tomorrow held. There was no fear in their dreams. After all, they were a lowly people who did not require much. They were not equipped to make the prudent decisions of the better-off. Instead, they naturally accepted all that life swung their way.

***

As the wagon rattled on, Esta held her little Bible close. She thought of her English teacher and the people at the Pathshala. The young girl asked God to help them find her. As incredulous as it seems, debt slavery, although an outlawed activity across most of the world, is still tolerated in some parts of Asia. Nearly half of the chattel slaves are under the age of ten. Ironically, the children sold into bonded labour lose their right to the knowledge and skills required for their own country's development. The vicious cycle of poverty and debt amongst the poor in these regions sadly shows little sign of declining. Greedy taskmasters still wield their trade on the backs of innocent children.

Like most children, Esta was oblivious to the wiles of evil people. She had been born into an Indian societal class known as the *Dalit*. These people are considered the lowest caste of their country's social order, also called the "untouchables". The term *Dalit* has for centuries been synonymous with weakness and humiliation. They are a people so degraded that they are ostracised from ordinary Indian civilisation for fear of them contaminating the protected traditional societies.

Esta knew that she was a *Dalit*. Generations of her family bore this shame like a malignancy deep in the marrow of their souls—passed onto their children. Her father, like many of the primary providers in the *Dalit* families, mollified his existence by drinking copious amounts of *handia*, a kind of rice beer. The man's alcoholism caused the family to become heavily indebted to his employer. Sadly, they were never able to settle their debt.

The *Dalit* and their children are indiscriminately preyed upon by the sleuths of debt slavery, an intergenerational practice rife with fraud. This custom keeps families in a cycle of liability for generations. The mounting debt is never alleviated, and the children of each succeeding generation are used to pay off their families' debt. Esta was sold because she was the only girl in her family. She would become part of a band of children worldwide who work for no pay in artisanal small-scale mining and quarrying to alleviate enduring financial burdens.

***

Esta mustered some courage to pull herself from her straw cocoon. Hers was not the only idea. Little heads began to peek from their hiding places beneath the grass. Their faces were expressionless. The wagon drawn by a team of strong mules slowed down as they arrived at their destination—a stone quarry that loomed austerely above the ground like a giant gravestone. The mine was located in the mountain that overshadowed Mark's farm and the Pathshala School. In Hindi, the driver ordered the children off the wagon, leaving them to stand and wait for their new owner.

A tall Indian man with a bony frame, eyes as black as a raven's, greeted them. He led the group of children to their meagre quarters behind the main entrance to the quarry. The new arrivals were given a list of instructions. It included the time they had to rise in the morning to work in the quarry, and the time for when their lamps had to be doused. Although the slaves working at the quarry were mostly adults, Esta noticed that there were also children toiling in the shadows beside them. She saw a girl younger than herself, tiny and insignificant, resting against the grey rock working with a stone anvil. She guessed the child could have been older, but it was difficult to tell. Streaks of grime and dust covered the slave while she chipped skilfully at a piece of rock. Esta was overwhelmed by the despair of the children who worked there. It was as if the harsh sun and relentless toil had drilled holes into their souls. Young boys not much older than thirteen stood in a disorderly row above the girl. They were using large power drills to carve stone from the mountain. Clouds of dust flew into their eyes and stained their shirts with the moisture from their thin bodies. They stared occasionally into the dirt-laden smoke like frightened birds caught in the fumes of a factory's flue.

Esta barely had time to store her belongings. She checked to make sure that the small Bible Grace had given her was safely tucked in her cotton dress. The man who met them at the entrance to the quarry eyed her suspiciously. He indicated that it was time for her and the others to begin their training.

The children were sorted into clusters of twos and threes. They were ordered to work alongside the experienced adults—the ones she had seen earlier. The man with the raven eyes was called Mogi. He appeared uneducated. Most of his instructions were delivered with strange movements and grunts to get the poor slaves to do what he wanted. Cutting stone from the mountain that towered over them was Mogi's sole ambition.

Esta did as she was told. She assessed the situation to see what her best chances of survival would be. How she longed for the smell of her grandmother's sweet pancakes and the irksome company of her younger siblings. They were always pestering the old woman who wiped their snotty faces on the hem of her apron to show them that she still loved them. Esta would scold her grandmother, '*Dadi Ma*, how can you clean their faces with the same apron you use to make our food?' Her *Dadi Ma* would affectionately reply, 'Esta, my child, you should worry more about what comes out of your mouth than what you put into it.' The old woman would lovingly embrace her granddaughter, then hurry her along to get the water ready for the family to clean up before their paltry meal. Esta would give anything to be near them all again.

Esta took a deep breath. Her recollection of the story of the Hebrew man sold into slavery by his own family was etched in her mind. It inspired her to turn to God for help. She positioned herself alongside her team. Picking up the anvil she was given, Esta followed the instructions of her group leader. Peace filled her heart as she tightened a grubby face-scarf one of the older girls had given her. The scarf covered her mouth and nose to protect her lungs from the dust.

Esta had been sold into one of the direst situations a poor girl could find herself. It seemed her days carving stone from the mountain had no beginning or end. Mogi woke them from their rest whenever he felt the need to make his slaves reach his quota. There were times when the sun had scarcely risen and they were forced to work the quarry. Once a week the slaves were given a few hours off. Esta used this time to read from her little Bible. She enjoyed the stories she read of courage and faith.

They inspired her and gave her hope of being found by the people at the Pathshala.

Esta shared a small hut with a young girl close to her age. They slept on floor mattresses opposite each other. Sometimes Mogi used both girls to prepare food for the others—mushy rice dredged in salt. Esta tried to talk to the reluctant girl as they prepared the meals together. She felt that they could both do with a friend. The girl, however, snubbed Esta's attempts, but Esta was determined not to give up. She decided, instead, to do what Teacher Grace had taught her at the Pathshala.

The English teacher had once told her that God knows what we need even before we ask. He has many good things to give his children—we need only make our request known and wait patiently for his answer. Esta decided to give her need of a friend to the One who knows best. That night, while a cool breeze blew off the grey mountain, Esta knelt over her straw mattress and thanked God for the friend she did not yet have. She pushed her mattress into the corner of the stone hut to watch the tiny creatures they shared their dwelling with scuttle about in search of food. Esta felt confident that her answer was indeed on its way.

***

There was nothing attractive about the quarry. The massive outcrop was surrounded by small makeshift dwellings which were permanently covered in grey ash. Whole families lived in some of the huts. The cramped conditions gave little relief from their daily toil to meet the high quotas of cut stone. Esta worked hard at her job. She prayed for the girl who remained hostile towards her. God knew how to soften a heart that had become impenetrable.

The Lord did answer Esta's prayer and it came to her in a most extraordinary way. Like some things with God, only through his intervention do we become open to receiving his kindness.

Mogi's greed meant he was constantly pushing for more stone from the quarry. His equipment was also old and outdated. It was not uncommon for the younger ones, especially the boys using the heavier machinery, to get injured. Most of the gas they used for the heavier apparatus was stored in special bottles which Mogi kept in an enclosed area. Mogi knew their exposure to the sun would be risky and could cause a sudden explosion at any time. Still, he did not provide appropriate protection for the bottles. He was happy when he did not have to pay for anything out of his own pocket.

The stone-slaves had to provide their own materials. Frequently they were seen trading scarves and pieces of old fabric with each other. They bartered relentlessly, as if they were exchanging items of high value, to improve their chances of preventing dust from reaching their lungs. So fine was the grey talc-like powder that it found its way through the pores of their skin. Developing eye infections and other breathing problems was not uncommon. It did not help at all that sanitation was poor. The child workers walked barefoot across the sea of rocky stone every day. Their feet, at such tender ages, were already calloused. The cuts would harden into scars which, ironically, provided some protection from the stony ground. The worst kind of injury sustained, however, was to the human spirit. The living conditions of the slaves and their daily toil was a constant reminder that they were from a lower caste. Their expectations were not to exceed the class they were born into. They were slaves—there to pay back the loans offered to their families by men like Mogi.

One morning, Esta prepared herself in the way that was customary for work in the quarry. She fastened her thread-bare scarf over her mouth and under the thick braid she had secured at the back of her neck. Most of the people at the quarry were not physically equipped for the work they had to do. Esta noticed that her surly roommate, Fatima, was especially weak. She wondered how the girl kept up with the hard labour each day.

Mogi gave Esta and Fatima instructions to join a team of workers in the deeper parts of the quarry. The girls bundled their tools in pieces of old canvas and tied them around their waists for easy storing. Their taskmaster wanted a team of younger slaves to start cutting at a special site where prized granite rock could be accessed. The two girls had smaller frames than their older counterparts and could slip through the crevices of the tall rocks without difficulty. The team set out as they were instructed, with Fatima keeping her usual distance from Esta.

Mogi was particularly pleased with himself that day. He had selected the best group to reach the granite. He would sell the stone for the production of products that would fetch a higher price. Mogi ordered some migrant workers who worked seasonally at the quarry to join Esta's team. These men were the only ones getting paid. Each year Mogi employed them during the dry periods before the rains fell, when it was virtually impossible to dig rock from some of the lower-lying quarries in the district. Not so for the chattel-slaves who worked tirelessly regardless of rain or shine, splitting the rocks from large boulders into smaller pieces of stone.

Esta kept up with the crew as they made their way across the ocean of chipped gravel. She hurt her small feet on the stone but pushed on regardless. The others glanced at her from time to time. Their faces were always sullen.

Esta stayed close to Fatima as they clawed their way into a rocky ravine. Clinging to the rocks that jutted from the cliff face, Esta edged her way along the ledge, keeping a watchful eye on Fatima. The girl appeared to be having some difficulty.

One of the migrant workers, who appeared more experienced than the rest, led them through a deep fissure which was flanked by two large boulders of cold slate. The man instructed Esta and Fatima to squeeze through an opening in the rock that could barely accommodate one of them, let alone two. Esta took the lead hoping that Fatima would follow.

Finally, she was able to make her way through the narrow gap. Esta was pleased to see that Fatima was close behind. The rest of the team did the same.

There they were met by a dazzling wonderland of granite—a speckled sea of quartz-like stone. The sun's sharp rays danced between the different shades of white and grey rock, resting awhile on some, playing hide-and-seek with the others. The band of workers lifted their heads for the first time since the start of their hike. They were awestruck.

When he had composed himself, the leader announced, 'This must be the place where the most prized rocks of the world come to rest. We will work here for a while.' He removed his tools gently from their place of storage. Then, as if he stood on sacred ground, he carefully motioned for the others to do the same. The crew got to work immediately, splitting the rock and stone with artisanal precision.

Some of the migrant workers who were physically stronger, dug at the narrow gap to widen it for the rest of their equipment to fit through. They needed to carve a secure path to haul the stone to the other side. Esta had become quite skilled herself. She worked deftly alongside Fatima. They sorted the cut rocks into different sizes, placing the medium pieces of stone between their feet. They then chipped away at the surface with their strong anvils to produce the granite that lay beneath the chalky covering. The rest of the men worked noisily above them. Their robust voices echoed dissonantly through the slender gaps between the boulders.

Although Fatima made no effort to speak to her, Esta felt that in the rhythm of their work they were developing a strong bond. All day long they filled the wheelbarrows and strong baskets made of rope with split and carved rock. The older men hauled the loads unhurriedly through the enlarged opening.

Not far into the afternoon, clouds filled with rain cast dark shadows over the area. A storm was gathering. Soon the rain fell, first in small splashes, then in larger ones, wetting the stones with their heavenly liquid. Because of the possibility of a storm, the migrant workers decided to shut down their power tools. In their haste, the men partially dislodged a boulder that had not been properly secured when they first began cutting. Water rushed under it when the rain fell, weakening its already precarious position.

Esta and Fatima were the last of the group to climb

through the opening that shielded the granite from the rest of the quarry. As Fatima clamoured behind Esta, the young Indian girl lost her footing. Looking for something to grab onto, she mistakenly chose the edge of the loose boulder, which immediately gave way. Esta watched in terror as Fatima fell onto her back while the large stone tipped and landed with a thud on the poor girl.

'Fatima!'

Esta quickly pushed through the gap created by the missing boulder. She shouted for help. Some of the younger workers and the team leader rallied to help. They gathered around the injured girl with their high-pitched solutions.

The rain was falling heavily now. Esta could scarcely see in front of her. She panicked, but then remembered Teacher Grace's words. It was a scripture from the book of Psalms. Her teacher had once recited it to encourage the girls at the Pathshala, *'For He shall give his angels charge over you, to keep you in all your ways. In their hands they shall bear you up, lest you dash your foot against a stone.'*

Esta knelt at Fatima's side, and took hold of the girl's hand. With her other hand she wiped the tears from Fatima's face. Esta hoped that the soothing gesture would bring some comfort to the girl. The two men tried in vain to move the rock. Fatima was sobbing now, but she kept her eyes on Esta. It was as if she knew that the only way she would survive the whole ordeal was to keep focused on the girl she had shunned every day. One of the workers gave Esta a bottle with some water in it. She held it to Fatima's lips while the men struggled to free her. The rock would not budge, though, and the rain only worsened the situation. Esta prayed earnestly to the Lord for a miracle. They needed to get help fast.

While she contemplated their options, Esta heard a mule braying in the distance. It was making its way up the stony bank towards them, pulling a cart behind it. It did not seem to be hauling a heavy load, only a few crates of bananas and other fruit bought from the valley below. An old man, a stranger to their world, led the mule. His long white hair and beard almost reached the stones on the ground. Letting go of Fatima's hand briefly, Esta asked one of the men to mind the injured girl while she breached the short gap to reach the old man. Esta addressed him as *babu* to show her respect.

The man looked at Esta. His eyes were the gentlest blue. He spoke to her in their native vernacular, 'Don't be afraid, I've been sent to help you. I was on my way home after delivering some fruit to a friend who has taken ill when my Master told me to take a different route.'

Esta's heart pounded with joy as the old man went on, 'My Lord told me that I would find a situation—quite a serious one—and that I should help where I could. What is it that I can do for you, my child?'

The man's compassion immediately won Esta's trust. *He speaks of his Master in the same way I think of my Lord.* She helped him lead the mule, with its cart trailing behind, to the outcrop where Fatima lay in agony.

Esta noticed that the efforts of the workers to console Fatima had helped—Fatima appeared calmer. They quickly unharnessed the mule and set to work. Securing part of the long rope across the animal's shoulders, they tethered the rest of the rope to the boulder. One of the men coaxed the beast to move in the opposite direction to where Fatima lay. Esta reassured Fatima, praying for her as the girl's dusty head rested in the palm of her hand. To

Esta's relief, Fatima opened her eyes. Then closing them a little, she whispered Esta's name.

'We must hurry, please,' Esta implored the men. They pulled the rope tighter and called again for the animal to move forward, but it would not budge. The old man, who had been watching quietly to the side, felt it was time to intervene. He raised his long stick, not to beat the animal, but to give it a signal to give a strong heave. It worked. The mule lurched forward, causing the stone to roll away—and with that, Fatima was freed.

The man hitched the mule to the cart again. He instructed the workers to lift the girl carefully. Gently scooping her in their arms they did as they were told, taking great care with Fatima's injured leg while they placed her on some old sacks in the wagon. The mysterious man secured the girl's leg with a makeshift splint. This he did with a thin yet sturdy piece of wood he had loosened from the side of his cart. Making her as comfortable as possible, the workers positioned Fatima against the side of the cart to stabilise her trip back to the base of the quarry. Esta sat next to the injured girl and thanked God for sparing the girl's life. Taking a mixture of herbs and a bottle with some liquid in it, the old man handed them to Esta along with some of the fruit.

Esta thanked him as she stored the items in the folds of her dress.

'Give these to the young one,' he said. 'They must be mixed together if they're going to be of any help.'

Looking up at the sky, the man crinkled his eyes as beads of rain began to hit the earth again. 'Take the mule and cart too, and all will be well—only trust in God.'

Esta waved at him as the young workers led the animal away. The old man did not follow them. Esta noticed that he had turned to walk in the opposite direction to where they were headed. He looked back at her as she called after him to thank him again for his kindness. It seemed as though his work was done, and he was needed elsewhere.

Esta watched as the old man raised his stick into the air. Then he disappeared as a dense cloud settled over the mountain.

The cart swayed from side to side as it bobbed over the rocky terrain. Esta's eyes rested on Fatima. These were her new friends now, bound together by the power of the miracle God had performed that day. She knew that the young men who had helped her to free Fatima would be changed forever.

Esta sheltered Fatima with her own body using the purity of the rain to wash the girl's face. Then the rain stopped, as if only for that brief moment it was sent to provide Esta with an antiseptic from heaven. By now Fatima was fully awake.

She whispered to Esta in Hindi, 'Thank you. And thank you to your God, who today has surely saved me.'

Esta smiled at the girl. She held her hand in a way that friends do when they run into the sunshine to play. Warm shards of light pushed through the clouds above them. Esta knew that the old man was right. All would be well. The mule steadily made its way towards the base camp.

Teacher Grace had once said, 'God is moved more by the heart that fully trusts in him for deliverance, than by the difficulty of a situation.' She did not know what the future held as the little cart wheeled its way into the compound. One thing she was sure of, though—her new friends were loved by the God of heaven.

***

The wagon rattled slowly into the camp. An angry Mogi was waiting for them. The sun was beginning to sink behind the small huts, casting an ominous shadow behind him. The migrant workers jumped from the cart before Mogi could stop them. They fled down the pathways that separated the dingy shacks. Esta would have to face the wrath of Mogi on her own.

The man's face darkened, the smell of alcohol evident on his breath. Esta clutched at the rope that hung loosely around the mule's neck, and prayed as the cart came to a halt. Mogi must not see Fatima lying in the back of the wagon.

Mogi stared angrily at Esta. He accused her of sabotaging his whole operation. Esta felt her body tremble as the man's ranting increased. Then she thought she heard another voice, still and clear, rise above Mogi's, 'You hold a gift in your hand.'

Esta turned from Mogi to look at the mule. She lifted the rope that was used as a harness, and handed it to him. The man immediately stopped his yelling. He looked at Esta in surprise.

'A gift. I have brought a gift for Mogi.'

In an instant, Mogi's countenance changed from anger to confusion. He grabbed the rope greedily from Esta's hand.

'Now that's more like it.' Looking askance at her he drawled, 'You've wronged me, yes, but you've also brought me a gift—to say you're sorry.'

Mogi lifted his bony hand into the air as if to pardon Esta. 'You'll go far with Mogi. Now go find a place to secure the beast—and that wagon.'

Esta was relieved. She was grateful that Mogi had not spotted Fatima asleep at the back of the cart.

Mogi turned from her, unsteady on his feet. He made his way back to his shack. Esta hurried the mule through a narrow passage between the stone huts at the lower end of the quarry. She knew of a tree nearby—few though there were. She used the rope to secure the animal and cart to the tree for the night.

It was dark. Esta worked quickly. Then, to her surprise she heard the doors of the little huts open. A few came at first, then slowly others joined them. The sound of soft pounding feet made their way towards her. The falling darkness hid their faces. The slaves used candles and homemade torches to light their way. Little flames moved through the air as if with wings. They worked silently alongside Esta. No one spoke, yet each knew exactly what to do. Tears spilled from Esta's eyes. There was no end to the miracle of love that day in a place where people thought God had forgotten them.

11

Light poured through the cracks of the little shacks that housed the workers. The smell of cooked rice and burning wood tantalised those who still slept. Their signature coughs could be heard wafting through the open windows. The slaves woke to ready themselves for yet another day of gruelling work at the quarry. Esta had been awake most of the night looking after Fatima.

The young girl was slightly sedated by the concoction the old man had given her. She had begun to speak a little, but her words were mostly incoherent. Comforting Fatima, Esta told her new friend that she needn't fear, she would take care of her. The workers brought what little they had to help Fatima recover. Miraculously, food made its way into Esta's hands. Among the gifts were some clean rags and water to bathe Fatima's wounds.

While this was happening, Esta found the courage to tell Mogi that Fatima had taken ill and that she, Esta, would be taking care of her. She also offered to put in extra work on Fatima's behalf to fulfil their daily quotas. Mogi checked in on Fatima frequently. Although he remained cautious about the arrangement, he seemed satisfied. There was, however, an increasing restlessness about the man that Esta felt was a separate issue to Fatima's accident. Could Mogi's mounting anxiety have something to do with his devious activities at the quarry?

For now, though, Esta remained prayerfully vigilant.

One morning Esta decided it was time for her friend to try to walk. She helped Fatima with her first steps. Esta thought it was appropriate to engage the girl in what would be their first real conversation. She had noticed from when they first met a large birthmark across the left side of Fatima's face. The mark was hidden behind a soft veil. Esta wondered whether this was the reason Fatima had avoided her.

Fatima smiled shyly, 'I'm ashamed,' she said. She looked down at her mangled leg and tightened the knot of the fabric that was fastened round her wound.

'What nonsense is this?' Esta replied, chuckling a little. 'There's nothing to be ashamed of.'

Fatima ignored her friend. 'How is it that you're still so kind to me after the way I've treated you?' She raised her head. 'I wouldn't be standing here if it were not for you and the old man. I remember his face clearly. It seems as if he was sent just to help me. I want to know your God,' she continued. 'Could you tell him for me that I would like him to be my friend?'

Esta was touched by Fatima's change of heart. She silently thanked the Lord for answering her prayers. It is God who creates this moment of truth for each heart. Esta had only helped to soften Fatima's heart through an act of kindness.

'Your God is more powerful than the many gods I've had to worship.'

Fatima squeezed her eyes. She made a funny face which caused Esta to laugh out loud. Her laugh could be heard across the compound, but she did not mind. Esta knew that the angels were rejoicing for the lost sheep that had been found.

'My dear sister,' Esta said, when she was able to catch her breath again. 'God sees your heart. Today he will surely come to live with you.'

They prayed together, two sisters of suffering, but also two daughters of the King of Glory. The veil Fatima wore to hide her birthmark slipped from her face as she prayed. Esta noticed the glow that replaced it—the mark seemed to pale in the light of God's love.

***

In the weeks that followed, Mogi turned a blind eye to the behaviour of the two girls. He seemed distracted by his own problems. The man thought he was losing his sanity. *I must stop drinking so much,* he scolded himself. His thoughts were muddled, and things seemed different around the quarry. Even the surly Fatima constantly smiled when she should clearly be miserable in her dreadful state.

Mogi grew fearful.

The power he had over his slaves had always made him feel strong. Lately, however, he felt awfully weak around them. He began rummaging through their small shack while Esta was out helping Fatima exercise her leg. There had to be some god they were praying to that made him feel this way. Mogi searched in vain—there was no statue or idol to be found. Esta had fortunately hidden her Bible in a torn section of her mattress. *Who was it, then, that the two girls prayed to every day?* He did not have an answer now, so he felt it best to lie low till he could figure it all out.

Esta enjoyed the times she was able to share with Fatima from the Bible that Grace had given her.

Sometimes they were joined by the others. At first, the people were inquisitive. One by one they came to her, to hear her read. Esta would read from her English Bible first. Then she would translate the scriptures into Hindi for everyone to understand.

Esta had to work hard to keep up with Fatima's required quota of cut stone, but God gave her strength even when she felt she would not make it. Mogi's erratic behaviour—felt by all the workers—worsened each day. This made Esta more apprehensive. She shared her concerns with Fatima. The two girls prayed earnestly for the slaves each night when the fires were dying and life in the compound had calmed.

The people continued to visit the shack where Esta and Fatima worshipped the unknown God. They asked the two girls many questions about their Saviour. Esta taught them the songs that Teacher Grace had sung to them at the Pathshala. Their favourite was a melody, a gentle contrast to the harsh stone they had to cut each day. Boldly, they sang with all their hearts, their voices rising above the compound.

It is among the poor and enslaved that God's love can be seen moving with great force. How wonderful for these people to feel free even in the midst of their circumstances—to have their burdens lifted from their tired hearts. This was the change Mogi witnessed at the quarry, and which worried him so. The slaves even appeared to be happy chipping away at the rock each day, as if they were working for a new master. Mogi became increasingly anxious.

***

There came a day when two men, who appeared to be on official business, paid a visit to the quarry. Their appointment would change the lives of the people working there forever. Esta watched the men from the small window of her shack. They made their way up the mountain towards the area where the labourers worked. A dry wind flapped around their jackets and lifted their ties over their shoulders. Most of the workers had already retreated to their huts as the gust was strong—little work could be done beneath a dome of heavy dust.

Esta watched as the men looked for Mogi through the cloud of sand. They eventually found him standing in an open area. His face was covered in dirt and his thick hair whipped around him as if caught in a whirlwind. A heated argument followed. Although she could not hear what they were saying, Esta sensed that the men were not happy. Finally, Mogi threw his scrawny arms into the air as if defending himself from an allegation. He wiped his mouth with the back of his hand.

Noticing that Esta was distracted by something happening outside, Fatima walked over to join her friend, her slight limp the only sign of her past injury.

'Those men are from the government.'

'How can you tell?' Esta asked.

'They've been here before—the time they wanted to close the quarry. Some people said the men do not want children working like this every day. They want them to be in school. Others say they come to the quarry because Mogi is not giving them enough money for allowing him to run his business here.'

Esta's mind raced. 'Why is Mogi continuing with slave labour then? Surely there are signed international treaties that prohibit using children as slaves.' She shook her head. Fatima was illiterate like many of her class. She did not know much about the rights and freedoms of people. Esta had learned about these things at the Pathshala.

The two friends were wondering about Mogi's contraventions when the entrance to their little hut darkened. The shadow belonged to Aadesh. He was one of the young migrant workers. Aadesh bent his tall frame to enter the shack which, typical of all the dwellings, was low and narrow. He had always been kind to the slaves. In his hand he held a bundle with bread in it.

Esta was relieved to see Aadesh. He handed the parcel to her, and she thanked him. She invited him to take a seat on a small bench—the only real furniture in their hut. Esta was keen to hear his views on the recent activities at the quarry—the migrant workers generally knew more than the slaves.

Aadesh eased the long strands of his fringe from his face. 'These men aren't as innocent as you think,' he said. 'They're extorting money from Mogi. In exchange for his generosity, they don't report his activities to the authorities.'

Esta looked sullenly at Aadesh, as if he represented the people who were exploiting the slave children.

'Hey, don't look at me that way. I'm just a messenger.' The young man leaned back as if to protect himself from Esta's intense glare.

'I'm sorry, Aadesh. I get furious when I think of how our people are being used to advance someone else's greed.' Esta spoke softly then. 'Perhaps Mogi's been holding some of the profits from these men. He's been acting rather strange lately.'

Aadesh got up to leave. He gave the girls a smile

and waved at them as he exited the shack. There was work to be done now that the squall of dust had eased. Esta felt sad that Aadesh had to leave so soon.

***

Darkness fell quickly, bringing an uncharacteristic chill with it. It was a night when men, like ravens, come to steal the poor and break the strong. The wind stole into the girls' shack like an uninvited guest with cruel intentions. Esta tried her best to find whatever she could to keep Fatima warm.

A group of men in dark clothing made their way up the grey hill. They raided the small dwellings as they searched for young and pretty girls. No lights burned that night, nor could the usual smoke be seen snaking its way from the little chimneys. Only the muffled cries of the female slaves could be heard across the quarry.

Mogi had arranged with some acquaintances who profiteered in kidnapping to abduct the girls he thought would sell well in Mumbai. No one else knew of his plans. Among the poor, this kind of evil is often the most common. The men worked quickly, plucking the girls from their shacks. They left the girl with the disfigured leg behind. She was of no use to them. One of the girls had a strange book in her hand, which was taken from her and tossed to the ground. Where she was going, they reasoned, there would be no time to read.

The girls were thrown into the bin of a truck. They were covered with a dark tarpaulin which was held down with iron rods. The slave girls huddled together, cold and afraid, too frightened to call for help. No one would hear them anyway.

The men had done their work, now the rest was up to Mogi. Satisfied with the evening's secret operation, Mogi felt he needed to complete the finishing touches to his plan. He would not be shut down without a fight. The officials, who represented the government—or so they had told him—had extorted money from him long enough. It was time for him to procure his own profits some other way. Selling the young girls who worked at the quarry to the people who trade in humans seemed the easiest solution to Mogi's dilemma.

Mogi made his way back to his shack. He lit a fire to rid his bones of the cold he felt. He tried to sleep close to the warmth of the fire, but the cries coming from those left at the compound made it impossible. He cursed the world and those who he felt were responsible for forcing his hand to commit such a heinous act. *Just a little while now*, he thought, *and it will be over.*

***

The compound was quiet as the morning light snuck above the grey mountain. Mogi rose quickly and set to work with his final plan. He felt as sharp as the slate stone that cast depressing shadows across his hut. He must hurry before everyone rose and he had a mob on his hands. Why had he not thought of it before? He made his way to an old shed where he kept the gas bottles that gave power to the heavy drills. There he found what he was looking for—some half-filled cans of gasoline which would serve his purpose well.

Mogi worked quickly as he poured the thick amber liquid into a container. He dragged it towards the enclosure that housed the gas cylinders. Taking an old rag from his pocket he pushed it into the opening of the canister. Then he lit the rag with a match. Quickly placing the container between some of the larger bottles of gas, he made a hasty retreat from the impending explosion. Thinking his plan had succeeded, Mogi did not see the roll of twisted wire lying across his path. The last thing he heard as he desperately tried to free himself was the detonation he had carefully planned. Mogi's fate was sealed. He would never own a slave again.

***

Again, Esta was taken from her people. As she lay in the dark at the back of the truck, she could feel the smooth skins of the female slaves against her own. They were trembling, but she did not feel afraid.

Esta, like the others, did not know where she was being taken. She gathered that Aadesh had been right about Mogi, although she would never know of Mogi's end. They were far from the quarry now. Esta thought of Fatima—frail and defenseless. What had become of her friend in all the mayhem? She decided to bring her fears to God. Esta had learned quickly that although man may fail you, God will always be with you. She recalled again the story her English teacher had shared of the young Hebrew man called Joseph. No matter what happened, God would be victorious in the end. Nothing on this earth could separate her from his eternal love.

12

Grace could barely see the quarry. Huge clouds of black dust blanketed the mine. She pulled the cotton scarf Aayshirya had given her tightly over her mouth and most of her face to allow her searching eyes some visibility. Aayana and Mark sat on either side of her, their bodies jigging in the back seat of an old sedan, the same look of despair on their faces. Grace could hear the crunch of stone beneath the tyres of the vehicle as it crept up a gravel road. Her mind flooded with what ifs. She worried about the fate of the many debt slaves who had worked there, but most of all her heart was filled with apprehension for Esta. *Where is my young Indian friend? Has she been hurt in the explosion?*

Grace felt two hands reach out to hold hers. They were Aayana's. The unspoken word of this comforting gesture was exactly what Grace needed. She quieted her thoughts while she recalled a scripture she had once read to the girls... *You will keep him in perfect peace, whose mind is stayed on You, because he trusts in You.* Grace glanced over at Aayana. She was grateful for the Somali girl who had come into her life at a time when she needed a close friend. Aayana was always at her side, like a guardian angel constantly watching over her.

As they approached the entrance of the quarry, Mark called out to the driver to go faster. The road had levelled out and they needed to find a safe place to park away from the smoke and chaos. Debris and stone lay in mangled heaps around the shanties. The smell of burning gas hung thickly in the air. Tears spilled from Grace's eyes as she thought of Esta working in the quarry every day. Her heart was heavy with concern that something terrible had happened to the young girl. Grace silently prayed that God would give her a sign that Esta was alive.

The driver manoeuvred their vehicle through the rubble to the area behind the small shacks. Grace looked intently at the rocky ground through the window. She noticed something, a small book, lying in the rough.

'Stop!' she called out. 'Mark, please tell the driver to stop the car,' she repeated. 'I recognise something. I think it's the gift I gave to Esta.'

When the driver finally brought the vehicle to a halt, Grace got out with Aayana.

Lying on the ground was the near-burnt remains of the little Bible Grace had given to Esta. She finally had the evidence she was looking for. The young Indian girl had indeed been sold into chattel slavery… but where was she now?

Someone shouted to them. It was the voice of a man used to giving orders. He gestured for them not to venture any further. It was difficult to get a clear glimpse of him as clouds of thick smoke laden with the pungent smell of gas filled the air. The man ordered the trio to join the others where it was safer.

Some ambulances had arrived to assist those who had been injured. The three friends did as they were told, but Grace continued to search for Esta as the medics carried the injured towards the standing vehicles.

Grace's search produced nothing.

From where he stood Mark noticed the troubled

look on Grace's face. 'Have you not found her?'

Grace shook her head. She felt Aayana take hold of her hand again.

'Oh, Lord,' Grace whispered under her breath as if she was talking to him alone. 'What has happened to our sweet child?'

Mark noticed a stretcher being carried towards one of the ambulances. In it lay the frame of a thin girl.

'Hold a minute,' he called out to the men, hoping that the patient lying on the stretcher was Esta, but quickly realised it wasn't. Mark thought to question her, instead. Perhaps she knew something.

Grace and Aayana stood beside him as he patiently spoke with the girl. Mark had a special way with the Indian people, and was also fluent in their native tongue. He was hopeful that the young girl would know of Esta's whereabouts. He noticed that she had a distinct birthmark across her face and that her right leg did not sit well with the rest of her body.

The girl looked up at Mark as he questioned her in Hindi. 'We're looking for a young girl. She's about your age and her name is Esta. We know she was taken from her family to work here at the quarry. Perhaps you know something about her?'

The child's face lit up when she heard Esta's name. Mark smiled at Grace. She spoke softly as she pushed her reply between short breaths.

'I do know of the girl you ask about. She's… my sister. Her brother is Jesus. He's the one who rescued me from a terrible accident. Esta's a friend of God.' Her eyes closed briefly each time she spoke.

Grace felt her heart fill with expectation. 'That sounds like our Esta. Do you know what might've happened to her?'

Mark translated for Grace. The girl replied, 'She's not here. She's gone. Last night men came and took slave girls with them to Mumbai.'

The girl's eyes filled with tears. Noticing her distress, one of the medics asked Grace and Mark to step aside. The men needed to get the girl into one of the ambulances immediately. Grace looked on as they took her away. Her heart sunk. She felt the thud of deferred hope twist deep into her like a sharp knife.

***

Most of the injured were eventually cleared from the quarry. The stone mine resembled a graveyard—devoid of industry and life. The three friends made their way back to the Pathshala. When they arrived they shared the sad news with Aayshirya, who tried to console Grace. The burden Grace had carried for Esta and the rest of the slave children seemed too much to bear.

Aayshirya explained to Grace and Aayana that over the years she had lost many girls from the mountain villages in this way. Her own heart had broken more times than she could recall, until she felt there were only pieces left to love those who were still with her. Aayshirya had prayed that God would send someone to help rescue these girls from the horrific life they had been sold into. Grace, she felt, was that someone. Aayshirya embraced her companions. She quietly sang a song of praise and thanked God for his mercy. Aayshirya asked him to deliver her people from these awful crimes.

They worshipped quietly together for some time. Grace thought of the broken people of the world. She prayed, not only for those who had been stolen, but for their loved ones also—the ones who had to go on without them. It would take much courage and sacrifice to be the solution for those who were hungry for their freedom. A life given for others was the gospel of Christ.

Grace knew she was at another crossroads in her life. So much had happened, yet she felt she must go deeper still, where most of the nation's exploited were found. *Could the Lord be using my need to find Esta as a magnet to draw me into the heart of India?*

Grace did not get her answer right away. Her intuitions did, however, stir in her a wish to leave the mountains. She would have to tell Mark about her plan to go to the great city of Mumbai. But would her friend agree? He had lost so much there and had returned a broken man. Would he risk letting Grace leave the farm to find Esta? Would Mark sanction Grace's pursuit of whatever else God had for her?

***

When they arrived back at the farm, Grace prayed more earnestly about the call she felt the Lord had given her. She did not speak to Mark right away. Instead, she decided to first share her feelings about the matter with Aayana. After freshening up, Grace went to search for her Somali friend.

She found the young woman shelling peas under a large tree. The tree had, for many years, provided an umbrella of shade for those who sought protection from the heat and rest from their labour. A light breeze tugged at the flaps of Aayana's peach-coloured scarf. She looked up at Grace as if she were expecting a serious message from her friend.

When Aayana eventually spoke, it was to make a statement rather than a question. 'We're leaving, aren't we? We're going to Mumbai to find Esta.'

Trying to disguise her surprise, Grace settled beside Aayana. She took some of the vegetables between her fingers and prized the little green pearls from their neat havens. She was glad that Aayana appeared willing to go with her. Aayana's solitude was not to be mistaken for timidity. Once she set her mind to something, she passionately pursued it.

Grace was, in fact, encouraged by her friend's boldness. More often than not, Aayana had confirmed the way the Lord was leading Grace.

'Do you think I'm chasing an empty dream, Aayana? Taking on a fight I can't win?'

Aayana drew her long limbs under her cotton dress and looked at Grace. 'In all our battles, Grace, we are more than winners because of Jesus. There are no other soldiers in this world who go into a fight having already won, except the true believers of God.'

'You're right. My own battles were only overcome when I decided to give my whole life to him. It's just that there are times when I'm afraid of my own weaknesses. What if I give up halfway? To search for Esta would mean placing us both in danger. It would mean risking our lives every day. It doesn't seem fair to expect this of you.'

Aayana placed her hand gently over Grace's. 'Even our failings must be given to the Lord. If he has called you for this work, he will also provide. He knows about the dangers and, of course, your limitations. Was he not a man like us, who walked the same earth—one who understands our weaknesses?'

Aayana took Grace by the shoulders so that her friend faced her. 'We must have faith in him. He will not let us down.'

Grace smiled. 'Then you're willing to go to Mumbai with me?'

Aayana nodded confidently. The determination in her eyes was all Grace needed. In rural Somali, everyday decisions centre around life and death. Her quiet resolve was Aayana's way of keeping her feelings tucked inside her heart so that when it was time to make a decision, it was easier for her to think about what was needed to survive.

'I'm here to serve you. Say what I must do, and I will do it.'

Grace thought back to the story of Ruth and Naomi. She recalled the biblical tale that Aayshirya had shared with the girls on her first day at the Pathshala. Grace had her Ruth. Now she was certain about the dream she had had of the young girls with light brown faces and shiny locks all that time ago.

Disregarding Aayana's composed presence, Grace leaned over and embraced her friend. All that was left to do was to find Mark and to see whether he would help them.

***

Grace looked for Mark that evening after dinner. She eventually found him in his study. Mark had been praying for Esta's return. Although he had worked through many kidnappings before, this one weighed heavily on him. His thoughts went to the red-light district of Mumbai and specifically to Kamathipura, the district where he and his late wife had established a rescue center in the heart of the squalor and misery there. They had called the shelter "House of Joy". Their ministry's objective was to help young victims heal and to discover their gifts and find God's purpose for their lives. He wondered now, as he sat pondering Esta's fate, whether he would be willing to let those he had recently grown to love, risk their lives to pursue rescuing hers.

Mark knew all too well of the peril that haunted the streets of Kamathipura, but he also believed that God's work was not finished there. The only thing that stood between him and the next step was Mark's complete surrender to the Lord's will. Obedience, he had learned, was better than sacrifice. It was the price of not being able to have true fellowship with God. This he could not do. He had come so far. He tried to push away the thoughts of doubt that occasionally visited him when he was alone.

Mark was sitting in this contemplative state when there was a faint knock at the door. It was Grace. She quietly made her way in. Mark loved the effortless way in which Grace connected with the people at the farm and the school. She was indeed a woman who could easily capture a man's heart. But in all the time she had been with them, he had kept his feelings to himself. Her heart, it seemed, was still devoted to someone who lived on the other side of the world.

Mark knew that Joseph had not communicated with Grace in a long while. It was just like the priest, he thought. Joseph would not fight for anything outside the will of God. Perhaps he had chosen to do so for Grace's sake. Grace had had her own issues with trust, but she had come a long way and had grown in her faith. Her capacity to serve others was exemplary, as a true Christian's should be. Only God knew what the future held. Joseph, Mark was convinced, would not do anything to jeopardise the Lord's dealings. As far as good friendships went, it was simple enough for him to share his feelings with Grace—yet, when it came to love, he held back. The whole situation seemed vexingly complex.

Mark smiled to himself and Grace frowned. He removed his reading glasses from the bridge of his nose and invited her to sit in the chair opposite him.

'How are you coping?' Mark finally asked. 'This has been a trying time for us all but I know it's affected you the most. You had become quite fond of the girl.'

As if knowing the reason for her visit, Mark shifted slightly in his chair before he continued. 'Finding Esta in the streets of Mumbai will be an immense challenge… not to mention the risks involved.'

Grace was not surprised that Mark had an inkling of what she was about to ask—the two had grown close. She decided to dive right in. 'Well, that's why I'm here. I'd like to discuss a possible plan to rescue Esta. I believe we can get her back.'

Mark could see the desperation in Grace's eyes. He sensed the longing in her heart.

'What I'm saying is that I want to go to Mumbai to look for her. Aayana will go with me.'

Grace searched Mark's face for any sign of agreement before she continued. 'I know it will be dangerous but I've made up my mind, and the Lord will be with us.'

Grace added cautiously, 'If we don't leave soon, the chance of not finding Esta at all will only increase.'

Mark knew how she felt so he held back his concerns.

'You mentioned before that the shelter you established with your late wife in Kamathipura was still operating. It would be a good place for Aayana and me to start.'

Although he felt strongly inclined to discourage Grace from such a crazy idea, Mark's heart softened.

He was quiet for a few moments.

'I'll help you, but only if you have full assurance that this is what the Lord wants you to do.'

Grace nodded enthusiastically. Her accompanying smile was radiant.

'Then so be it. You and Aayana are going to Mumbai.'

***

The next few days were taken up with arrangements to get to the city, specifically to the House of Joy. Mark knew he would have to leave Grace and Aayana there once he had them settled. He was in no position to leave things the way they were in the hinterland. As far as the shelter was concerned, an elderly lady currently ran the establishment. Pandita had often appealed to Mark for extra hands, so it was not without reason that Mark felt oddly excited about Grace and Aayana going there. He would have to send word to the woman immediately, explaining the situation and letting her know that they would be leaving right away.

While they waited for their travel documents, Mark took it upon himself to provide Grace and Aayana with information about the red-light district of Mumbai, and in particular Kamathipura. He was careful to explain the challenges that lay ahead. Grace and Aayana committed these to the Lord in prayer.

There were times when Grace questioned her desire to go to Mumbai. She wondered what she was getting herself into. One morning, while hanging her washing on the communal clothesline, she voiced some of her concerns with Mark.

'The powerful cycle of poverty that encourages human slavery is what troubles me the most. What do you know about the *Dalit*? I believe Esta was born into this caste of untouchables.'

Mark knew how important it was for Grace to know as much as she could about Indian society so he tried his best to help with her questions. 'That's true, although the use of the term *Dalit* to classify people was outlawed in India… about the mid-twentieth century. Sadly, though, the reality of the casting society still exists in the minds and behaviours of the poor. There is some good around, though. Family is important to the people here. A patriarchal view of marriage still exists in the rural areas where marriage is for life and divorce is unheard of.'

Mark handed Grace a few clothes pegs. While she shook her wet shirts before fastening them to the line, he went on. 'Some of the traditions here are in fact quite good for family life, but most are devastating. Esta was probably promised in marriage from a young age—a decision conjointly made by the families concerned, and one that wouldn't be easily broken. This in itself is not a bad thing,' he went on, 'as it helps to strengthen family bonds and secure financial stability for generations.'

Mark paused for a moment while he handed Grace the last of her wet clothing. 'There are some horrific marriage practices that still exist among the poor, though, like the killings or suicides of young Indian women, known as dowry deaths.'

Grace felt her heart sink. 'How much worse can it get? I was forced into a marriage I didn't want. But when I think about it, my own experience was not nearly as horrific as what these poor women have to go through.' She sighed. 'What causes these circumstances?'

Mark's expression was empathetic. 'The groom's family relentlessly harasses the bride-to-be in an effort to extort a greater dowry from her and her family. Another tragic reality is that these people are seldom avenged by the police.'

Grace admired Mark for his capacity to empathise with abused women all over the world. He took the empty basket from her. Then putting her hand in the crook of his arm, Grace walked with Mark back to the homestead. She had always enjoyed Mark's company. Grace knew she would miss the farm, the school, and its special people.

They made their way down the well-trodden path to the house. Grace was still haunted by the fact that there were young brides being burnt to death—perhaps as they spoke.

'What drives these women to take their own lives?'

For the first time during their conversation, Grace noticed the emotion in Mark's reply.

'Undoubtedly, the constant and often brutal harassment for more money by the groom's family brings these women to the point where they feel they don't have the mental capacity or will to cope with it all. Consequently, India has one of the highest dowry-connected deaths in the world. These practices are not limited to a specific religion either,' Mark concluded.

Grace thought that much like Joseph had at The

Cielo, Mark strongly empathised with the downtrodden—a passion God puts in your heart when you have allowed him to heal your own.

Mark opened the door to the first bungalow where the community's laundry was sorted and washed. Some young women were busy working there, singing while they did their chores. Grace wondered whether it would be the same at the House of Joy.

Not before he clasped her hand in his to pray did Mark leave Grace. His decision was made; he must let her go. This was the will of God concerning Esta and others like her. For a second time, Grace had to leave behind those she had grown to love. To obey the call of the One who loved her first was the only path she was determined take.

13
Red-light District, Mumbai

Grace entered Mumbai through a small portal that betrayed its vastness. The city rose like a torn picture from a child's pop-up book. With Mark and Aayana close at her side, Grace did not feel as vulnerable as she had when she first arrived in India. They edged their way past tiny urban caves streaked with urine. The constricted streets and half-lit verges were as deterring as they were fascinating. Inching their way in sporadic stops and starts, the group moved deeper into the heart of the red-light district—Kamathipura in particular.

Mark felt certain that the traffickers would have taken Esta to be used as a sex slave in the dingy lanes of the old district. Grace admired his rapport with the people. Mark's good-natured charm, first-rate command of the language, and his compassion won them over at the outset. The driver of their *bajaji*, a kind of automated rickshaw, was clearly well rehearsed in navigating the narrow streets of the area. They lurched vigorously from side to side as they pushed on. Every obstruction was a potential challenge for the man, yet he excelled at getting them through safely, albeit with some measure of self-importance.

Mark explained to Grace and Aayana the demographic arrangement of the prostitution areas. They learned that there were several red-light districts in Mumbai. It would take weeks, if not months, to track Esta's whereabouts. Consequently, every second was precious to them. Grace struggled to quell the mounting anxiety she felt. She knew Mark's main objective was to settle her and Aayana. Once this was done, he would have to get back to the outreach farm. The incident at the quarry had left the area unhinged. There would be many looking to him to establish stability again.

The shelter would serve as a secure base from which Grace and Aayana could work and carry out their search for Esta. As they snaked their way through the streets, Grace was anxious to know more about the secret life of the street workers. She would have to understand how the area functioned if she were to be of any use to the people living there. Of one thing she was sure—life here was far removed from the life she had known. She wondered how she would ever truly empathise with the women who worked the streets each day.

Mark on the other hand was preoccupied with his own thoughts. The old Indian woman, Pandita, who currently ran the establishment was not well. She had been weakened by a recent bout of cholera that had erupted in the district. Pandita was frail, and Mark hoped that he could take her back with him. He would have to wait, however, for the right time to reveal his intentions to Grace and Aayana.

Grace thought of Mark as they entered the area. It was in Kamathipura that he had lost his wife. She wondered what impact returning to the place might have on him. Mark concealed his feelings well.

Finally, Mark instructed the driver to stop alongside a cement curb in front of a large building. Although it had always been an impressive place, built in the centre of the squalor that surrounded it, Mark was surprised at how unremarkable the House of Joy now seemed. He stayed seated for a short while, looking at the building before gathering himself to help his two companions.

They climbed from the *bajaji*. Grace's first reaction was to survey the sturdy house. She immediately thought, *An unknown destination is sometimes inflated to fit one's wishes. In reality, it is often less than magnificent.*

Grace had imagined the place to be filled with an unperturbed traffic of people. The house was, however, quiet. She got the distinct impression that the place and the people had been through a difficult time. Although Mark had told Grace and Aayana that the elderly lady who was looking after the place was not in good health, he had not elaborated on the situation. Grace had no idea what awaited them.

The only reason the House of Joy appeared different to the other dwellings that lined the lane on either side was because it stood the tallest. Its roof, unlike the other houses, was not garlanded with brightly coloured marigolds unevenly scalloped together.

The streets were hushed and devoid of human activity. Only a stray dog could be seen. The chirruping from the myna birds nestled in the eaves of the dirty gutters were the few sounds to be heard. Grace felt her heart sink.

She assumed the streets were quiet because most of the people worked at night. Grace noticed a better sign to the establishment fastened across the main entrance. On it was written "House of Joy". *Perhaps*, thought Grace, *there is a semblance of life about, after all.*

Mark left the women standing at the entrance while he paid the impatient driver. The man had already dropped their luggage on the curb. Grace scanned the vertical windows of the shelter. She spotted little dark faces from the corner of her eye, peeping inquisitively through the half-drawn curtains.

Mark eventually joined Grace and Aayana before he knocked on the large door. There was no response, so he gently pushed it open. The commotion of visitors at the door brought an old lady followed by a beautiful woman, to greet them. The women shuffled slowly—their sandaled feet scraped the stony floor.

Mark's face lit up when he saw Pandita. He gently pushed past Grace and Aayana and pulled her into a warm embrace.

'Pandita, Pandita.' He repeated the woman's name and held her at arm's length for a moment before holding her again.

'Mister Mark!' Pandita rasped, clinging to him.

She took a step back. 'You're looking well, my son.'

The woman playfully tugged at Mark's waist. 'It's been too long! How is life in the mountains?'

Pandita was quite conversant in English. This was a relief to Grace. She was touched by the warmth she witnessed between Mark and the old woman—the kind often witnessed between a mother and her son.

Pandita touched Mark's face gently with her thin hands as if savouring a moment she might forget. Then she turned her attention to Grace and Aayana.

'And who do we have here? Are these the lovely angels you said you'd bring with you?'

Mark introduced Grace and Aayana to Pandita. He made certain she was able to hear their names clearly. The two women immediately warmed to her. Grace knew then that although the exterior of the establishment appeared dull (and perhaps with reason), warmth and kindness graced the interior. She took a closer look at the Indian woman standing close to Pandita. She was striking. Her exquisite features were set in a heart-shaped face, but there was something different about her eyes. A milky halo filmed the irises. She did not look directly at them either but stayed close to Pandita. Grace was certain the woman was blind. Pandita drew her companion closer to introduce her. 'My dear friends, the lovely lady at my side is Alisha. Alisha hasn't been with us for very long. You may have noticed our dear sister cannot see, but she does have a sharp mind.'

Pandita's head moved gently from side to side as she spoke. Although Alisha did not speak, her silence was welcoming. The old woman suddenly broke into a raking cough, and Grace noticed Mark's concern.

'Don't mind me,' she said, somewhat self-consciously. 'This cough comes and goes. It's like an impolite neighbour visiting me when I least expect it.'

Pandita led them down a narrow passage that seemed damp. It opened into a spacious sitting room that faced a set of tall windows. The windows let some light in, though it was hard to believe that any sunlight found its way down the narrow lanes and alleyways that were characteristic of the Kamathipura district. Light is, thankfully, a determined caller. It will penetrate even the darkest of places.

They entered the living area. Pandita suggested they all take a seat. Once they were settled, the young woman who Pandita introduced as Alisha perked up. She gave some instructions to the younger girls who had gathered inquisitively to greet the newcomers. Alisha spoke to them in Hindi. Grace and Aayana, who sat beside each other on the dusty sofa, greeted each girl warmly.

Grace felt as if she had been transported back to her early days at The Cielo. She tried her best to commit the girls' names to memory as they were introduced to her. Experience had taught her, though, that as she became familiar with the character of each child, their name would be easier to recall.

There was a ripple of giggles when the girls were introduced to Aayana. Most of them had never seen an African woman before. The Somali girl laughed along with them. Soon they were all sharing sweet milky tea together. Mark began to relax too. He chatted spiritedly to Pandita, sharing all his news with the old woman. As they drank their tea, Grace looked over at the man who had become her close friend. She would miss him. *Will my journey through life always be filled with transient friendships?* she wondered. *Will the Lord eventually settle me somewhere, with someone?* But these were questions for another time. Right now, there was work to be done and a young girl to be found. In the meantime, the catch-up with Pandita continued late into the afternoon.

Grace felt herself drift from the conversation in the living room. She contemplated her new life and the possibility of finding Esta. She took in her new surroundings and the other dwellings she spied through the tall windows. The House of Joy appeared to be higher than two stories. She wondered if there was more to the large building that seemed to sway of its own accord.

Most of the other buildings in the area were not built with reliable materials, but the people inhabited them as if they were immortal. Walls merged with other walls. Roof edges touched each other like chocolate slabs melting in the sun. The foundations of the dwellings appeared to be joined by the arms of a large phantom that held everything together in chaotic unison. It was a melting pot of concrete floors and human activity. In fact, some of the buildings were notably crumbling. The shelter, though, stood strong in the midst of it all, as if it were held erect by some unseen force. Grace could feel that God was at work in the House and that many miracles had occurred there.

She was brought back to the conversation by a gentle hand on her shoulder. It was Alisha. By now the sun had begun to set and its fading crest could be seen through the tall windows. Alisha asked Grace and Aayana to follow her. They were trailed by a stream of giggling girls whose dark braids bobbed around their faces. Alisha led them to their shared bedrooms. Every inch of the house was precious to the people who lived there. Although the sleeping arrangements appeared cramped, it was cozy and safe.

Mark would not be staying for long. A bed with clean linen was prepared for him in a tiny loft. A further surprise for Grace was that Alisha could speak English. Grace was touched by the way she mothered the young girls, speaking to them in their native tongue when she needed to be understood.

After dinner with their new family, Grace and Aayana left Pandita and Mark to talk alone. Alisha, who was assisted by one of the older girls, began to chat more freely with Grace and Aayana. She showed them around the first floor of the house, pointing to the things she could not see. The woman was frequently interrupted by some of the more inquisitive girls. They nagged Alisha with one question after the other about where the newcomers would sleep.

The girls remained intrigued with Aayana. Never had they seen a person of her physical stature. Some of the girls ran their small hands over her ebony skin. Aayana did not mind it one bit. At one time she even stretched out her arms with a welcoming grin so that they could all feel her skin. They laughed at her thick African accent, and Aayana—who had eventually settled on one of the mattresses—told them stories about her village.

There was a quiet hush in the dimly lit room when Aayana finished. Grace took her friend's hand in her own. She knew Aayana longed for her family. The ache was deep, and it never left her. Aayana turned to Grace and gave her a reassuring nod— the kind that said not to be concerned; that she was quite fine. She was, in fact, enjoying all the attention. It was seldom that a girl from Africa was held in such awe.

The three women talked late into the night. Little by little the younger ones eventually trotted off to bed.

Grace was struck by Alisha's testimony. She was especially interested in the young girl Alisha referred to as Little Saamaree, the little Samaritan, who had brought Alisha to the House of Joy. Alisha had never learned the girl's real name, but Grace secretly hoped that she would get to meet her one day.

Grace thought Alisha quite remarkable. Although her loss of sight had left her disadvantaged, Alisha's love for God shone through her spirit.

'I'm here now,' Alisha said. 'I've found the true God of all humanity. Although I've suffered many trials, I would rather know and love him as Lord than have a thousand men tell me how beautiful I am.'

Grace was moved. God had given Alisha spiritual

insight that was rare—even among seeing folk.

***

Tired and quite spent from the journey, Grace decided to retire. She said goodnight to Aayana and her new friends. Grace looked out of the small portal of their bedroom before climbing into her cozy bed. She recalled the conversations she had had with her mother as they gazed at the moon together. Now, the silvery pan was not just a symbol. It cast an eerie light across the sky. It seemed more foreboding than usual. *What was it about Kamathipura?* Grace wondered.

Despite the weight of human suffering that hung willfully in the air, Grace would find more daughters here who needed her. She prayed a prayer of thanksgiving, then closed her eyes to sleep. Perhaps Esta would catch the whisper of Grace's prayer in the constricted lanes of the red-light district.

***

Morning squeezed its way into the cracks of the shelter like a stray dog rummaging for food. Grace opened her eyes. She immediately sensed the weariness of human despair through the gaping holes in the house. But there was also a certain peace that rose like a gallant soldier to ward off the arrows of shame that pierced the alleyways and dimly lit brothel houses. She reached for her Bible, the book she carried with her wherever she went. It was the one Joseph had given her. Reading one of her favourite passages in Isaiah, Grace was reminded of the prophet's words that God was true to his Word and he had given his Son to a dying world to prove his love.

Grace read for a while before she drew back the scant bed covers. She quickly dressed while the others slept. Quietly, she made her way downstairs. Some of the windows were still covered in old bed sheets which were used to keep the night prowlers from looking in. She could hear soft voices coming from the ground floor.

She made her way to the kitchen. The faint smell of coal coming from the stove was inviting. It filled the space with its warmth. The previous evening's meal of vegetable curry cooked with pungent spices still hung in the air. It was a meal they had all enjoyed together. Grace would always remember her first meal at the House of Joy.

Mark and Pandita were seated beside the warm stove. They were surprised to see Grace up so early. The old woman greeted her warmly. 'You're up with the myna birds, as the saying goes around here. Was your sleep not a good one?'

Holding a closed hand to her mouth, Pandita coughed. Grace placed her own hand gently on the woman's shoulder, assuring her that all was well.

'I had a pleasant night's sleep, thank you. Alisha and her charming girls have taken great care to ensure that Aayana and I are comfortable. I was a little troubled when I woke, though... the kind of disturbance that only God has the answer to.'

Grace sat beside Pandita while Mark got up to pour her some of the tea that had been brewing on the stove.

He handed Grace a cup. 'It's good that you have these promptings. They'll be of help to you. There are many challenges in Kamathipura. The spiritual ones are the toughest. There are many persecutors of God's work here.'

Mark grew serious. 'Gangsters and traffickers are against us rescuing the women and girls from the streets. It puts them out of business. The more we help and empower the victims, the more we threaten the economic welfare of these ruffians.'

He got up to pace the floor. 'They're at war with the House of Joy. They're angry and vengeful. There's also a lot of unrest amongst the different religions of the district. The Muslims and the Hindus often engage in violent clashes. Each faction is trying to drive the other out.'

Mark sat down while Pandita continued. 'The fear you sense, Grace, has latched onto the people who live in Kamathipura. This has been the case for many generations. It's like a predator that sinks its teeth into its victim, leaving it maimed and weakened before another attack. If it wasn't for God's love, those who come here to seek help would surely be damned for eternity.'

Pandita held a frail hand to her mouth, trying to stifle another raking cough. Mark rested his hand on her back. 'I think the time's right, before the others wake, for us to share with Grace what we've decided.'

The old woman nodded. Grace braced herself. Things were about to take a turn and she did not know if she was ready for it.

Mark hesitated as if searching for the right words. 'Grace, you know we decided to leave you here to assist Pandita with the hope of also finding Esta. I was going to go back to the farm on my own, but I've decided to take Pandita with me. She's not well and I cannot allow her to continue to stay here in her condition.'

Grace felt her heart race.

'We're not sure what the problem is. It could be that Pandita is suffering from one of the more serious lung diseases that affect many people in this area. I need to get her to a drier climate—a place where she can receive rest and better treatment.'

Grace knew Mark was right. Pandita was frail. She would need special care to overcome her illness. The woman had given herself wholly to the work at the shelter. She had run her race well. Now she needed to be rescued. Grace understood the predicament Mark was in. Her heart beat rapidly at the prospect of him asking her to take charge of the work at the House. Had this been God's plan for her life right from the start—when Joseph had rescued her from the militia and brought her to the orphanage? Questions flooded her mind. *Not of your own. Not of your own.* Grace listened to the voice that quietened her feelings of inadequacy.

Eventually, Mark confirmed Grace's hunch. Pandita took Grace's hands and prayed. She prayed for strength during the times Grace would feel like giving up. She prayed for a fire in Grace's soul during the times she would feel the flames dying. She prayed for the fruit that Grace would bear in her Christian walk, and she asked that Christ himself would be the one to prune so that she would bear more fruit in the months that lay ahead. Above all else, Pandita prayed that Grace would have the wisdom of God. It was the wise who could see God's plan for the lost. God had prepared Grace for this time.

***

Grace learned a great deal from Mark and Pandita in those early hours around the warmth of the stove. The old woman took it upon herself to give Grace as much information as she could. Grace would need to recognise the challenges she would be facing at the shelter.

It was difficult for Grace to accept that as the girls of the shelter slept safely in their warm beds, countless others were being abused or sold on the streets of Mumbai. She was astonished to learn that India was among the highest countries in the world where young children are routinely trafficked.

Mumbai, formerly known as Bombay, is India's fifth most densely populated city. India was built on what was once an archipelago of seven islands previously ruled by the British. The Maharashtra State with its great city has the largest and oldest red-light district in India. In the nineteenth and twentieth centuries, it was believed that a vast number of women and girls from continental Europe and as far as Japan were trafficked into the Kamathipura area of Mumbai. Here the girls were used to serve British soldiers and Indian men. The situation grew worse till women from as high up as Nepal were being trafficked for this purpose. Grace was interested to know how the local girls, especially those from the rural areas, had come to the red-light district to find work.

'Poverty is what draws them to Kamathipura,' Pandita said. Her eyes were soft—those of a woman who had seen much suffering in her time.

'The people here, and especially those in the countryside, are extremely poor. Their beautiful daughters are forced to relieve the financial burdens of their families. They come to Mumbai in the hope of finding work in restaurants or as housemaids. However, they are pressured and sometimes even kidnapped to be sold and groomed as sex slaves in the prostitution industry.'

The old woman dabbed at her eyes with the hem of her dress. Grace felt her heart soften. Would she ever have the strength of Pandita?

'Kamathipura consists of about two dozen avenues, and the living conditions for most who live here are cramped and squalid.' Mark picked up the conversation, allowing Pandita time to rest.

Grace reflected on what her friends were telling her. It was as if time had stood still in the area. She had noticed tall buildings in the distance when they first arrived. They were being modishly erected above the squalor, like princes of plenty ruling over their poor subjects. She closed her eyes and felt ashamed to be called human. The life that God had breathed into humanity appeared to have little value here.

'Today, there are countless brothels in the overcrowded red-light areas of Mumbai, with prostitutes being handed out on the streets like candy from a basket. In fact, this building used to be a thriving brothel long ago. My late wife and I bought it for a good price when the madams and pimps fell on hard times.'

Mark looked at the floor of the warm kitchen for a moment. 'The streets of Kamathipura are a playground for traffickers. Some of the girls who are kidnapped against their will are held in boxlike cages when they are first trafficked into Mumbai. They become bonded to their captors through terrible acts till they are broken and have no will to run away.'

Kamathipura was a place of immense pain—a district where the insignificant and vulnerable are preyed upon for the pleasure and greed of their abductors. Grace realised that the only way anyone could truly help was to be the eyes and hands of God. She felt honoured to be sitting among such company.

Grace thought of Esta. *Could this have been the young girl's fate? Was Esta kidnapped from the mountains and sold into the sex trade?* As if reading her mind, Mark raised his head to look at her. 'You must take heart, Grace. In the centre of it all, God has raised his perfect standard of love against this weight of oppression on the poor. He works through ordinary folk like you and me to bring deliverance and give hope to people who are barely able to make it through to the next day.'

***

They continued in earnest conversation for a while in that warm musty kitchen. Eventually Grace heard the rest of the girls. One by one the younger ones came to greet their elders.

'Namaskaram,' each one said shyly, bending their dark heads as they tootled off to help prepare breakfast. Coal was collected from a large metal bin to light the fires for cooking. Ceramic jars were filled with clean water so that the bread-making process could begin. Some of the girls took the water to a room behind the kitchen, the entrance of which was covered with a thick muslin curtain. They began washing themselves. Their laughter and chatter immediately brought the House to life.

Grace noticed that there was not much given to education at the establishment. She made a mental note to make it her first priority. Pandita turned to her, intrigued by the passionate expression on the young woman's face. 'My dear child, you are going to enjoy it here. Not in the way others have loved it, but in the way God purposes your heart to love it.'

Grace smiled affectionately at Pandita. In the short time since their acquaintance, the old woman had understood that Grace needed to have time to discover truth in her own way and that she was not easily persuaded by the opinions of others.

'I see that the flame already lit by God in a place far from here will ignite into a fervent fire within you. The daughters of the house are going to spoil you with their love and devotion. Yes, Grace, you will be happy here.'

Satisfied that the shelter was going to be in good hands, Pandita took Grace in her arms. Grace knew that much work lay ahead. She was, however, grateful that God had given her Aayana and Alisha. Their support would be invaluable in the months to come. Such are the adventures God gives to his called ones.

After they finished breakfast, Mark asked that everyone remain in the dining room—he had an important announcement to make. He explained to the women and girls of the House that he would be taking Pandita back with him to the outreach farm in the mountains to take care of her there. Grace, with the help of Aayana and Alisha, would take over the leadership of the shelter. There were tears and hugs all round as the girls embraced Pandita. They understood that the woman who had looked after them for so long needed to be cared for by others. Some of them wept loudly for the grandmother they would sorely miss.

Mark gave them all some time to take in the new changes. He added that the schoolmistress at the Pathshala, a woman by the name of Aayshirya, was in fact a relative of Pandita's. He was certain that Pandita would be overjoyed rekindling their lost years when the two women were eventually reunited.

Things soon calmed and the older girls left to help Pandita pack what little belongings she had. Some of the others pulled away from the cozy gathering to prepare a meal for the two travellers—a long journey lay ahead.

Time was needed for goodbyes, which Grace encouraged. She was touched by the close bond between the people at the shelter. As the others busied themselves with the preparations for Mark and Pandita's departure, Mark took the opportunity to have a word with the woman he had grown so deeply fond of.

'It's all been quite overwhelming for you, I'm sure.' Mark stood close to Grace so that only she could hear him. He led her into the street just outside the shelter—it was a little quieter there. The sun shone brightly and some of the people were out and about. Large grass mats were being thumped vigorously over balconies, and the doorsteps leading into the many dwellings were being swept with small brooms. Others, who had worked the night, chose the shadows as their companions.

Grace tucked the free bits of the scarf Alisha had given her to cover her head into the neck of her cotton dress. Her attire was plain these days, but Mark was captivated by her radiant smile.

Grace lifted her face to feel the warmth of the sunshine. 'I have so much to learn, and I feel inadequate. But I do know that this is where God wants me to be.'

Grace added playfully, 'And I have help! I can hardly say I'm on my own.'

Mark reached for her hand. Although he spoke calmly, he found it difficult to hide the emotion he felt. 'You must keep in touch with me. Write to me as often as you can. My heart and prayers will be here with you all.'

Grace squeezed his hand. 'I'll do that, but you also

have your work. I don't want to bother you.' She added before he could protest, 'Do you think we'll find Esta? I know the chances are poor… but I feel that we will.'

Mark fixed his eyes on her. 'Believe, Grace. God knows all things. Pray for his mind on this matter. Don't give up hope of finding her.'

Grace hugged him. They stood there for a moment, two friends holding each other. Finally, Mark remarked lightheartedly, 'You know, you have more than what Joy and I started with.'

Mark could feel her warm tears dampen his shirt. He wanted to stay in Kamathipura, but this was not what God had prepared for them. Mark eventually pulled himself from Grace. He felt at peace about everything. The guilt that he had carried over Joy's death finally lifted. There truly was a reason for all things—even in having to say goodbye.

PART IV

Blessed be the God and Father of our Lord Jesus Christ,
the Father of mercies and God of all comfort, who
comforts us in all our tribulation, that we may be
able to comfort those who are in any trouble…
2 Corinthians 1:3-4

14
House of Joy

Grace looked into her teacup. She enjoyed savouring the fragrant Indian spices rising from the sweet brew. It had been some weeks since Mark and Pandita's departure, and there was still no sign of Esta. Grace remained hopeful, though. Alisha and the girls at the House spoke of a young Indian girl they called Little Saamaree—how she had not visited them for a while. The child's description had piqued Grace's interest at the time, but with so many things to manage each day, her curiosity had faded.

During their first weeks at the establishment, Grace and Aayana were introduced to the relentless vitality and impoverished reality of the people who lived in the district of Kamathipura. Despite the frequent turmoil often associated with caring for the physically destitute, Grace was content. It gave her immense joy to watch her adopted sisters and daughters ready themselves each day for the learning environment she had created for them. It remained a challenge for her, however, keeping the girls' education as structured as possible. Her school, she had come to accept, would not be a conventional one. Grace had to make do with the little resources she had to adequately instruct the girls.

Some of the older girls had had the privilege of learning to read and write. This was a blessing as they were able to assist the younger ones. Grace found the

Bible to be an excellent resource as it housed a wealth of stories and topics to teach from, and they became central to the endless discussions she had with her students. Together they discovered worlds, different yet similar, to the situations the girls themselves had overcome through the love of Christ.

Grace converted one of the first-floor rooms into a classroom. Although it needed a good paint, it was spacious and safe. Themes such as female hygiene and health were covered. Communication, English, and creative arts were her students' favourites. Aayana supported Grace wholeheartedly. The Somali woman enlisted the help of one of the older girls in making little desks that were mounted to the walls of the room—forty in all.

Aayana was good with her hands. She was not afraid to tackle anything that was akin to men's work. The two women took turns to teach, as extra hands were always needed when a new girl came to the shelter. Wooden blocks were purchased from the street vendors, and colourful patterns depicting Indian culture and rural life were crafted and painted on them. These were hung on the walls to brighten the room.

Alisha too, was a constant inspiration. She helped Grace and Aayana translate from English to Hindi when they shared from the Bible. The Indian woman had a deep love for spiritual truth. Her lack of sight seemed to have been replaced by a heightened sensitivity particularly of the girls' needs. She shared tales of life in pastoral India with them. The students sketched the stories she told with brazen colours—the sun, rice paddies, and warm fires. The girls produced on canvas and paper what they thought life in the country would resemble. Many of them were born on the streets—they knew little of what it was like to live outside of Mumbai.

Extra help was always needed at the house. Grace tried to keep the girls in their usual routine, but she felt that if they were to grow as a community and see to the needs of those not only at the shelter but also on the streets, there had to be some changes.

For the day-to-day running of the House, schedules were drawn up. Some of the girls were put in charge of the more challenging chores, others had to slot in for the lesser duties. Grace changed this arrangement from time to time to give the younger girls an opportunity to learn from the older ones. Everyone had an opportunity to lend a helping hand with the smallest and greatest of tasks.

The coal stove needed constant attention. Bread had to be baked early in the morning before the sun was up. The girls on kitchen duty would have to prepare the basic dough for breadmaking the night before. Electricity was generally in short supply in the district, and the people at the shelter went to great lengths every day to conserve energy. Most of their nighttime reading or studying was done by candlelight or kerosene lamps. Breakfast was held after morning devotions, and the majority of the girls came together to pray and worship before the sun was up.

For Grace, the time spent in corporate prayer and then sharing the Word of God was the most important event of the day. Besides school, the rest of the time was taken up with an endless stream of cleaning and sorting laundry. Maintenance of the old building was expensive, and the women did what they could. Occasionally, Mark sent money for repairs and fuel, but for the rest it was a battle Grace was happy to yield to prayer. The paltry meals served at the establishment consisted largely of vegetables cooked in aromatic spices and herbs. The broth was served on rice the consistency of porridge. Most of the girls were vegetarians. It was difficult to procure anything fresh in the area, and meat was too expensive. Some of them had taken to growing small pots of herbs which they kept on the sills of their bedroom windows. Grace promoted the sacredness of life throughout the establishment. She believed that they were children of the light, and where there was light there was Christ's love also.

One morning while the three women prayed together, there was a sharp knock on the door to the House. Grace had insisted, for safety reasons, that they keep this access as the only one to the establishment. When the knocking grew louder, the women hurried to the door to see what the fuss was about. However, they were ever cautious as there were some in the district who wished to harm them, so they did not open the door right away.

Grace slid the iron latch to one side. This allowed a slight gap in the door for her to take a peek outside. Unable to decide if there was anyone standing in the street, she motioned for Aayana to assist her. Aayana's height was advantageous in situations like this. The Somali girl looked for the enquirer but she too could not see anything—the street was quiet.

With her ears finely tuned to what was going on outside, Alisha pleaded with the women to keep searching. She was sure she had heard the faint whimper of a child on the other side. Although it was risky at that time of day, the women decided to open the door. There, lying motionless on the doorstep, was a young Indian girl, barely clothed and no older than ten years of age. Grace immediately thought of Esta, and her heart stopped. Taking a closer look at the girl, Grace quickly realised that she was not Esta, but another wounded daughter of Kamathipura.

The girl's dress, torn and damp, clung to her body. She was shivering—not only from the breeze that whispered eerily down the lanes, but also from the trauma she had clearly suffered. Too distressed to speak, the child cried softly. Grace briefly scanned the lane. Out of the corner of her eye, she noticed the figure of an elderly woman turn into one of the adjacent streets. The woman's yellow sari was barely visible in the pale light of the morning.

Grace bent to help the others with the child. Before she could mention anything of the fleeing woman, Alisha spoke up. 'Describe the woman you just saw, Gracie.'

Amazed at Alisha's instincts, Grace began to respond, but Alisha seemed to already know who the woman was. 'She is the old witchdoctor of this division—the *Daayan*. She lives on Third Avenue. I sensed her presence. She's been bringing girls for us to help for some time now. I've heard her say to the people on the streets that there is a healing light around the House of Joy... that people are rescued here.'

They lifted the girl gently from the street and carried her into the House. The older girls were called to heat some water on the coal stove. Others gave a little leftover vegetable broth with rice from the previous evening's meal for the girl to eat. Grace and Aayana threw some blankets together and made a bed in Alisha's room. Grace emphasised that the child would need someone to stay close to her for a while—someone who spoke her language and understood her needs. She assigned Alisha for the job. Although space was limited at the shelter, the rest of the girls made sure that the traumatised child's recovery was as comfortable as possible.

Everyone rallied around the girl. They were all well-rehearsed in caring for fallen daughters of Kamathipura. They had once been there themselves. Hearts and hands joined to help where they could. Serving at the House of Joy meant laying down one's life for your neighbour. God's love and care through his people would prove that he was their healer.

***

By noon the young girl had been cleaned and her wounds wrapped in bandages. Proper medical care in the district was hard to come by. Doctors were generally overworked and underpaid. Grace felt that Alisha should have some time alone with the child as she was the one who spoke the girl's language—a mix of Hindi and a local dialect.

Alisha enquired gently of her name, where she came from and, most importantly, what had happened to her. After spending some time alone with the child, Alisha softly sang a song of thanksgiving. When the girl's eyes finally closed, Alisha left the room to speak to Grace and Aayana. They gathered in the living room of the House, where most of their worship took place. Aayana served tea and Grace was the first to speak. She was anxious to know more about the new girl.

'Did she tell you her name?'

'I'm afraid, despite my promptings, the girl didn't share much. Perhaps we need to give her more time. Even a name of our own… for now,' Alisha suggested.

Aayana's face lit up. 'Let's do that. We love to do that in my country. The character of a child directs the name to be chosen."

'That's a good idea,' Grace remarked. She patted the Somali girl on her hand and then turned to Alisha, touching the young woman on the shoulder. 'Did she say... anything?'

Alisha turned towards Grace. 'Yes, she did. I'm afraid our daughter has suffered much in her young life. It's a miracle that she survived and was brought here. Her mother was a prostitute. The child grew up on Thirteenth Street. It's one of the more notorious areas in Kamathipura. She had two siblings who lived with her and her mother in a place no larger than a small room. They lived in squalor and the place scarcely had enough room for her and her family, let alone the many customers her mother served.'

Alisha sighed. 'The children stayed on the streets all day. They begged and hustled while their mother worked in the cramped room. They didn't attend school at all.'

Grace fought back her tears as she listened to the horrific account of the girl without a name. She interrupted Alisha briefly. 'Did she say how they all survived?'

Alisha took a deep breath and spoke like one who had heard the same story countless times. 'She's just like many of the street-children in Mumbai... and other parts of India too. They are the forgotten ones of our country—they are the proof of just how wretched life is for the poor. Her mother died, and she and her brothers and sisters had no choice but to live on the streets. They spent all of their time there. They slept in dingy alleyways and scrounged in bins for their food... and they got really good at hustling. Once, they got hold of an old sheet of canvas and made a street-cave out of it for shelter from bad weather.'

Aayana thought of her own life back home. Before the warlords came to ravage their villages, they had been safe and happy—mostly because they were surrounded by family who pulled together during hard times. Aayana asked, 'Was there no one to take care of them? What about their family?'

'Some friendly prostitutes, mostly the older ones who are more sympathetic to street children, gave our daughter and her siblings scraps of food when they could. Sometimes she would beg on her own from the passing trade, and this eventually led to her being separated from her siblings. Two of her brothers had joined gangs as a way to survive the streets.'

'What became of her?' Grace asked.

Alisha leaned closer. 'A young girl on the streets of Mumbai is much like a wounded creature amongst predators. Her father was a poor flower vendor. Because his daughter was beautiful, he knew he could fetch a good price for her from one of the brothel owners. The girl accepted her father's proposal. He promised her that she would be well cared for that she would wear beautiful clothes and glittering jewellery. Her new life would be better than the one she had on the streets.'

Grace thought of the way she had given in to marry Antonio. She had felt like a trapped bird at the time. She wondered if, in his way, the father thought that he was saving his daughter from an even worse fate.

'How old was she when she started working in a brothel?' Grace asked.

'She was just ten when she was sold into the sex

trade.'

Alisha turned to where she felt Aayana was seated. 'You may have noticed it's difficult to determine the age of these girls. They look like young women once they're wearing makeup and their arms are covered with fake gold bracelets past their elbows and with their colourful saris smothered in cheap perfume. She became a slave in exchange for freedom from misery.'

Alisha hesitated before she went on. For the first time during their conversation, Grace noticed her eyes fill with tears. 'Worst of all,' Alisha tried to compose herself, 'our daughter made a decision on her first day of working on the streets that she no longer existed. Someone else had come to live inside her. This is the reason she decided to have no name. She kept her true identity hidden from everyone. She's a broken young soul who feels she doesn't belong anywhere. What would be the point of owning a name?'

Alisha pushed on, 'Our daughter, dear sisters, is very ill. She has that awful disease so many of the girls become victims to in this business.' Her voice broke as she remembered the struggles of her own past.

Aayana took hold of Alisha's hand while she spoke. 'An even bigger tragedy we face on the streets is that when a brothel owner knows you are ill, they will throw you out—much like they will an old pair of shoes. A gang of young men found her on the street... she did not say what things she suffered at their hands.'

Grace wiped at her own tears. She thought again of the cherished story Joseph had shared with her about the king who found a bride in a gutter for his son. Christ came, she thought, to bind the wounds of the hurting and to heal those whose hearts were broken.

Grace finally asked Alisha, 'Are you sure about the woman who brought the child to us?'

'Yes, she's an old witchdoctor, who showed compassion for the child. The Lord used the kind heart of this woman from the dark world.'

Grace carefully considered Alisha's words. It dawned on her that God, who is the Father of lights, shone his light wherever he chose, even if it meant that he would use a minion of darkness to do his work. There was no other help around. Had he not worked in the heart of Pharaoh to release his children from slavery in Egypt? The abundance of God's grace and mercy overwhelms the human soul. It cannot be understood with the natural mind. *Now the Lord is the Spirit; and where the Spirit of the Lord is, there is liberty.* Though her body was perishing, the child's soul would surely be saved.

***

The days that followed were centred on the recovery of the girl without a name. Others came to the House for help. Some needed prayer, some comfort and care. Those who were in danger as a result of the increasing attacks of gangsters and religious extremists sought protection at the establishment. The people there ministered the love and healing power of God. Some of the girls they helped never returned to the House. Most of them received Christ and went back to the streets to preach the gospel to those who had not heard of him. There were countless stories of miracles during that time. Many were delivered from the shackles of sin. No matter where the women and girls traversed, they remained the daughters of the House of Joy.

The work at the shelter was expanding. But for the grace of God, Grace and her team would not have managed. They had become the burden bearers that the apostle Paul spoke of in his second letter to the believers at the church of Corinth. Of the hurting and downtrodden, they would take their petitions in prayer to God—a banquet of souls ready for harvest. They were the surrendered vessels through which God would touch broken people all over the area of Kamathipura.

Grace worked tirelessly alongside Aayana and Alisha, ministering and caring for the people who came and went. The House, in the meantime, remained a safe haven for the young women and girls who stayed there to escape a community that was constantly under siege. Here they were protected from being brutally pressured till they complied with the rules of the pimps or brothel owners. They were being rescued and led to find their salvation in the Good News of Christ.

And here they learned to dance. Alisha taught the girls to abandon themselves completely in true adoration and worship to God. They learned to express their gratitude and thankfulness to him in their work, their creativity, and their rest. Love shared with others multiplied in their hearts, for it was the love of God. They learned that all things beautiful and pure did not only exist inside the House but that it could also be found in the streets and alleyways of Kamathipura—a lone flower growing in the midst of crumbling alleyways, an old prostitute wiping the tears of a child who had been abandoned, and the warm sunshine that shone on the broken people of the district.

Grace never stopped praying for Esta. However, the hope that their paths would cross someday seemed more distant than ever. In the meantime, she continued to preach and teach about the liberty that could only be found in Christ. There were still many people who clung to the ancient beliefs of the caste system. These ideas saturated the architecture of the buildings and infrastructure of the labyrinth. It affected the way the people treated each other.

The days were long and hot. There were few electric outlets and fans for cooling, and often the heat became unbearable. Water had to be rationed daily for each person. Near the centre of Kamathipura, where the lanes converged, was a pump that reminded Aayana of the one she had had back in her village. She quite happily helped the younger girls fetch clean water from it each day. They would fill a large stone pot that was kept in an area just outside the kitchen and carry it back to the shelter.

***

Grace asked the Lord for a name to give to the girl he had brought to them. Even though she had made a miraculous recovery, the child remained weak. She seemed unable to do much except join the family during their morning and evening worship times. As the Lord would have it, an incident occurred where Grace's prayers were answered regarding her special request. It was around the storage of the shelter's water that this miracle occurred—and under the most unusual circumstances.

A strange custom of Indian folk, especially those of the poorer class, is to feed any living creature they come into contact with in their day-to-day lives. This is a deep-seated practice despite the prevailing reality of starvation amongst the poor.

Within the corridors came the whisperings of a cobra that had taken residence in the House. These reptiles are known to be highly venomous—even life-threatening. Alisha suspected the younger girls had been feeding the creature. Small lizards slipped through the cracks in the roof of the House when the rain fell. The snake was living behind the large stone pot that housed the family's fresh water. Small rodents were attracted to the fraying vegetable baskets and musty tins which stored rags for cleaning, and were easy pickings for an opportunistic snake.

Grace and Aayana discussed with Alisha the possibility of the fiend living amongst them. The Indian woman advised that it was best to first let the brute rear its ugly head before they did anything about it. Grace decided to remain quiet about the snake although she was of the opinion that the quicker it was discovered and destroyed, the better for everyone. Aayana, on the other hand, refused to take a passive stance on the matter. She vowed that she would not rest until the creature, if it truly did exist, was flushed out or killed.

Grace prayed for wisdom.

One evening, in the midst of all the apprehension around the cobra, the family seated themselves for a meal of aromatic rice and vegetables. It was unusually cool. Grace wondered whether this was a sign of the anticipated monsoon season. The sight of the girls chatting together and exchanging stories around the day's activities warmed her heart. The nameless girl sat between Alisha and Aayana, and Grace marvelled at how happy she seemed.

Suddenly, and to everyone's surprise, the child

leapt from where she was seated. With lightning speed, she grabbed the long knife that lay next to the *kofta* bread Aayana had made. The girl ran from the table towards the room behind the kitchen. She focused on the stone waterpot. Some of the girls followed her. There beside the urn, swaying fiercely from side to side, was the cobra. With speed and agility, the girl slit the throat of the snake... and left it lying dead on the floor.

Loud gasps and shrieks came from the girls. This was followed by nervous laughter that rippled like lit firecrackers around the room. Grace sat frozen in her seat throughout the whole incident, unsure of whether she should join in the commotion or not. The girl returned victoriously to the table with the dead cobra slung over her arm, the rest of the girls in tow.

Grace was the first to speak. 'Well, that settled the rumour!'

They all laughed. The family at the House accepted the fact that events like these— uncommon to well-off folk—were to be treasured; they brought light relief to relentless hardship. Some of the girls had removed themselves as far as possible from the dead snake. Others drew inquisitively closer. Grace gave Aayana a quizzical look, and the Somali woman stifled a giggle.

Alisha, who had sat quietly throughout the whole ordeal, got up from her chair. She made her way to the girl. 'Where do you get your bravery from? Today you've saved us all.'

The girl smiled at Alisha, then turned to face Grace. She spoke in her native tongue, and Alisha routinely translated.

'One of the girls told me about a story that Teacher Grace had read to her. The story was about a man called

Moses.' She hesitated before continuing. 'The man was sent by God to save his children from being the slaves of a wicked king. Teacher Grace said that many of God's people died because of this bad king.' Alisha felt for the young girl's shoulder, and encouraged her to go on. The child's eyes lit up as she continued. 'Moses was in the royal court of the wicked king whose magicians were trying to prove that their magic was stronger than the power of Moses' God.' She moved on her feet as she tried to contain her enthusiasm. 'Moses threw his rod to the ground in front of all the magicians. It turned into a terrible snake that gobbled up all the other snakes. When I saw the cobra, I knew it would harm us and that it had no place amongst God's people.'

The girl looked cautiously at Grace. 'God gave me skills to survive on the street. This is not the first time I've destroyed a vicious snake.' A wave of laughter followed. This only encouraged the girl to go on. 'I had to be rescued by you so that one day I could save you all.'

Alisha leant over and embraced the child while the others gathered around their new sister. It was at that moment that Alisha thought of a name for her. In light of Aayana's earlier suggestion, she gently offered, 'I think the name of our new sister should be "Saanp Hatyaara". In Hindi it means "snake killer".'

In the end, "Hatyaara" stuck. Although it may have offended some people on the outside, those at the House of Joy knew their story was worth more to them than anyone's disapproval. Grace thanked the Lord that even though the situation could have been dangerous, the outcome had given Hatyaara a certain confidence and faith in him.

The evening drew to a close as the excitement

abated. The women and girls cleared the table, happy that the threat of danger was over. Aayana offered to get rid of the snake. Grace had learned not to question the Somali girl's methods of disposing of creatures that were potentially harmful to them. What remained an ongoing mystery for Grace, though, was the frequent mention of the girl they all referred to as Little Saamaree. *Who is she? Why has she not come to the House so that I can finally meet her?*

***

Grace could not sleep. Esta's whereabouts haunted her. At times, when they all shared a special moment together, she thought of her young friend. Grace made her way to one of the tall windows of the room. It had a ledge that was like a small bench. She sat there for a while, enjoying her private view of the street below.

A gentle breeze rarely felt this time of the evening slipped through a small gap in the window. The sky above seemed expansive. Grace could not tell whether it was the sign of the coming rains or the name given to their new daughter that made everything seem inordinately clear to her. Such was the love of God—its length and breadth unfathomable. One thing Grace was certain of, God was at work even when prayers seemed unanswered—the solutions were in fact on their way. God is always ready to respond graciously to our faith in him.

Grace noticed some older prostitutes sashay down the street, their chit-chatter wafting up. She prayed for them. The older ones were generally more difficult to reach. Even though a pane of glass separated her from them, she knew that there was nothing in this world that could separate them from the love of God. Each day had to be taken as it was. Grace could not say what tomorrow held—it was in his hands. The fight she now fought was no longer one of self-preservation.

As Grace spoke to God in the way she had learned, she felt that it was time to make some adjustments in the way they were reaching the women and girls on the streets of Kamathipura. Grace realised that there were many who would not come to the House of Joy of their own accord. The believers at the shelter would have to take the Gospel of Christ to them.

The time was right to go out into the lanes and alleyways of Kamathipura to preach the gospel of Christ to those who had not heard of his love. It was good that they were a light in a dark place, but what of the many who were too broken or afraid to come to the light? Grace remembered Joseph's words to her, 'We are the eyes, the hands, and the feet of God. That is why we must go.'

The kingdom of heaven was in the hands of the worshippers—the life of Christ rested in the palms of the believer who touched those who were hurting. Before she retired for the night, Grace looked up at the moon and thanked God for watching over young Esta. She still believed that he would make a way for them to find her.

***

Over time, work at the establishment became more challenging. As if driven by an unseen fire, Grace and her young disciples pushed on regardless. Their work grew and began to take new directions. Grace arranged for the women and girls at the shelter to wear white saris. An old woman who came to help at the House from time to time was also a seamstress. She made the dresses to Grace's specifications. Skilled in embroidery, she stitched a small red cross in the centre of each garment.

Soft fabric straps were worn around their waists, and leather sandals were worn to protect their feet from the debris in the cobbled lanes. Aayana and Alisha made pouches which were fastened to their belts to hold the money they would give to the poor. Any food the establishment could spare was taken with them. They set out early each morning when the myna birds began their first chirruping. At times, when the women were invited, they entered the dilapidated dwellings of the residents. They even ventured into some of the cages where they ministered to the girls who had possibly been abducted. Their presence, however, made the gangsters and brothel owners angry. While some of the proprietors to these establishments welcomed the gospel, others did not.

Grace and her followers were given the name "Angels of Joy" by the people in the district. Grace arranged baptisms for those who gave their lives to Christ. This was indeed a challenge as water was scarce and the inhabitants of the district were prohibited from conducting any foreign religious rites in the nearby rivers. These waterways were strictly reserved for the ruling religion of the area—that of the Hindu people. Violating these laws could elicit a violent reaction from them. The people of the various districts often took matters involving the law into their own hands. This would usually involve a brutal punishment. Grace shared her concerns with Aayana and Alisha. Together they prayed to God for guidance to follow the instruction he had given in his Word to baptise those who had welcomed him into their hearts.

It was Alisha who found a solution to their dilemma.

One day after a heavy downpour and after having spent some time on the streets, Grace and her Angels of Joy scurried back to the House to take shelter. They were completely drenched. That is when Alisha came up with a creative way to have the new believers baptised.

'We must gather the people just outside the house when the rains come. Let the water wash over them while we baptise them in the name of the Father, the Son, and the Holy Spirit.'

Grace sanctioned Alisha's idea. The people of the district watched in amazement as the new converts lined up in the streets. The heavy rains poured buckets of heavenly water over their heads while Grace and her disciples baptised each one of them.

Along with all the blessings the people at the House received, there was mounting unrest between the Muslim and Hindu religious supporters. At first, the clashes were only small skirmishes between the faction groups. Religion rose against religion. Hatred spilled through the dense alleyways and lively corridors of the district as each group wanted their adversary to be driven from the area. The people at the House of Joy prayed earnestly for those who were affected by the constant fighting. At times the hostility seemed to subside—only to flare up again.

Grace prayed for Esta. There was still no knowledge of her whereabouts. She had begun to enquire after the girl on the streets while Alisha translated for her. The more Grace spoke of Esta, the more Alisha felt there was something familiar about the girl Grace was describing. Every night Grace and Aayana prayed that they would find their young friend.

In the meantime, Grace marvelled at the miracles

God was doing in the lives of the young women and girls at the House of Joy. Hatyaara was thriving, even though signs of the virus she carried had weakened her body. Grace's heart swelled with joy when she heard the young girl sing sweet songs of praise with some of the other girls before they went to bed. She often thought of ordinary folk who usually prepared for the rest they needed at the end of each day. For those living on the streets, however, this was a time of immense suffering at the hands of brutal profiteers. Grace imagined a picture of Esta. Her thick glossy hair and dark eyes were shining in the dark. It was a vision of hope, and Grace felt confident that the Indian girl was somewhere near—alive and radiant.

***

Esta drew closer to the warmth of the fire her little band of friends had made in the old bin near the flower stalls. The market was quiet now. Most of the weavers had returned for the night to their families in the dimly lit shacks of Kamathipura. Esta had not visited her friends at the House of Joy for some time. The streets had become unsafe as a consequence of the constant clashes between the Muslims and Hindus. For her own protection, Esta stayed close to where she worked and took shelter. Although the people at the House were always in her prayers, Esta's curiosity had recently gotten the better of her. She had heard, quite by chance, of an English woman who had taken over the leadership of the establishment. She wondered what could have happened to the old woman, Pandita. Rumours had wafted down the lanes to her part of the district. It was said that the English woman was like an angel—she walked with her disciples among the poor and destitute, blessing them with food and medical care. The thing that piqued Esta's interest the most was that word on the street had it that the woman's hair was like the colour of ripened corn—spun with gold.

***

Like so many nights at the House, Grace concluded her work by ensuring all were settled and safe. She made her way to the kitchen—the back door and windows were often left unlocked by the younger girls after they had washed up. Just as she thought, she found the door to the street was closed but not locked. Before securing the entrance, Grace turned to see Alisha carefully tip-toe into the kitchen. The Indian woman often made herself a cup of tea when the girls had finished washing. While Grace offered to help Alisha with the tea, the door from the alleyway was pushed open.

'Saamaree!' Alisha cried. 'I knew you were near! Come inside, my child, there is someone I want you to meet.'

Grace was struck by Alisha's extra-sensory abilities. Although sightless, Alisha was able to perceive the people near her, even those she had not seen in a while. Grace was just about to point this out to her friend when the visitor caught her attention.

Could it be…?

The young girl looked cautiously at Grace, unable to speak for a moment. Then suddenly it dawned on Esta that the woman standing in front of her was in fact her dear English teacher from her old school in the mountains.

'Teacher Grace!' Esta threw her arms around Grace, almost knocking her teacher off her feet. They fell into each other's arms, laughing and crying together.

Alisha sat on the wooden bench near the stove and raised her hands to quietly thank the Lord. What was lost had been found; what was taken had been graciously returned.

15

Abdul hung his head low. He was tired. Too many gangs were wrestling for control of the Mumbai streets. Some of his older relatives had not escaped the effects of the riots in the nineties. The police had cracked down on gang activity in the area causing them to split and spill into other parts of the city. The dark alleyways connecting the maze of slum dwellings were perilous—this he knew too well. He had become artful at dodging the tangled cables that hung inches above his head. Abdul knew how to move stealthily up and down doing business in the narrow corridors of Kamathipura.

Surprisingly, the shadows that danced against the walls of the hovels with their flickering televisions and smells of fragrant curries brought comfort to him. He took a drag on his cigarette as if it were his last. Using his free thumb, he massaged a deep scar in his left cheek.

Abdul had come a long way and life had been comfortable till now. He raised his head to peer over the street at the crude building that used to be a brothel. It was now flagrantly known as the House of Joy. *How ironic,* he thought. The House still brought joy, but not for the clients he had recruited his girls for. Everything had changed since the Christians took over. There had to be something there—a mysterious force. It was transforming those who had once worked for him. He straightened his back to ease the ripple of anger that welled in him.

Abdul was afraid that the establishment would bring more attention from the authorities than he cared for. He had worked hard at maintaining a fine balance between friends and enemies. His motto had always been, "Have no friends, have no enemies". One never knew when you might need either to get you out of a spot of trouble.

For now, Abdul felt threatened. He folded his arms across the orange shirt he regretted wearing. The people at the House must not see him. There was a sound coming from one of the upper rooms. It was a song of some kind. He could see his profits dwindling before him like the ashes that were left after he had made a wood fire.

Abdul turned on his heel, his mood grim. The words of the song dug deep into him like the talons of a harrier. He felt weak. The young man had learned, however, that when one felt this way, it was a sign from the gods to stand up and fight—but not alone. Abdul would gather his fellow gang members to help him with his mission. It was time to take back what was his. He felt certain that his friends would understand that they were also affected by the new developments at the shelter. If they did not immobilise it, they would all be doomed. Abdul resolved to tackle the crisis the only way he knew—incite anger amongst your friends. Together they would bring the House down.

***

Abdul had been engaged in a battle for as long as he could recall. He had never known the love of his mother, who had died when he was a child. The rest of his family lived in rural India. Most of the young man's childhood was spent avoiding his father's angry fists. One day when he was barely twelve years old, Abdul ran away from the small farm his father had owned. Jumping a train with others like him—runaways who hoped to escape the abuse of family members and the relentless cycle of poverty—he arrived in Mumbai at the start of the monsoon season.

The train was a means of escape for Abdul. The trains that formed part of a massive network crisscrossing India symbolised a far-off place where he could dream with the other children. They shared stories with him about the opportunities that waited for them in the great city. Whether through ignorance or avoidance, they never spoke of Mumbai's underbelly where treacherous grown-ups and gangs preyed on the children escaping their rural misery. Abdul had nevertheless been excited.

The station was frenzied with hundreds of commuters boarding and disembarking. People with evil motives waited for the runaways. They lured the children with empty promises and illegal substances. Even the seemingly kind old ladies he came into contact with had ulterior motives. Abdul had, however, since he was a child, wisened to people's flaws—a quality his father despised in him and for which Abdul had paid a heavy price. Tradition at the expense of posterity amongst the lower caste often causes conflict between family members.

This quality had worked in Abdul's favour, though. He was able to avoid being enticed from the station platform by the pimps and gangsters who loitered there. Instead, Abdul had followed the other bright minds who collected plastic bottles from rubbish bins and places where people thoughtlessly threw their trash around the tracks. Although it was dangerous, Abdul had worked hard to collect as much of the garbage as he could. He had sold the discarded items to dealers for a meagre yet doable sum. At the end of each day, Abdul would be exhausted. Finding an old plastic sheet with which to cover himself, he would wedge his body between the steel tracks that lay amongst discarded lintels in order to get some rest.

On other occasions, Abdul joined boys who had made several old rusty carriages that lay half on their sides their home. The windowless coaches had no other purpose than to serve as a shelter for the destitute children who were coming to the railway platforms in their droves. Abdul had jokingly called his carriage "The Hotel". His wit had brought him some respect amongst the other children. Abdul's ability to avoid being lured by adults who patrolled the platforms in search of unsuspecting children had also earned him the name "Rat".

There came a day, though, when Abdul grew tired of scavenging for a living. He began to look for other ways to improve his income. One day he noticed a gang of boys jump onto one of the moving carriages. Forming a tight circle, the young ruffians prevented the passengers from gaining access to the eighteen available seats. The commuters were tired from their day's toil. Unable to find other seating in the already overflowing train, and to avoid further harassment from the thugs, the people quickly paid the fee the boys demanded.

Abdul was careful not to get too close to the gangs who controlled the station. In this way he was able to pilfer their ideas without raising their suspicions. In the months that followed, Abdul selected trains not frequented by the other criminals, for his illegal activities. Although he was able to recruit only a few boys to join his gang, Abdul quickly became a strong leader amongst them. Having a tendency for vice, Abdul soon rose in the ranks of the wider criminal hierarchy. Before long the more experienced gang leaders noticed his blatant guile. Consequently, Abdul was hired by them for more sinister activities. His job was to lure young girls from their poor villages to the red-light district of Mumbai. Here the girls were sold off as prostitutes to brothel owners. These activities brought Grace and her work at the House of Joy in direct conflict with Abdul's new occupation. Most of the time Abdul promised the fathers, who were poor farmers, domestic work for their daughters in the city. Nonetheless, he did not find his new job that challenging, and was surprised at how the fathers handed their daughters over so readily. Some of the families who had many daughters found Abdul's proposition indeed more lucrative than farming.

***

Grace began each day at the House with an expectancy of what God would do through her and her helpers. The women and girls at the shelter had suffered inordinate trauma. Their healing required human attachments that would help them to trust people. Accordingly, each day was addressed as it was presented. Everyone helped where they could. If there were problems that could not be solved, Grace would personally take them to the Lord at the end of the day to pray for guidance, just as Pandita had advised her.

A consistent life of faith is what helped the women and girls at the shelter grow in the forgiveness and love of God. Much like the sun that rose each morning to cleanse all that had been soiled the night before, the destitute souls were washed by God's mercy.

Grace was led to pray when she felt troubled. Although unsure of the source, she had of late felt a sinister presence lurking near the establishment. She had been warned about the clashes between the gangs and the constant conflict between Muslim and Hindu... perhaps this was the reason for her apprehension.

Grace had become used to the knife fights and skirmishes in the streets of Kamathipura. She kept the women and girls locked in the shelter when news of such outbreaks reached the House. This time, though, her concerns were disturbing. To confound matters, Grace had recently noticed a young Indian man, who wore an orange shirt, peeping through the tall windows of the shelter. Although the people at the House were quite used to curious onlookers, the man's presence still troubled her.

***

Abdul wiped his mouth with the back of his hand. The chicken leg had left a greasy trail on his face. He took his time finishing his meal. Still eating, he eyed the men he had gathered in his small koli. They were restless. Some had had prior engagements. Others felt uncomfortable meeting so close to the House of Joy.

Abdul used their unease to his advantage. It was easier to stir an already agitated group.

Eventually he stood up.

'Make fast, Abdul, make fast!' one of the gang members shouted from the back. The man spoke rapidly in Hindi. 'We have a big mission tonight. Some girls are coming in from the mountains.'

'Make fast, Abdul!' the rest of the men shouted together.

Abdul paced the floor thinking of a way to persuade the men to join him. They had to get rid of the shelter and the woman who had become a threat to their business.

Abdul explained the situation and his concerns to the men. He went on to tell them that the woman with the gold hair was, in reality, stealing their profits. She was enticing the girls from the clutches of the gangs and madams who ran the brothels with lies about a better life.

Abdul threw his hands in the air and accentuated his words for dramatic effect.

'In fact,' he proclaimed, 'the House of Joy is destroying the livelihood of the whole district!'

With that the gang of men rose from where they were sitting. Arming themselves with sticks and knives, they left Abdul's koli and took to the streets of Kamathipura—to the place that housed the Christians. Abdul did not follow the men, who were too enraged to notice his absence. As they continued their march, other men with nothing better to do joined them. The mob grew larger as they snaked through the alleyways like a determined serpent towards the shelter.

***

Alisha was awakened by a loud noise beneath her bedroom window. She shared one of the rooms on the first floor with Aayana, who was still asleep. Putting her gown on, she slipped down the stairs that separated the upper floor from the lower area where most of their work took place. Clutching the railings so that she did not miss a step, Alisha ran to Grace's room. She nearly stumbled over the spare mattress which was permanently kept on the floor of the bedroom for Esta when she needed shelter for the night.

Grace was already awake. Alisha greeted her anxiously, 'What's happening in the streets? It sounds like a furious crowd outside.' Alisha's voice was still trembling.

Grace walked over to her. She steered Alisha away from the window, then drew the curtains a little. A gang of men chanted angrily in the street below. Grace's worst fears were upon them. Mark had warned her that the greatest threat to the survival of the people at the House of Joy would mostly come from the gangs or other religious parties that inhabited Kamathipura. The rescue and care of the young women and girls would always be in direct conflict with their mission.

Grace closed the curtains. The two women began to pray. They prayed for God's protection and for his ministering angels to guard the house. As they knelt together the door to Grace's bedroom flew open. Aayana and the rest of the frightened girls rushed in to join them, their bodies crammed into the confines of the small space.

They fell to their knees at once and joined their sisters in prayer. Their voices could be heard rising above the chanting below.

Unbeknown to the Christians, a young Indian man, wearing an orange shirt and standing separately from the mob, stood aghast as he looked up at the house. A white light so bright it could not have come from a human place surrounded the shelter. Abdul's heart raced. He slunk into his koli. Too afraid to move, he wiped at the beads of sweat that had gathered across his brow.

The next morning was unusually quiet—the silence

one usually feels before a storm is about to break, when the wind has calmed but refuses to leave.

When Grace woke, she routinely committed the day in prayer. She felt confident that God would warn her before there was another riot. She made her way to the kitchen knowing that Esta would probably stop by to fill her in on the recent unrest in the area. Grace would have loved to have had Esta stay with them permanently. She accepted, though, and even rejoiced in the fact, that the young girl had become their Samaritan of the streets. Esta frequently brought young girls and women who had been sold into slavery to the establishment to find refuge.

Grace brewed some coffee on the coal stove, a luxury she rarely allowed herself and which reminded her of her beloved Colombia. She sat close to the warmth of the hob. She closed her eyes to meditate on some scripture verses she had read that morning. God had encouraged the prophet Isaiah about the coming salvation of his Son. He would bring comfort and beauty to the poor. He would give to them his joy to replace their sorrow. Just as Jesus calmed the sea that was threatening to tip the boat of his disciples, the beloved Shepherd would also calm her own heart.

Grace sighed. She gazed out the window of the warm kitchen and spotted Esta dodging the debris of rock and glass in the street. The girl's unflagging spirit ignored the wreckage as if the rioting had not occurred at all. It dawned on Grace that Esta had just given her the best illustration of peace in the heart that defies understanding.

On the other side of the street, Abdul also noticed the Indian girl making her way towards the shelter. He lit his paraffin stove and placed some *chapati* in a pan to warm. His mind raced. There had to be a way to rid himself of the Christians. So far none of his plans had worked, and what of the bright light he had witnessed? There had been no explanation for it. Perhaps he was hallucinating—the result of a tired mind. Whatever the reason, he must put these doubtful intrusions out of his mind. Although his recent experiences were by far the most challenging, Abdul would find a way to shut the House for good. Perhaps the solution was right in front of him.

Back at the shelter, Grace greeted Esta as she entered the warm kitchen from the alley that separated Abdul's koli from the shelter. They hugged. Since finding Esta again, Grace's attachment to the girl had deepened. She thanked God each day for answered prayers. Even though their relationship was unconventional, Esta was like a daughter to Grace. All the girls held a special place in her heart, but as far as Esta was concerned, the bond between them had cemented from their first meeting at the Pathshala.

Esta called Grace "Maan"—mother, in Hindi.

'It's good to see you, Maan. I heard what happened and came as quickly as I could. I'm sure the situation has troubled you.' Esta continued without waiting for Grace's response. 'I know the man behind all of this. His name is Abdul Farooki. He wants nothing more than to see the destruction of the shelter.'

Grace thought she must say something in defense of the shelter, but her strength had left her. Esta threw her arms around Grace as if she were saving her from some terrible calamity. Grace gently motioned for her to sit for a bit. She served the girl some of the coffee she had made.

'Thank you for coming to us, my child... for being our eyes and ears in the streets. I know it's not easy for you. My heart aches each time you have to leave. But…' Grace's voice faltered, 'it's not to us you belong.'

Grace squeezed Esta's hand before she went on. 'Now, this Abdul. Why do you think he has such an obsessive interest in what we're doing here?'

They spoke for a long while, like a mother and daughter will when facing things in the world that are too great for them to bear alone. Grace shared her concerns with Esta who, in turn, acknowledged Grace's apprehension. Esta promised to take care of herself. She described the situation at the station platforms—how hundreds of young children, especially girls, were being exploited by traffickers. Esta went on to say how she had heard of Abdul Farooki, and how those at the stations feared him. He was the leader of a notorious gang and would stop at nothing to get what he wanted. They sat for a while in the silence that followed. Grace did not it know then, but Abdul would use with cunning industry the thing dearest to her heart to carry out his evil plans.

Sensing the need to move on, Esta rose from her seat and excused herself. 'There is a train coming from Thane. There are bound to be those who need help when they arrive at the station.' Esta had previously told Grace that she had connected with a loose network of charities and organisations that worked relentlessly to dismantle the giant web of trafficking at the stations. Sensing the girl's urgency, Grace released her with a warm hug. It was one that always left Grace with a sense of uncertainty. She was never sure when or if she would see her daughter again. With God's help, Grace had found Esta. His will for the broken people of Kamathipura was all that mattered now.

They said their goodbyes. Sensing the prospect of

danger close, Grace called for a meeting with Alisha and Aayana to discuss Abdul and his evil plans. They would also pray for God's leadership in the matter, which was far more serious than they even realised.

An old brass bell that hung in the centre of the living room was still in working order. Grace used the bell to alert the women and girls if there was an emergency at the shelter. She pulled on the bell as hard as she could. Its sound reverberated throughout the establishment. Little by little the girls came through to the living area. It was quite early, some of them were still in their sleepwear.

Calmly, Grace addressed them all. She had learned by now that, unlike girls raised in safe homes, she could be as direct and informative about the situation as she wanted. These girls had been through so much already. This time, however, they had the support and care that should have been theirs from the very beginning.

'Come a little closer,' Grace entreated. 'There's something important I must tell you all. The gangs of our streets led by a young man, Abdul Farooki, are threatening to shut us down by whatever means they think possible. Their threats are real, not just empty words.'

Grace looked through the window as she spoke, searching for the villain, Abdul. A glint of resistance shone in her eyes. 'I've been praying with our older sisters about the situation, but we've not had a word from our Lord as to what we should do. We're waiting on him for guidance. As you know, our Saviour knows all things. He will give us wisdom to resolve this terrible situation we find ourselves in. For now, we'll have to take extra care. There'll be some new rules added to our daily schedule to ensure that you all stay out of harm's way.'

With Alisha and Aayana's help, Grace put together

a schedule that was aimed at keeping their work and ministry low for a while. This was one of the most difficult undertakings for Grace since her journey to India. She had long felt a burning desire to conquer every inch of India for God. Now that same fire was appeasing her, demanding that she stand back to see God's miraculous hand at work on their behalf.

There would no longer be walks in the streets. Most of their ministry—for only a short while, they hoped—would be indoors. Lights out would be earlier than usual, to keep the hoodlums from looking through the windows. Candles and low lanterns would be used in case of an emergency. The girls were instructed not to run any errands alone. *Always have a group of sisters with you for safety* became their daily maxim.

'Do not cease to pray for one another and for the beautiful people of Kamathipura,' was the advice Grace gave to her family. Through prayer the soul gave up its own will in order to hand all things over to God.

***

The weeks rolled on without event. The women and girls at the House went about their daily chores, quieter than usual. While Grace and the older women were locking up one evening, an unusual incident occurred. Aayana had shared from the Book of Esther, and the meeting had closed with songs and prayers of thanksgiving. After everyone retired, Grace did her usual rounds to ensure that the girls were settled safely for the night. She felt comforted to see them sleeping peacefully—heads turned to one side against their soft pillows, their velvety skins shimmering in the moonlight. The look of peace and contentment on their faces stirred Grace's heart. Like Esther, they too would be used to help others like them find freedom. He had replaced their ashes for beauty.

As Grace looked at their sweet faces, she saw a vision. A large heap of rubbish appeared in front of her. It was a place where people had thrown their waste for years. She saw a man make his way towards the dump, riding a magnificent pale horse. The man wore a white robe, and on his head was a crown of thorns. In his left hand he held a cluster of stars. With his other hand he took from the pile of rubbish a broken bottle, a discarded shoe, a tattered frock, and some shredded paper. From this seemingly soiled collection of unwanted materials, the man fashioned a person. He poured his own light into his creation, which was at once surrounded by a brilliant glow. Pleased with his workmanship the rider began to form other people from the heap. He adorned them all with the stars he held in his left hand, as if he were sprinkling gold dust on them.

The rubbish eventually faded, and in its place stood a vast meadow of green. Flowers pushed through the lush grass producing a spectacular kaleidoscope of brilliant colours. Children came to play in the meadow and to drink from the sweet stream that ran through it. Grace immediately understood—that whether they were here on earth or with God in heaven, he would make all things beautiful in his time.

Before turning in, she checked on the younger girls who slept in a small area adjoining her room. Hamila, Tshwari and Yuditha shared the same sleeping area. Their door was ajar, and inside a lantern glowed softly in the dark. Grace entered the room quietly to put out the small flame. It was then that she noticed one of the beds was empty. Hamila and Tshwari were sound asleep, but there was no sign of Yuditha—and the child's bed was untouched. Grace tried to recall if she had seen the girl at Bible study. She came to the conclusion that she had in fact not seen Yuditha at all. Grace panicked—the child was clearly missing.

Grace quickly made her way to where Aayana and Alisha slept with some of the other girls. The two women were praying together but they looked up when Grace entered their room.

'Sisters, Yuditha is missing from her room.' The panic in Grace's voice brought the two women to their feet.

Alisha put her arms around Grace and tried to console her. 'I'm afraid the recent threats to the House have unsettled us. Don't be so concerned; she must be around here somewhere. The doors to the House are well barricaded. Let's think of where a little one could wander off this time of night.'

Grace thought of the time Yuditha was first brought to the House of Joy. It was only a year ago that she had held the body of the tiny girl in her arms. Yuditha had arrived by train with other youngsters looking to escape their impoverished lives in the mountains. She was amongst the youngest of the children Grace had heard of. Like many others, Yuditha had been trafficked. The girl's situation, however, had had a different outcome.

The madam, under whose control Yuditha eventually found herself, had had family who owned sweatshops throughout the greater Mumbai area. Yuditha was handed over to them to be trained as a carpet weaver. The woman thought she was doing the child a favour by keeping her off the streets. Yuditha did not earn a wage, but was given a little food each day and a space to sleep on the factory floor. She had become the victim of a large network of child carpet factory workers—almost a million worldwide. These children remain illegally employed to this day, making hand-woven rugs sold to wealthy people.

The factory where Yuditha worked was monitored by an inspector who was paid by the owner to keep from reporting his dubious activities. The man would call ahead to arrange a visit. This gave the owner time to make the factory appear safe and to hide the child workers. He told the weavers who remained what to say if the inspector asked any questions. During preparations for one such visit, Yuditha managed to run away. Her dehydrated body was found near a rubbish dump by a group of sisters belonging to the House of Joy. The women had taken Yuditha straight to Grace.

Grace had become particularly gifted in nurturing back to life little ones destined to die on the streets. For now, however, the mystery around Yuditha's whereabouts grew more perplexing.

Aayana, who was always one for action rather than words, swept passed the two of them and made her way down the stairs, Grace and Alisha close on her heels. Grace took hold of Alisha's arm to guide her as they tried to keep up with the quick pace of the Somali woman. Aayana took them straight to the kitchen. She noticed that one of the smaller windows in the kitchen was ajar. The gap was too small for a person to get through but was unquestionably the perfect portal for a small animal. Aayana placed her hands squarely on her hips. She tilted her head to one side and gave them a look that implied she had solved the mystery of the missing child.

Grace feared the worst. Perhaps Abdul and one of his no-good gangsters had taken Yuditha. 'Aayana,' Grace's voice was strained, 'if you have any idea what has happened to Yuditha, you must tell us. There is little time to spare.'

'I can't say that I know exactly where she is, but I can certainly tell you what she's been up to.' Aayana sounded officious. She continued with her deductions. 'Yuditha has found a friend. This new friend is like a cat, but it's not a cat. It's the baby of a cat—you understand?' Aayana turned to Grace, a look of frustration on her perfect features.

Alisha answered Aayana before Grace could respond. 'It's a kitten, Aayana—a baby cat is a kitten.'

'She must be hiding somewhere, playing with the creature. Yuditha knows Grace has forbidden this… for our own protection. I think the temptation was too great for her.' Aayana sighed, happy to have concluded her verdict in her best English.

Grace realised that this could quite possibly be the reason for the girl's disappearance. Aayana mentioned that she had on more than one occasion reprimanded Yuditha about the kitten—that the child should not leave the window open for the cat to climb into the house. Yuditha had disobeyed and had left a small opening for the creature to get through. The child had taken to feeding her new companion some diluted milk she had saved in a small cup after dinner each night.

Grace was relieved at the prospect of Yuditha being somewhere in the House playing with the kitten. The challenge now was to find where she had taken it, or rather—where the kitten had taken her.

'Follow me!' Aayana ordered the women.

Grace decided to first settle Alisha somewhere comfortable before they went traipsing around the old house in search of Yuditha. She seated the Indian woman near the open window of the kitchen in case the child turned up. Gingerly, Grace followed a somewhat impatient Aayana to the other side of the house which was mostly immersed in darkness. They ascended the stairs—the old boards creaking with their every step.

Aayana led Grace to the far end of the first floor. Then, just as Grace felt it was growing too dark to see any further, Aayana lit a lantern to help guide their way up a narrow set of steps at the end of the corridor. Grace wondered how the small stairwell had managed to elude her throughout her stay at the shelter. Perhaps, she thought, it was due to the fact that the women and girls never ventured this far. The second floor of the establishment had some loose floorboards and had therefore been out of bounds. There had only been sufficient funds to secure the ground and first floor levels of the establishment when Mark and his wife ran the shelter. Grace continued to trail Aayana. In spite of the lantern's light, it was still dark. She had come to appreciate that her Somali friend was like no other woman she had ever known. Grace trusted Aayana's leading completely. Aayana had no trouble navigating her way along the passage that led from the small staircase. The Somali girl was curious by nature and had a heightened sensitivity to the movements of all living things. It was because of her natural instincts that Aayana had noticed Yuditha's keen interest in the forbidden area of the house while the eyes of everyone else had missed it. It was the perfect place to play undisturbed with her little companion.

The moon cast frosty shadows against the peeling

walls that flanked the stairs, tricking the two investigators into feeling that there were strange people eyeing them in the dark. Although Grace felt her imagination was surely getting the better of her, the fact was she was not mistaken. They were not alone—and they were certainly not expecting the discovery they made when they reached the landing.

16

Abdul lit another cigarette. He knew he should quit but the foul substance had already taken hold of him. Besides, how could he focus on such things when there were more important issues at hand. He had to rally his gang together again. The small fires that they had been lighting were just not good enough. Their actions seemed to upset the people who inhabited the other buildings in the street more than those at the House of Joy. The woman called Grace had got to him. He was used to fighting till he was the last one standing. Only now, victory eluded him—something he would admit only to himself. A further hindrance maddened him—the people in the area held the woman in high regard.

'She has a certain peace about her,' he had heard them say. The woman walked freely up and down the lanes, helping the downtrodden with her following of young women. They bandaged the wounds of the beaten and comforted those who were hurting with their prayers and spiritual songs. They even gave food and money to the poor. There was a quality about the woman with the gold hair that could not be explained. Her feet, it seemed, barely touched the uneven paths that connected the broken lanes.

One person had asked, 'Could it be that angels are carrying her?'

Yes, it was time for something drastic, something

effective and permanent. Abdul had always relied on his sharp mind to get him out of trouble. This situation, however, was more than he could handle. Besides, there were enough men in his gang who were loyal enough to do his bidding. Surely it was time to pull the rug from underneath the light feet of the English woman.

***

Esta touched her cheek with the softness of the marigolds she had collected from Mr Shankar. The flower merchant had given her instructions to deliver the blossoms to a widow who sought comfort after the death of her husband. The woman would put the flowers at the feet of her idols when she prayed for his departed soul.

But first, Esta had to make some other deliveries. Her final stop would be closer to the shelter when the sun dragged its warmth from the alleyways. The Indian girl still bore the smile on her face that marked an amusing start to her day. It was an incident that had taken place at the flower market. One creature that owners of flower bazaars consider a mortal enemy to their beautiful baskets of blossoms—that dreaded adversary of all—was a rodent with a tail twice as long as its body and eyes, like the prayer beads the vendors wore around their necks. On that specific morning the giant rat, or so it was described, was found by one of the female flower sellers in a basket of rotting cut stems and bruised petals.

The animal had peeked at her from the basket with its murderous eyes and sharp whiskers. She had explained the episode with exaggerated animation. The accused was one of the largest creatures she had witnessed of its kind. The woman didn't stop there. The rat, it would seem, was probably quite accustomed to nibbling at the toes of humans. This would, of course, place all the weavers in immediate danger. The woman called for them all to run for their lives.

The ominous news spread quickly, and before long within the calm of that morning, pandemonium broke out as women and girls ran helter-skelter through the narrow pathways between the rows of endless flower baskets. Esta had looked on from her vantage point—a makeshift resting place she had fashioned for herself in the soft part of a tarpaulin Mr Shankar had stretched out for her over some wooden poles. She had not laughed so much in a long time. The only other time she could recall laughing till her sides felt like they were splitting open was with her cousins in the mountains of her beloved Thane.

The disorderly behaviour of the vendors did not subside quickly. Brooms made of dry straw went flying and baskets of fragrant flowers were overturned onto their delicate blossoms—only to be flattened by the screaming mob. Some of the older women, armed with sticks and lethal energy, tried to flush the poor creature from its hiding place. Unfortunately, with all of the original commotion, the creature was now nowhere to be found.

Esta decided then and there that it would be wiser to leave the scene and carry out Mr Shankar's instructions on her own. She could not wait to tell Grace and the girls at the House about the hilarious event. She skipped through the lanes until she came to a short flight of stairs that led to a section of the district she seldom visited.

Esta held the carefully wrapped flowers close to her chest. This would be her last stop before the shelter. Still mulling over the earlier events of the day, Esta thought of how God must have enjoyed painting the flowers in her hand and the characters of her people.

***

What was it that he really did not like about the English woman? It dawned on Abdul that there was more to it than the fact that she was an increasing threat to his profits. He had tried to avoid what he inevitably had to consider. It was the woman's teachings. He was irked by the spiritual lessons that spilled like pearls from her lips as she read from a book that rested in her hands. She had even dared to compare the clothes of this man, Jesus of Nazareth, to the humblest of Abdul's own religious people who wore sandals and simple garments. The woman acknowledged that the *maharishi* gave of themselves unconditionally—but she had quite brazenly said that this Jesus person was the true and only Son of God. He alone was the sacrificial lamb God had sent to earth to take away the sins of the world.

Abdul had never considered himself religious. He had always relied on his own cunning to survive the streets of Mumbai. It appeared to him, however, that the need for religion was in everyone—deep and hidden. It even caused men to go to war with each other over it. It bothered him entirely that the English woman had said it was possible for her God, who was holy, to live in man. How could this be? He knew how wicked he was. These lessons of hers were surely blasphemous.

One such teaching, through what the woman had called a parable, cut him to the heart. It had gnawed away at him till he thought he would lose his mind. Abdul assumed that after the recent rioting, the English woman would not have dared to preach on the streets, yet there she was with a beautiful Indian woman at her side.

Grace had preached on a subject she had referred to as "the Good News", while the Indian woman translated for her. A small gathering had drawn close to hear them. The first light shower of the monsoon rains had begun to fall but no one moved away. The people seemed to drink in her words. Abdul had watched the audience closely from the shadows of one of the brothel houses. He had noticed something flicker in the eyes of the listeners. It was a light that emanated from an understanding that had already been prepared in their hearts.

The woman had shared the story of her own life and how Jesus Christ had forgiven her sins. She had followed her testimony with a parable. Abdul had been engrossed. Her words were like fiery darts piercing the hearts of the people. The story she shared had been similar to the one in the book she held, except she had used Indian people to replace the characters.

'One day,' she had said, 'there was a man travelling from a far place. He came from the mountains of Sahyadri to visit with his family. As he was nearing the outskirts of the great city of Mumbai, he looked up at the sun. The man reached for some water in a container secured to his waist. He was tired and thirsty. Suddenly a gang of young men who had been kidnapping young girls and robbing old women confronted him. The thieves attacked the man and took from him the little he had—some gifts for the family he had not seen in a while.'

The English woman had adjusted her sari to protect her face from the soft rain before continuing. 'The gangsters left the poor man in the dirt... alone and at death's door. A priest wearing a bright robe happened to walk past the dying man. He was visiting a temple in the nearby village. Too afraid of the thieves who hid in the mountains, the priest refused to stop for the victim. Another man also walked by. This man was selling pots and pans from his rickshaw. He had no time to waste on someone who was not a potential customer. He ignored the wounded man and went on his way.'

The woman's tone had suddenly lifted. 'Just then, a Hindu man came along. The man was a taxi driver. He was driving a bajaji and whistling a *raga*. Although his bajaji was old, it moved very fast.'

Grace had adopted her best Indian accent. Although she was unable to speak fluent Hindi, her audience was clearly enthralled with the tale. Even the blind woman standing beside her had laughed.

'The taxi driver suddenly came to a halt. His eye caught something lying in the road. Was it a bird? No, it was too big for that. Was it a deer? No, the body had no horns.' The teacher had shaken her head briskly to emphasise the man's dilemma. 'Although it wasn't a safe area, the taxi driver decided to investigate the situation. As he drew closer, he noticed it was the body of a man—badly hurt. The injured man's clothing showed that he was a religious person... of the Muslim faith.'

Abdul had looked on while the English woman's audience had drawn back with a gasp. Some held their bony hands to their mouths while others gently nudged each other and smiled. Grace had confirmed that the wounded stranger was indeed someone of a different faith to the Hindu people. The woman at her side had also emphasised this fact while she translated the parable.

Keeping his eyes fixed on Grace, Abdul had listened in horror. His uncle had been killed during the Hindu uprising against the Muslims in the district some years ago. The war between the two religious groups had been a brutal one, and many had been killed or wounded. Abdul's uncle had been one of the countless fatalities. The streets of Kamathipura cried out for the vengeance of those whose lives were taken. The English woman would dare to make light of it?

Grace had continued with her parable, oblivious to Abdul's presence. 'The taxi driver was moved with compassion. He quickly returned to his vehicle and took from it all that he had—a bottle of water, bandages, and some neem healing oil that is pressed from the fruit and seeds of the neem tree. His wife always made sure her husband had these necessities in his vehicle, 'For just in case, Henri'.'

The English woman had moved her head from side to side as she imitated the wife. 'Henri is not the man's real name,' she added, 'but it would've been if he were English.'

A ripple of laughter had broken out, and a young man piped up, 'What happened then, Teacher Grace?' This was how most of the people in the district had come to refer to the leader of the shelter. The man had rubbed the base of his chin in anticipation.

It had dawned on Grace that most of the people who were listening had never heard the words of Jesus. 'Henri had such a big heart. He did not allow his knowledge of the man's religion to prevent him from showing compassion.' Grace's voice had softened considerably for effect. 'Using most of the neem oil, Henri bound the man's wounds with the bandages his wife had given him. The injured man began to stir. Henri could tell by the terrified look in the man's eyes that he was afraid of him.'

The woman they called Teacher drew her story to

a close. 'Of course, the man was overwhelmed when he realised his rescuer was kind and only wanted to help. Henri helped the man into his bajaji, making sure he was comfortable. He rushed his new friend to the nearest hospital where he was taken to the emergency unit. The doctors there helped the man to recover.'

Grace had lifted her hands in worship. As more people gathered to hear her, she thought it an appropriate time to ask them all a question. 'From the actions of the three men, dear people of Kamathipura, who was the one that showed love to this poor Muslim gentleman?'

Abdul had scanned the audience for their response. His mouth became dry as he listened tremulously to the woman with the golden hair.

The people had shouted their answer in unison, 'Henri!' The teacher had chuckled along with them. She embraced some of the people who were standing close to her. 'This is what Jesus meant when he said that we must love all people… as much as we love ourselves. Even our enemies.'

She had gone on to tell them. 'If your enemy is hungry, give him something to eat. If he's thirsty or needs a place to rest, provide this for him. In so doing, you may be ministering to the angels of the living God.'

The teacher had smiled at the people, the glow on her face warm and caring. 'We were all once enemies of the cross of Christ, strangers to receiving the love of God. God reached out to us by sending his only Son to die for our sins. He came to make us whole that through him, we can be born anew.'

Abdul had listened in disbelief. The rage he felt when he had first heard the woman's words was about to explode in him. He had silently slipped from the crowd, making sure that no one suspected his heightened agitation. He had turned his head to look back one last time as Grace and Alisha began to pray for the people who had gathered around them. There had been much excitement, as if they had all been taken by a feeling of great joy. The English woman had finally concluded her message by saying to her new converts, 'You will know that you are followers of Christ if you love one another—even your enemies. This is a peculiar, yet outstanding quality of a true Christian.'

***

Abdul was fearful—with the type of terror that alters your mind, tempting you to degenerate into the most iniquitous of deeds. He was amazed when an opportunity for the vengeance he sought like a ravenous wolf came to his doorstep. As if by chance, the gods had smiled upon his most corrupt intentions. It came to him like a gift wrapped in a dainty parcel.

Esta quickened her steps. It was growing dark and she had one more errand to run. A song she had learned at the shelter filled her heart. The melody wrapped itself around her soul as if to protect her from some future tragedy. She sang softly to herself, feeling the sudden need to find the place she had been sent to.

The young girl entered a shadier part of the maze of alleyways that connected the rows of dimly lit slum dwellings. She looked for the door of the house. Mr Shankar said she would find it easily, even if it was dark. It was painted bright red and had a fading picture of the deceased pinned to it.

While looking for the photograph on the door, Esta

was suddenly grabbed from behind and dragged from the main pathway. Her kidnapper pulled her into a dark alley. Abdul's face was the last thing Esta saw as darkness descended. She felt herself drift while streaks of light flashed before her—sketchy images of the day she was taken from her beloved grandmother to be sold as a debt slave.

Abdul had occasionally seen the girl on her way to the House of Joy. She always appeared to be carrying some great news. There were even times when she had another girl from the streets with her. He had observed how the English woman had welcomed the girl with an open embrace, and how the two of them had chatted together for hours. Abdul concluded that there was indeed a strong bond between them. Being the astute person he was, Abdul felt that to inflict pain on the woman—where it hurt the most—would be the best way to break her and finally bring down the House of Joy. It would be better than any other plan he could devise.

***

The landing that uncovered the dark passage was narrow. This was unusual for the type of design reminiscent of the older brothel buildings in Mumbai. If it had not been for the lantern Aayana held high above their heads lighting the way, the overwhelming darkness would have prevented them from venturing further. They shuffled furtively along the passage till they came across a tiny recess. The alcove was hidden in the wall. It appeared to have been purposefully constructed as an emergency exit. What lay behind the unique space was a mystery to Aayana and Grace. Realising they could go no further, which was curious in itself, Grace glanced questioningly at Aayana, who was clearly begging for an adventure. Grace gave her the go-ahead to investigate the small space.

Aayana raised the lantern above her head to take a closer look. Hidden in plain sight, her light revealed an opening in the back section of the wooden cubicle. It was covered with a large square board made to appear as if it was part of the original wall. Grace drew closer to touch the board. The frown on her face deepened. 'It's a trapdoor of some sort.'

Grace traced her fingers around the edges of the access. Suddenly she felt the board move against her hand as if someone was pushing against it. Always quick to respond, Aayana pulled Grace from the immediate area in front of the trapdoor. There was a noise on the other side. It grew louder. The thumping was that of a hand or foot. Grace looked on in horror as the board gave way. Bits of old paint and splintered wood came with it. Then the whole sheet finally gave way with a loud bang. Aayana and Grace jumped to the side to avoid further calamity.

In the brief stillness after the clatter, the two friends were shocked to see a tiny head emerge from the gaping hole. The face belonged to a little grey kitten. Its body was covered with fine grey fur, more like the colour of silver in the flickering light. The kitten turned slightly to observe its new world, its eyes like shiny marbles.

Then a second body appeared. Grace watched in astonishment as the missing Yuditha followed after the kitten. The child scooped the little feline in her hands, then landed feet first in front of Grace and Aayana. Yuditha was covered in dust and cobwebs. She clutched the creature firmly as if at any moment it would be snatched from her. Yuditha coughed and gasped as Aayana and Grace helped steady her. Grace could sense that Aayana was about to give their little adventurer a good scolding, so she quickly placed a finger over her lips, signalling for the Somali woman not to frighten the child.

Aayana conceded, and Grace was the first to speak. 'Gracious me, Aayana. Here we are taking a stroll and look who we've bumped into, our Yuditha and her new friend.'

Yuditha, still holding the kitten, glanced sheepishly at the two women. She decided to keep her eyes on Grace, away from Aayana's menacing glare.

'I'm sorry, Teacher,' she said in Hindi. Yuditha threw her arms around Grace, allowing the kitten to escape from her hands. The animal stopped at the top of the stairs to wait for her.

'I know you're sorry, little one.' Grace found her stern resolve yield to mercy. 'Just remember, sweet child, if you don't let us know where you are, we'll all worry about you, and this will make our hearts very sad.'

Grace stroked the girl's dusty head, and held her close to the hollow beneath her neck. Grace did not know why it happened then, but for a brief moment the cherished image of the inscription tattooed beneath the priest's collar flashed in front of her—*To love: Life's highest gain*. It was as if Joseph was reminding her of God's love for all his children. The Lord holds each one of us in the softness of his heart where he wipes our tears away.

'I don't want to make you sad,' Yuditha finally offered with a penitent look. Grace placed the child gently on the floor and winked at Aayana, who gave a sigh of relief.

'Sister Aayana will take you back to your room.' Grace turned to Aayana. 'I think we should call the new addition to our family "Silver". Don't you think it is quite an appropriate name for Yuditha's little friend?'

Aayana flashed a sincere smile, which showed her white teeth in the soft glow of the lantern. 'I'll get a bowl of milk ready for Silver before Yuditha lets him out the window.'

The child wiped her eyes with the sleeves of her nightclothes, and placed her small hand in Aayana's. The Somali woman looked at Grace. She said something kindly in her native tongue as she handed Grace her lantern. Although she did not understand what Aayana had just said, Grace assumed all was forgiven. She looked on as Aayana led the little girl towards the top of the stairs, thinking how special they both were. When one so young has suffered inordinate loss, they will look for someone or something to connect to. The human heart is created by God to trust again, even if it means breaking the rules from time to time.

Grace called out after them—she would follow, but meanwhile her curiosity had been stirred. She raised the lantern above the hole in the wall and peered into it. It was wide enough for one adult to crawl through, and sufficiently elevated for a small child to stand in it. Grace was astonished to see that the opening led to an extended passage. It was obviously hidden high above the old building all these years. She was unable to see its end. Her lantern did not allow much light, except for what was directly in front of her. Should she dare to venture further? Her curiosity got the better of her. Better still, Grace felt as if an invisible hand was guiding her. She entered the opening and crept stealthily along the passage.

Grace was surprised to discover an intricate labyrinth of dark corridors stretched out before her. Small doors which led to tiny rooms were the only breaks that interrupted the maze. Some of the doors were open, others were shut. She continued to creep along the main passageway. As she did so, she made another discovery. Through a tiny portal in one of the rooms near the end of the corridor, Grace noticed that the passage eventually connected with the neighbouring brothel that shared a wall with the shelter. A rustic door built into the wall was possibly an entrance to the other building. Was the design of these corridors a secret maze of passages where one could remain hidden from danger? Grace contemplated this possibility. The corridors and hidden rooms must have been used in times past when there had been police presence in the district due to gang warfare. Grace had heard of horrific tales where the owners and workers of the brothels were tortured. Some had even lost their lives during the brutal raids.

These corridors hold secrets, Grace mused. *They must have been the victims' only means of escape from the dense underworld of Kamathipura.*

***

Grace made her way back to the first floor of the House, still mulling over her recent discovery. The labyrinth of secret corridors that connected the old brothel houses together high above the streets below had fascinated her. She stopped outside Alisha's room. The Indian woman was already asleep. Nestled close to Alisha was little Yuditha. The evening's events had probably been quite overwhelming for the young one. The child had sought comfort in the arms of her older sister.

Grace sighed when she saw a little grey head with two shiny eyes peep at her. It was Silver. His chin rested confidently on Yuditha's neck. *Oh my,* Grace thought, *there are some things in life best left as they are. In time, the reason for their being will be made known.*

With that comforting thought, Grace closed the door and made her way back to her room. Before she closed her eyes, she read from the Bible and prayed for the man called Abdul. As she spoke to the Lord, she remembered the words of Jesus, *Blessed are those who are persecuted for righteousness' sake, for theirs is the kingdom of heaven.*

Grace closed her eyes to sleep. Almost instantly she had a dream that troubled her when she finally woke. Grace dreamed that she was travelling in a place so dark that she could not see in front of her. Blurry silhouettes of old buildings raced past on either side of her. The shadows grew tall and their points became sharp. Some of the family from the shelter joined her as she raced on. Grace did not recognise their faces in her dream but she knew that they were all dear to her. Then, out of the shadows a ferocious animal appeared. It was foaming at the mouth, its teeth flashing. From behind, a second canine appeared, then a third, and a fourth. The pack grew in strength, and advanced on Grace and her people. Grace tossed in her sleep but still the dream raged on. When it appeared that the creatures would surely devour them, Grace looked up to see a gigantic basket descend from an open heaven. The carrier scooped Grace and the people from the shelter out of harm's way, lifting them high above the clouds. While they were being hoisted away Grace glanced at the creatures below as they gnashed their teeth at the retreating basket.

In the calm of her spirit, Grace heard a gentle voice say, 'Surely I will deliver my children from the fiery furnace, for they have set their hearts upon me.'

The dream continued and Grace watched as they were carried through a white maze of clouds. Together they soared through a web of secret passageways. There were angels waiting at the ends of the corridors. Some of the people were taken from the basket by the heavenly beings. They looked back at Grace as if to say goodbye. Grace had never seen her daughters look more radiant—still she could not see their faces. A voice, deep and compassionate, called out to her: *He who overcomes shall be clothed in white garments, and I will not blot out his name from the Book of Life; but I will confess his name before My Father and before His angels.*

***

Abdul pranced around the small room like a peacock preening its feathers. What better opportunity could he have had than the one given to him earlier that day. The English teacher thought she was the only one the gods smiled upon, yet here he was with the best gift of all.

Abdul had succumbed to a degenerate mind where thoughts and hearts become darkened and where the truth of God is exchanged for a lie. His young victim was hidden away. She was in an area below the mysterious catacombs of the brothel building that shared a wall with his koli. His uncle had shown them to him one day. Abdul remembered longing for his uncle's affection, since he had received nothing from his own father. The older man had failed, however, to take the boy under his wing.

He remembered his uncle saying to him just before the man's passing, 'Abdul, don't tell anyone about these secret corridors. Our ancestors built them as hideaways before the brothel owners moved in. They were used to protect them from people who intended to harm them. You never know when such an opportunity might be put to good use.'

Abdul had since discovered that not a soul in Kamathipura was willing to speak to him about the secret passageways anyway. They avoided the subject for fear of the dead spirits believed to be lurking there. For now, though, he was certain that his uncle was not such a failure after all. His revelations had helped Abdul hide Esta from the outside world. He had hidden the child in a narrow cubicle above the flight of stairs he used to reach his small koli. It had a trap door with a small ladder that allowed him to secretly enter and exit whenever he needed to check on her.

Abdul thought about the ransom note he would write to the English woman. He licked his dry lips and rolled a pencil between his fingers. He must write carefully. Only a few words were necessary, but they must get right to the point. The shelter must close or he would take the girl from Grace for good.

***

Grace pushed her head through the small window that served as a look-out into the lane next to the shelter. The day had passed quickly. With the light fading, she waited for her customary visit from Esta. The young girl, who was usually punctual, had not arrived at the time she had promised.

Where can she be?

Something was not right. Apprehension had settled over the district. Grace grew anxious. She turned from the window and smiled faintly at Yuditha and Silver. It was time for them to turn in. Grace had softened to the pair and was constantly stretching the rules for their sakes. Silver ran in and around the legs of the little girl, tempting her into chasing him.

The kitten had made its way into the hearts of all at the shelter, but he belonged to Yuditha. Grace knew this was one of the better decisions she had made in a while. She had even purchased a thin red collar for Silver so that Yuditha could distinguish the kitten from the multitude of cats that scavenged the streets outside. Grace walked over to Yuditha while some of the other girls were preparing for evening worship and prayer. They were already singing a song in Hindi about the height and depth of God's love.

'Come, my child. You must prepare for prayers and bedtime.' Grace scooped the soft kitten to cuddle him. As she did so, she felt something sharp against her neck.

'Hmm, what do we have here? It looks like a note.' Grace pulled the folded paper from Silver's collar, taking care not to tear it. 'Yuditha, you must have missed seeing this when you were playing with Silver.'

'What does the note say, 'Teacher?' The child seemed thrilled at the prospect of a love letter.

Grace smiled at Yuditha. 'I tell you what, if you let me read my letter alone, you can give Silver an extra helping of milk tonight.' She signalled one of the older girls to collect the two friends, then she made her way to the living room to read the message alone. Before settling on one of the long sofas, Grace gave it a good whack. It was not unusual for the couches to be covered in dust—the old building allowed every bit of windswept particle into the interior. Grace was anxious to read the poorly written letter. The message was short and to the point. She read it for a second time… and felt her head spin. If what she read was true, then Esta was in great danger—and Grace was certain that she had interpreted the message correctly. Abdul had indeed kidnapped Esta. He meant to shut the shelter down, and if Grace did not cooperate with him, he would harm Esta in some way. Grace let the note slip from her hand. She placed her head in her hands to fight back tears and rising panic. For the first time in a long while, Grace clenched her fists in anger. She cried silently to the Lord, 'You cannot allow your servants to suffer this way.' Tears tumbled onto the tiny patterns of lace on her dress. Everything around her began to distort till all Grace could see in front of her were her own failures. She began to sob uncontrollably.

Then the door leading from the far end of the living room suddenly opened, and Aayana and Alisha rushed in. They could see that Grace had been crying. And as if matters could not get any worse, they brought news that could not wait a moment longer. Alisha placed her hand over Grace's, and was the first to speak. 'My dear sister, we have a serious situation on our hands. The Muslims and Hindus are headed this way. Their fighting has flared again. It's intensifying as we speak. They are burning down buildings… even ordinary folk are fleeing the area.' Alisha struggled to control the mounting fear in her voice.

Aayana drew close to Grace, who looked at them both through a veil of tears. 'It's true, Gracie. A great mob was spotted making its way towards the shelter. The men are carrying weapons with them.' The Somali woman's expression was grim. 'The Hindus want all Muslims and Christians out of the district immediately.'

Alisha composed herself. 'There is nowhere to go. We're completely surrounded. We'll have to do something immediately to protect the people here.'

The gravity of the situation began to sink in. It dawned on Grace that they would have to gather the whole family together and think of a safe place to hide till the chaos subsided. Amongst the members of the House, the younger daughters were the most vulnerable. Their immediate safety was Grace's priority. As she got up from the sofa, Aayana noticed the note which had slipped from Grace's hand. She read the brief contents to Alisha. They immediately understood why Grace had been crying—but they felt powerless. There was no way of rescuing Esta under the current circumstances.

***

Just that morning Grace had meditated on the words Jesus had spoken to the multitudes who followed him. These were the teachings of Christ duly recorded in the gospel of Matthew. He had taught his followers that the kingdom of God was like a mustard seed. Though the smallest of all the seeds, when it is fully grown, it is greater than all the herbs of the field, and in fact grows into a magnificent tree where the birds come to roost in its branches. Grace had thought of her own failings in light of the strength of her two dearest friends. Grace and Aayana's faith had been full of zeal before they arrived at the House of Joy. Now, refined by fire, it had become a bastion of hope for those who were weak and in need of help. This principle was central to God's kingdom and to their ministry. Here, the beat of his heart could be heard—the call to lay one's life down for another.

Grace dashed for the living room and pulled on the old bell as hard as she could. Although she had done this many times before, she wondered whether this would be her last. Alisha and Aayana helped Grace by rallying everyone together. They closed the doors to the main room, then gathered together to pray. Their voices rose above the angry protests and commotion that soaked the streets outside.

The sudden sound of a male voice and quick-moving footsteps interrupted their gathering. Grace was immensely relieved when she saw the doors being pushed open by her dear friend and benefactor. Although they still communicated, Grace had not seen Mark since she had taken over the shelter. But here he was… when they needed him most.

Mark's heart melted as he made his way towards the huddled group of women and girls. News of the Muslim and Hindu clashes had spread to the mountains. He had immediately treated the information as urgent and was determined to get to the House of Joy as quickly as possible. Some old friends from his time in Kamathipura had helped Mark make his way past Mumbai by boat. Mark had navigated the medium-sized vessel down a watery *wadi*, known as the Oshiwara River. Although the journey had been long and tedious, it was the safest way to get to the district. From there Mark was able to secure his passage into the area without being noticed. An old friend, Falak, who sold cabbages from his cart for a living, had hidden him below the vegetables in an empty crate. Mark had instructed Falak to wait for him in one of the adjoining lanes near the shelter, as an evacuation of the people living there was highly probable. Mark was concerned about Falak's reliability, however, as the rioting was rapidly closing in.

'I'm so glad you're all safe!' Mark's words had no sooner left his lips when he was bombarded by the women and girls who were overjoyed to see him. Reluctantly, Aayana and Alisha tugged them away and rallied them to a separate area of the room so that Grace could speak to Mark in private.

It was good to see Mark again. Grace rested against his chest while Mark placed a large hand on her head. He let her stay there briefly before he remarked, 'Even Kamathipura has always had a sense of normality—nothing is constant anymore.'

It felt as if their lives were unravelling around them. They could hear in the distance the sound of drums and voices intensifying into a terrifying crescendo. Grace took Mark by the sleeve so that he could hear her hushed words. She explained to him that on top of it all, she had received news that Esta had been kidnapped by a man who had been harassing the people at the House for some time. She was beside herself with worry for the child's safety.

Mark was speechless. He had been thrilled with the news that God had made a way for Grace to find Esta in Kamathipura—only to now hear that the girl had been taken from them again. There was no way of consoling Grace. Esta's kidnapping, it seemed, was just one piece of a larger trial they were facing. Although it was difficult for him, Mark felt it necessary to bring Grace's attention back to the impending danger. They had experienced numerous incidents like this before. These had blown over… however, things seemed different this time.

'I must get you all out of here,' Mark said with urgency. 'The rioters have a hatred for those of any faith other than their own—especially Christians.'

He looked out the window and into the street. 'It might even be too late.' Mark was angry with himself for allowing Grace to come to the House of Joy in the first place. What if he also lost her? Could he forgive himself a second time? Grace touched his arm with the little energy she still possessed. Mark must believe that God was still at work. Was this not the case with Elijah and the prophets of Baal who sought to destroy the prophet of God? In the end Elijah found himself alone and forsaken. God, however, had not left the prophet without help or a way out.

Grace took Mark by the hand and led him to where the group of women and girls were waiting for further instructions. The uproar of the angry mob was drawing closer. Aayana and Alisha formed a tight, almost impenetrable unit around the girls. Had it not been for the quiet prayers of her sisters and daughters, Grace felt her heart would have failed her. They would have to move immediately and quickly, but where to? Grace's thoughts were barely expressed when there was a loud explosion. A window in the living area smashed near them—then another. Within minutes the House of Joy was on fire.

17

Fire has traits that fascinate. It is equally hypnotic and treacherous. Once ignited, it unleashes an appetite like that of a ferocious tiger devouring everything in its path till its hunger is satisfied. A great fire came to the district of Kamathipura—a grim sweeper—leaving many casualties in its wake. It ignored the desperate cries of the people caught in its infernal grasp. Buildings already weak from their original constructions toppled like rows of dominoes—the hiss of half burning lintels could be heard for miles.

Small creatures that scavenged the streets during the day looked for shelter from the intense heat. There was none to be found. Already a huge cloud of black smoke had settled over the entire district. The fire that destroyed the House of Joy was started by humans—men who were angry with a religion different than their own.

A pathway of flames sped across the wooden floor towards the circle of people who were pressed together. The younger girls began to cry. As the flames licked their way towards them, Mark realised that there was no way out. He called over to Grace, who had scooped one of the little girls off the floor. The noise of the crumbling door frames was deafening. Grace could barely hear Mark above the commotion. Then, at that critical moment when all seemed lost, Grace remembered the secret corridors above the house. Perhaps they could make their way through the hidden passages to the other building that hopefully had not yet been touched by the fire. They had no other choice.

Grace prayed that the other building was still intact. She signalled for Mark to follow her with the rest of the group. Aayana and Alisha fell naturally into line at the back of the women and girls. The youngest ones were placed in the middle with two of the older women in front. Grace led the way with Mark, who kept a watchful eye on everyone. They were both thankful that the stairs leading to the first and second floors were still intact. By now the heat and smoke were unbearable but the group pressed on till they reached the landing at the top of the stairwell.

Mark ordered them to not look back. He was afraid fear would make them freeze. They moved forward, holding each other tightly… and no one noticed Yuditha slip from the grasp of one of the older girls. The child had caught sight of the kitten balancing on one of the rails of the staircase. She cried out to Silver. Above the sound of the crashing lintels, no one heard the little girl's cries for help as she plunged into the sea of flames.

In that moment, Grace decided to look back. She froze briefly with shock, but then immediately rallied to try to save Yuditha. Spinning instinctively on her feet, she rushed towards the railing. Noticing Grace's attempt to rescue the child, Aayana, with the speed of a lioness, caught Grace by the waist and pulled her back to safety. The first part of the stairs that led to the second floor had begun to crumble. Grace staggered to the front of the line as she choked back her tears. Her dream had come to pass. It was the only assurance she clung to right then. God had with him in heaven a precious daughter of suffering.

***

Mark kicked at the trapdoor that led to the labyrinth of corridors. Together he and Grace led the women and girls into the passages. The older ones went through individually, and the younger ones in twos. Grace asked Alisha to lead the way from then on—the Indian woman's extra-sensory awareness was more reliable in the dark. Most assuredly though, Grace could feel with them the strong presence of the Lord, a shield and light guiding their way.

They crawled on their hands and knees past the hidden rooms, pressing on to where Grace had seen the exit to the adjacent building. Heat and smoke rising from the fires made it difficult for her to find it. Thankfully the brothel buildings, although tall, were also narrow and tightly packed together. Eventually she caught sight of the door.

With a few strong shoves, Aayana and Mark had little trouble opening it, the door already weakened by the inferno below. One thing that pleased them was that the increased light from the intense fire pouring through every crack made it easier to make their way in the dark.

Grace's prayers were answered. The neighbouring building was still unaffected by the fire. The group knew that the building would not stay that way for long so they pushed on, hoping to find a gap that would lead them to the lower section of the brothel where they could find a way out. Grace could sense that the younger ones, although terrified, were also tiring.

Alisha suddenly brought their flight through the corridors of the new building to a halt. She spoke to Mark, keeping her voice low. 'I think I've found something. I can feel it but I can't see what it is.'

Mark constricted his eyes as a flimsy grid in the floor became visible. It was made of weak metal and had a handle in its centre. He took hold of the lever and lifted it. Then he smiled broadly. *Had Alisha found a way out?* Everyone was curious to know.

It was impossible to talk above the roaring fires from the other buildings. Grace edged her way to Mark. He took her by the hand and led her through the hole in the floor while motioning for the others to wait. A thin ladder connected the upper floor of the passages with the level below. The cramped elevation was dark.

Grace climbed down the ladder and planted her feet firmly on the floor. Then, without warning, she sensed the presence of someone else in the small space. Grace was certain that the whimper she heard was coming from a child. Mark turned his attention to helping the rest of the group down the ladder, so Grace decided to pursue the tiny cry on her own.

She fumbled around in the dark, feeling her way along the wall till she felt something soft and breathing. The child—a girl—was slumped against the wall. Grace gently touched her long hair which was matted and caked with soot. It was difficult to make out her features in the dark but, for a brief moment, Grace had a sense of familiarity.

Grace was just about to call for Mark when she realised that the whole group was standing in the room waiting for her. Mark made his way over to where she was comforting the mysterious girl. Without a word he took the child in his arms and lifted her over his shoulders, determined to get them all out.

***

They would still have to make their way to the ground floor before they could exit the building. To their surprise, however, they were already there. The loft where they had just been was part of a dwelling that had obviously been added as an afterthought or adjunct to the main building. The structure, although constricted, spanned two floors. Still carrying the girl over his shoulder, Mark led them to a small door which he had noticed in the far corner of the annex. He opened it and was excited to discover that it led onto an alleyway next to the shelter. As they all stepped into the light, which was magnified by the glow of the fires, the last thing Grace noticed draped over a chair in the small koli was a grubby orange shirt—the likes of which could quite well have been that of Abdul Farooki.

Their flight had inadvertently taken them through a labyrinth of corridors that connected with the building directly opposite the shelter. Mercifully, the building was not yet touched by the flames.

It was difficult to keep everyone together once they were out in the open street. Noticing the group's discomposure, Aayana immediately took charge, and it was not long before they were all together again.

Mark scanned the street. By now the House of Joy was practically a pile of ashes. Some of the girls began to cry as they looked at the ruins—everything they had loved and the little they had owned was up in smoke. The older women tried to console them. Mark saw this as an opportunity to divert the group away from the fire to a place at the end of the alley. The area was hidden in the deep shadows of the taller buildings. He told them to wait for him while he looked for Falak, still carrying the mysterious girl over his shoulder.

'Falak. Falak!' Mark called as he scoured the main street. The commotion from the rioting mobsters was still piercing the air. It seemed, though, that most of the angry mob had left the immediate area after they had burned the shelter to the ground. Mark called for Falak again. Just when he was about to give up hope of Falak's appearing, he heard the familiar squeak of the man's cart.

Falak drove his mules hard. He steered his wagon towards Mark with a loud 'Jaldee chalo!'

Mark was relieved to see him, and hoped that Falak had kept to their arrangement—to secure a boat for them.

***

It was a miracle that Falak's wagon accommodated them all. Some of the smaller girls tucked themselves into the empty wooden crates. The older ones wrapped some of the cabbage bags lying in the cart around their bodies to conceal themselves. Grace wedged herself between two of the wooden crates near a pile of limp leaves. She was about to cover herself with them when she felt the gentle weight of a small body pressed into her lap. Mark handed the unknown child to Grace before turning to make sure that the rest of the women and girls were safely secured in the cart. He then sat next to Falak, and the two men gave a resounding, 'Jaldee chalo!'

The mules pushed forward with their heavy burden. Although Grace knew their journey was far from over, she was thankful for the opportunity to take a good look at the girl huddled in her lap. She gently pushed the girl's dishevelled hair from her face—and saw that the mystery girl was, in fact, her Esta.

Powerless to shout her feelings of gratitude for fear of drawing unwanted attention to Falak's cart, Grace quietly but joyfully nodded instead. Just when she thought that after losing Yuditha there would be no hope of ever finding Esta, God had given Grace another miracle. And it was little Yuditha who had been instrumental in helping them find each other again.

Grace looked at the sleeping girl. Esta seemed so small and frail in her arms. She gently cleansed the child's face with some of the water from a small container Mark had left with her. Grace was unaware of the extent of God's influence in Esta's life, how the Indian girl's first journey into slavery had been in a wagon similar to the one they now travelled in. However, this time things were different. Falak's cart was taking them all to freedom.

Grace looked at the sullen sky and thanked the Lord for his kindness. Her smile was one of relief as the cart pulled away from the burning streets to make its way towards the Oshiwara River.

***

The river—one of the tributaries of the Indus basin from where the great city of Mumbai can boast its water supply—was a disappointment to Grace. Its lacklustre water lapped against the small vessels that sat on its shore. The group of exhausted women and children readied to embark. Falak was true to his word and, so it appeared, were countless others wanting to escape the devastation in Kamathipura.

Mark was eager to get them out of the area as soon as possible. He searched for Falak, who appeared to be negotiating a deal with one of the boatmen. People were climbing into various-sized vessels in their droves. Some, in their haste to leave, toppled the boats with their weight. During the chaos, Falak was able to nab a small craft. It was a miracle that they had all managed to squeeze into the cabbage cart—but that, Mark mused, was on dry land. Could God do the same for them on water? He had helped his servants in times of old out of the toughest of situations. Surely, he could do the same again.

So it was that, through a not-so-minor intervention, the small vessel left the shores of Oshiwara. There were gasps of amazement and wonder from those left standing on the shore. They witnessed the little boat chug into the murky waters of the river with twice the weight it was made to carry.

***

The Oshiwara River was once a great tributary that originated in the forested freshwater lakes of Mumbai. Drenched in industrial effluents and sewage, it was now little more than a narrow water channel. The pitiable state of the river was the result of the numerous slums and industrial plants that impinged her banks, spewing their toxic waste into her waters. For the little group that huddled together in the small vessel, their journey along the waterway was like entering the mouth of an angry beast. Occasionally, they saw a dead dog or cow float by. The river would eventually cut through the Yeoor Hills before making its way to Thane Creek, where they would have to board a train for the mountains. From there they would head for the outreach farm.

Esta stirred in Grace's arms. Grace gave her some

water to drink. She opened her eyes and offered Grace a faint smile. One of the women began to sing a song of the Lord. Her voice filled the boat, with its melody lifting the flagging spirits of the occupants. Grace listened to the song, thinking it may be Aayana who sang so beautifully.

As the words of the song trailed in the wind that pushed their little boat forward, Grace scanned the faces of the group for her two closest friends. They were nowhere to be seen. This was unusual as Aayana was not easily missed, especially in a space of such small confines. Grace strained her neck, not wanting to lift her body any more than she should in case she woke Esta. A sense of dread came over her.

A strong hand took hold of hers. It was placed there to provide Grace with the reassurance that all would be well. Grace took a sharp breath. 'They stayed behind, didn't they?' She closed her eyes to come to terms with the deep sense of loss she felt in her heart.

Mark looked ahead while he replied. 'Alisha was the one who decided to stay behind. She had already made up her mind about staying before we fled. You were so taken up with the marvel of finding Esta. When I pointed this out to her, she saw it as an opportunity to keep her decision from you. Alisha felt you had been through so much already—you looked so happy. She told me that she knew you'd understand that her place was in Kamathipura—with her people. The Lord would need someone to remain—people to rebuild the house and continue the work when things settled.'

Grace nodded slowly. She looked away. 'And Aayana?'

Mark squeezed her hand before he responded. 'Aayana was adamant that Alisha would need her help.

She told me that I shouldn't try to persuade her otherwise. When Aayana sets her mind on something, there's little one can do to change it—of course, you know that. We had to leave the area so quickly… it was impossible for me to argue with her. I do recall, however, her calling out to me. She said something about a caterpillar and a herb garden, that I should mention this to you… that this too you would understand.'

Grace remembered her first real conversation with the Somali girl. They had shared with each other, while preparing the family's meal, their personal stories, how God had brought peace to their once tumultuous lives. She recalled the time she had almost crushed the brightly coloured worm she had found crawling on a spinach leaf and how Aayana had rescued the creature from her. Yes, Grace understood. Aayana had been called by God to push against the boundaries of oppression—not only for her sake, but also for the sakes of others.

Grace pulled the veil of her thin sari over Esta to shield the girl from the sun. The tears that spilled onto her cheeks embodied her own feelings of love and loss. She rested her chin on Esta's small head. Then she closed her eyes again. Her sisters were never hers to keep. From the very beginning the Lord had fashioned them for his own purposes. As for Grace, she had the rest of her daughters with her. And Mark, he was taking them all home.

***

Their journey through the Yeoor Hills was quite breathtaking. It was as if God was specially there to soothe the waning hearts of the people in the boat. Here and there large patches of emerald moss covered the craggy outcrops. Their visible tips were mostly shrouded in mist. They passed many sacred Hindu sanctuaries that had been carved from the walls of the hills. The shrines were covered in broad-leafed vines. No one made a sound. Grace guessed the experience was overwhelming for some of the women, who had only known the streets of Kamathipura and the confines of the shelter for most of their lives.

Esta finally woke. She held Grace tightly, afraid to lose her again. She repeated over and over, 'I knew you would find me, Maan. I knew that God would lead you to me.'

Leaving the creek for the mountains of Thane was somewhat of a relief for the weary travellers. Here they were able to stretch their bodies and eat the food Mark had gotten while they boarded their train. The younger girls amazed Grace. They ran up and down the aisles of the hefty locomotive, tugging at each other as if the trauma of the last few days had not occurred. The girls tried to get Esta to join them, but she was happy to sit beside Grace and feel the warmth of the sun through the train window.

After making sure that everyone was eventually seated, Mark sat himself opposite Grace. He looked at her closely. 'What a mission it's been. I must admit at one point I wondered whether we would all make it out of Kamathipura alive.' He sighed. 'How're you coping? We haven't had time to talk, what with you losing Yuditha, and then Alisha and Aayana in a different way. You've had so much to deal with, I can't imagine how…'

Grace reached out and took hold of Mark's hand.

'If it wasn't for you constantly watching over us, none of us would be here. You, my dear friend, would've been our greatest loss.' Grace turned to Esta and brushed the top of the girl's head with a kiss. She kept her hand tightly clasped in Mark's.

***

The subsequent events were vague in the memories of Grace and her family. They arrived at the outreach farm tired and bedraggled. Their traumatic ordeal in Mumbai and the long journey to Thane had taken its toll on all of them. The sun had relaxed over the mountain that had so fascinated Grace on the first day she had arrived in Thane—a place of tragedy for the young girls who had been trafficked from there.

The smell of wood fires welcomed the evacuees. They were comforted and cared for by the people who had waited patiently for their return.

Hot showers were arranged and there was food for everyone. Grace helped with the younger girls till Mark eventually pulled her aside. He asked for one of the female volunteers to take Grace to get a shower and to finally rest in her old room—ignoring her protests. Grace was eventually grateful for his insistence when she finally yielded to the soft pillow beneath her head. Mark had obviously noticed that she was on the verge of folding.

Dawn was never more beautiful to Grace. She forced her eyes open to take in the first soft rays of the morning. How long she had been asleep was a question for another time. For now, she felt warm and protected beneath her covers. An older Indian woman was sitting in the chair beside her bed, waiting for Grace to wake up. The woman reached down and gently touched Grace on her cheek. Grace immediately recognised the soft eyes and loving smile. It was Aayshirya.

'Oh, my dear Gracie, we have worried for you. It's good to have you back with us. I've been checking on you every day now, praying for your recovery. The doctor's only instructions were for us to leave you to rest.' Aayshirya clasped her hands together with delight as she spoke to Grace. She was evidently overjoyed to see her friend again.

Grace sat up slowly and gave Aayshirya a hug. Despite her chignon of grey hair, the woman had aged gracefully. 'It's wonderful to see you again. I've missed you and the entire family here. How are things with you... and the Pathshala?'

Aayshirya took Grace's hand. 'We're all well and continuing with the ministry of the Lord. Things have improved since the quarry closed. The girls are somewhat safer now. How happy I was to see that you found our Esta... that you've brought her back with you. I never doubted that God would answer your prayers to find her.' Aayshirya chuckled before she added, 'I'm sure there is quite an adventure behind that story, but it can wait for another day. We must work hard to get you strong and healthy again.'

They talked—two friends sharing tales of faith and fortitude. They spoke of the beautiful people God had given and taken, and of Grace's work at the House of Joy. Aayshirya told Grace that she would be leaving for the Pathshala in the morning. She was sure to see Grace soon though. Feeling unusually sad, Aayshirya left Grace to rest.

The light outside was fading and the myna birds had quieted their chirruping. The old headmistress did not press Grace about the possibility of returning to teach at the Pathshala. Instead, she closed the door quietly behind her. For some reason, Aayshirya could not shake the feeling that this would be the last conversation they would have together about the school. Unbeknown to the Indian woman, Grace's return to the area had stirred in her a deep longing. A hope she thought had been buried forever.

***

The following weeks passed with some difficulty for the survivors. Recovery from their ordeal was slow. Grace was grateful to Mark and the people at the farm who gave of themselves unconditionally by way of care and prayer. Grace spent most of her time recuperating in the sunshine shelling peas, just as she had done with Aayana under the large tree. She kept encouraging her daughters, who were overwhelmed by their new home.

Although most of her work at the farm became mundane, it was also comforting for Grace. It kept her mind alive with the pleasant recollection of the Somali sister she sorely missed. Esta, on the other hand, recovered quickly. Grace was filled with pride as she watched the girl minister the Lord's love to the young and old alike. The Indian girl tackled her daily chores with great enthusiasm, genuinely enjoying her new family at the farm. It was as if Esta had returned to the mountains of Thane a whole new person.

Esta's family came to see her when they heard of her return. What a joyous occasion it was for her dadi ma and brothers to reunite with her. Surprisingly, Esta's father was also with them. Grace was pleased to see that the man had sobered considerably. Mark winked at

Grace from where he observed their generous reunion, confirming that he had had something to do with it.

Among Esta's family members was the boy, a grown adolescent now, who had been betrothed to her. Esta smiled at him—shyly at first. It was not long, though, before the two of them were sitting side by side on one of the low boughs of a tree near the centre of the celebrations. Esta read to the boy from the new Bible Aayshirya had given her. For Grace, this was perhaps the most precious outcome of all. Although there are sometimes forces beyond our control, God's merciful plan for our lives ultimately delivers the best for us.

Grace felt a pang of loss on learning that, in just a matter of months after the old woman's arrival, Pandita had passed from them to be united with the Lord. Aayshirya, in that short space of time had been blessed by her reunion with Pandita. It is recognised in these parts of the world that people who have forsaken the traditional beliefs of the majority are often ostracised by their families. Some are fortunate enough to escape being stoned to death. So, it was with much joy that Aayshirya received Pandita when she arrived. Their time spent together was like that of two old friends regaining, through their happy exchanges, the lost memories of their childhoods.

While Grace had been in Mumbai, Mark had erected a large shed on the farm's premises. Here he trained young men and women in various artisanal skills. Grace visited with the trainees and admired the work they were doing there. She was especially fascinated with the people who worked with the clay that had to be shaped before being baked into various-sized vessels for storage. Grace thought of the verse in the Bible where the apostle

Paul encouraged the believers at Corinth in his letters to them... *But we have this treasure in earthen vessels, that the excellence of the power may be of God and not of us. We are hard-pressed on every side, yet not crushed; we are perplexed, but not in despair; persecuted, but not forsaken... always carrying about in the body the dying of the Lord Jesus, that the life of Jesus may also be manifested in our body.*

Mark had done well. He had fought the good fight, demonstrating this scripture in his life. Grace thought of Aayana and the beautiful Alisha. Like clay jars, they had become carriers of the light of Christ, chosen to shine in the veiled places of the world. The Potter drew to himself his most precious vessels. Theirs was a life poured out as a drink offering to others.

***

Grace placed the empty shell of the pod she had opened into a separate bag. She lifted her hands and cried out with joy, 'Praise to you, oh gracious, Lord! You make all things beautiful in your time.'

As she sat there in the sun, a shadow fell near her. Mark crouched beside her while he took a handful of the pods. 'Everything's arranged. Another goodbye, but I'm sure this time it'll be your last.'

Grace reached out to her dearest friend. She stretched her arm across the width of his shoulders. Mark felt warm and strong in the sunshine. Her eyes filled with tears. She would miss him the most.

18
The Cielo

Grace cradled the bundle of life asleep in her arms. The baby had been found at a rubbish dump near the orphanage. She stroked the infant's soft head, then counted the little one's fingers and toes. They were all there—just as God intended. The child would, however, struggle to walk perfectly when the time came for him to do so. Grace was content, however, with the knowledge that being created in God's image did not mean being completely whole.

She had learned that God's love is perfected in weakness. The tent that houses the human spirit is, at best, tenuous. There can be no other reason for its existence than to be wholly occupied with God and living for Christ.

Aayana had sacrificed that which was most precious to her. Her loss had become the force God used to save others. Alisha had lost her sight, but her blindness had been used to help women and girls turn their hearts to Jesus. Esta had experienced the loss of her freedom, and yet she had helped others to find theirs. Each one had been crippled in some way by life's atrocities, yet perfected in the demonstration of love's highest deeds towards humanity. The war on human suffering would, in the end, be won only by love.

Grace looked across the courtyard from the room

where she had learned so much during her early days at The Cielo. Mama Sofia would have taken the little one Grace held in her arms and loved him as her own. The nun had died while Grace was in India. Sofia was buried next to a tree near the orphanage's vegetable garden. The tree, a large acacia, lavishly stocked white blossoms on its boughs. The flowers reminded Grace of the faithful habit Sofia was so fond of wearing.

Sofia had once said to Grace, 'It's an honour for me to serve in God's kingdom, but the secret to a happy life is to be a branch for Jesus.'

Grace thought that this was indeed how Sofia had lived—as a fruitful branch, weak but strong, poor yet rich.

'Ah, there you are,' a male voice called to Grace as the door opened. Joseph's arms circled her waist. His lips touched her temple and stayed there a while. Sensing the infant stir in her arms, Joseph pulled back.

'Where did you find this little one, Señorita? I will have to expand every corner of The Cielo to accommodate them all.'

The priest placed his hands squarely on his hips, pretending to be annoyed. Grinning, he pulled Grace close again. 'I wonder why I feel compelled to do that.'

'Because, sweet husband of mine, you're very much in love with me.'

Feeling utterly content, Grace placed the child safely in Joseph's arms.

Author Bio

Debbie Watkins is a professional by day and novelist by night. She is a qualified English and Special Needs teacher who has had the privilege of helping many children reach their potential.

Through the stories she writes Debbie seeks to put a human face to suffering. Debbie's goal is to not only expose the causes of pain and trauma in the world, but to also speak of the deliverance and redemption that is found through Christ.

Debbie resides with her husband in New Zealand. This is her first Christian novel.

www.ingramcontent.com/pod-product-compliance
Lightning Source LLC
Chambersburg PA
CBHW020134130526
44590CB00039B/165